Lonely Soldier

Lonely Soldier

The Memoir of

an American Soldier

in the Israeli Army

Adam Harmon

PRESIDIO
PRESS

Ballantine Books • New York

Published in the United States by Presidio Press, an imprint of The Random House Publishing Group, a division of Random House, Inc., New York.

PRESIDIO PRESS and colophon are trademarks of Random House, Inc.

Library of Congress Cataloging-in-Publication Data

Harmon, Adam.
    Lonely soldier : the memoir of an American soldier in the Israeli Army / Adam Harmon.
        p.   cm.
    ISBN 0-89141-874-1
    1. Harmon, Adam.   2. Jews, American—Israel—Biography.   3. Soldiers—Israel—Biography.   4. Israel. Tseva haganah le-Yisra'el—Biography.   I. Title.
    DS113.8.A4H37 2006
    956.94005'4092—dc22
    [B]   2005058656

Printed in the United States of America on acid-free paper

www.presidiopress.com

9 8 7 6 5 4 3 2 1

First Edition

Design by Joseph Rutt

For the family that molded me,
the two nations that nurtured me,
and the woman who fills my life with love

Acknowledgments

I would like to take this opportunity to thank those who enabled me to experience the life described in this book, as well as those who provided me a way to share those experiences with others.

First and foremost, I thank my parents, Phil and Carol Wilks, for their unstinting support and guidance over the years. Along with my sisters—Wendy, Susan, and Deborah—they provided a strong foundation of love and encouragement that made moving to Israel seem risk-free and made every challenge seem surmountable.

I can't thank the Barelli family enough for their overwhelming generosity. Feeling welcomed and at home in Israel is largely due to their warmth, kindness, and compassion.

I also thank the members of Kibbutz Tzora for welcoming me to their community.

None of this would have been possible if the 202nd Battalion, the

Alpinistim, and the 9203 reconnaissance unit hadn't instructed, protected, and accepted me as one of their own.

I thank friends like Karen Berman, Roni Edri, Stuart Gold, and Uri Resnick for the materials they provided and for the feedback that has improved the book's accuracy.

I am ever grateful to Scott Miller at Trident Media Group for suggesting that my personal history may be of interest to others. I am indebted to him and thank him for his encouragement, counsel, and hard work.

Without the interest and support of Ron Doering at Presidio, my experiences would never have been transformed into a book. I have learned a great deal through our collaboration. His keen eye and expertise were critical. I greatly appreciate his vital contribution.

Also, many thanks to my copyeditor, Laura Jorstad. Her attention to detail and thoughtful remarks led to a much-improved book.

I would be remiss if I didn't acknowledge my father, in his capacity as first reader of every page written. His feedback has been an invaluable part of the writing process.

Finally, without the support, encouragement, and patience of my wife, Jennifer, I probably wouldn't have even completed the first chapter. I can't thank her enough, but I will try.

Contents

The Path to Israel

It's June 27, 1984. I've just completed my sophomore year of high school and I'm flying to Israel for the first time with thirty-two other teenagers from all over New England. Arthur Starr, the rabbi from my synagogue in Manchester, New Hampshire, leads the group.

When we first board the El Al flight, most of us are strangers. But after sharing hotel rooms, living out of buses, camping, hiking, and traveling across the country, we are now more like old friends. For five weeks, we literally touch more than two thousand years of Jewish history: from preserved ancient sites like the Western Wall, Solomon's mines, and Masada to places of more recent importance such as Ammunition Hill, Yad Mordechai, and the Golan Heights.

It's 9 PM and we're at a large park in Tel Aviv. Along with thousands of Israelis, we watch a troupe dance to Israeli folk music. Each new song and costume change celebrates one of the many immigrant groups that have come from across the world to make Israel their home.

While foraging for food, I stray from the group. Snacking on a falafel and completely absorbed in the performance, I lose track of time. Karen, a member of my group, passes by. Probably because it's unusual for any of us, and especially me, to be sitting alone, she asks if I'm okay. With more emotion than I mean to express, I say, "I'm fine. It's just so beautiful. One day I'm going to live here."

The idea of living in Israel was probably planted by all the Israelis who keep asking if we plan on moving to the country, but I can't pinpoint the time, the place, or the reason behind my answering that question in the affirmative. Prior to this trip, Israel was a place on a map and a topic for discussion. Israel is the first safe haven Jews have known in two thousand years, but I don't need sanctuary. I lead a relatively idyllic life in the United States, and thoughts about my future don't usually extend beyond the next day.

I've traveled across America and been abroad. Like most teenagers, I'm prone to infatuation with new and exotic locations, but this is different. It's not rational, but Jerusalem feels more like home to me than New Hampshire. I don't love the United States any less, but I feel like I belong to Israel and the place belongs to me in a way that I've never experienced before.

When I return to the States, a glass Coca-Cola bottle filled with sand from near the Western Wall and ancient pottery shards from Masada, an Israeli flag, dozens of pictures, lasting relationships, and my growing youth group involvement all serve as constant reminders of my experience in Israel. More importantly, my family nurtures my interest. My parents and siblings are my closest friends. Their positive feedback and support is critical to Israel becoming an increasingly important part of my life.

I'm not surprised by their response to my admiration for Israel and my expressed desire to live there one day. If I had told my family that I wanted to climb Mount Everest, they would ask questions and help me find a mountaineering school. They would fear the dangers associated with climbing and would share their concerns with me, but they would do everything they could to support my decision in the end.

Combine this with the fact that my family has taken pains to instill within me a strong Jewish identity. Ever since I can remember, we have been involved in our small but thriving Jewish community. We aren't particularly religious, but we go to synagogue regularly, keep kosher at home (although spareribs and cheeseburgers are okay when stepping out into the world), and every Friday we celebrate Shabbat with special conversation-filled dinners that last for hours.

Israel plays a central role in Jewish life. Our history is one of exile and return to this Promised Land. Israel, as a modern and thriving nation, embodies my people's greatest hopes and serves to calm our worst fears. Knowing this, it's easy to see why my family was happy to let me take another trip to Israel. During the following summer, I sign up for two months of traveling and learning Hebrew. When I return to the States, most other members of the program remain to study at an Israeli high school for a year. Long before the summer is over, I am envying those who are able to stay. The trip reinforces my growing belief that I would enjoy living in the country. I realize now that Israel feels like home because almost everyone I meet acts as if I'm part of their family.

In Israel, there is an assumed connection between me and everyone else. People speak candidly and interact with a warm familiarity that is very different from the emotional distance typical of New England. I find their knowledge of Israel's history, the way they love their land, and how much they care for their community very enticing. The typical Israeli's everyday appreciation for his or her country reminds me of America on special holidays like July 4. I bet America was more like this in the heady days of the Revolution and immediately after World War II.

When I return to New Hampshire at the end of the summer, I am seriously considering moving to Israel. It is no longer just a fanciful idea. I want to explore what that means, want to know what actions I need to take, and want to start considering the consequences. When I tell my family, they are eager to discuss it further and expressly support the idea.

My parents and I differ only on the timing. They want me to complete my undergraduate degree before I move, and I want to leave after my senior year in high school. I know I will have to serve in the military and want to join when I'm eighteen just like my Israeli counterparts. I don't completely accept the argument that having a degree will give me a significant head start in the future, but I accede to my parents' wish. I am accepted at American University and the school lets me defer for a year. This enables me to take part in a Reform movement program called College Academic Year.

The nine-month-long program in Israel combines academic study and work on a kibbutz. It is mainly for college juniors and seniors who want to study abroad, but I am one of several freshmen who join. For my family, the program is a perfect compromise. The first kibbutz, Deganya, was established in northern Israel in 1909. The founders of Deganya created an egalitarian community that combined the socialist ideal of common ownership of all property with the ideal of direct democracy. All decisions relating to work and life were made as a community, where every kibbutz member had an equal vote.

Life centered on agriculture. Work days were long and arduous, but the kibbutz members valued cultural activities and saw dancing, singing, and dining together as a vital part of community building.

Deganya would be the first of more than two hundred kibbutzim built across Israel. Now, nearly a century since Deganya was first established, the kibbutz movement has evolved and adapted to meet the changing needs of subsequent generations, but the original intent of creating a close-knit community remains the primary goal of every kibbutz.

I will live and work at Kibbutz Tzora. This kibbutz was established by members of the Israeli proto-military known as the Palmach along with new immigrants from South Africa during the Israeli War of Independence in 1948. When it was built, the kibbutz was situated on a hill that overlooked the road to Jerusalem. Its location is no longer a strategic asset, but the kibbutz remains well known in Israel as a vibrant community.

By the time I first arrive, the kibbutz has made a successful transition from being supported primarily by its agricultural fields to a diversified economy that includes a furniture factory and fashion design. In addition, many members of the kibbutz are members of the Israeli professional class. They work as doctors and architects in Jerusalem or Tel Aviv, but their paychecks go directly to the kibbutz.

After a few days, the thirty members of the group are divided into different work groups. Some are sent to the community kitchen; others go to the factory. Most of us go to the fields. We start in the vineyard and learn how to pick grapes by hand. Even though I often missed the school bus growing up because I overslept most mornings, I have no trouble waking up before dawn to go to the fields. Field work is hard physical labor, but it encourages long, stimulating conversations. Working opposite sides of the vine enables me to get to know the members of my program, the Europeans who work on the kibbutz in exchange for room and board as a way to travel abroad cheaply, and the kibbutz members who work alongside us.

While we harvest grapes, avocados, and almonds, conversation topics range from local gossip and Israeli current events to geopolitics, philosophy, and literature. For me, this lifestyle is heaven. I love waking up early, working hard during the week, chatting most of the day, enjoying meals in the cafeteria with the entire community, and spending the night drinking and talking with my friends. The fun doesn't deflect me from my responsibilities. Each morning, I'm awake and ready for work.

By winter, I am convinced that I will be happy living in Israel. At different intervals throughout the year, my parents and sisters visit me. They can see that I'm happy and continue to support my desire to move to Israel after I complete my undergraduate degree.

When the program is over, I travel in Europe on my own for several months. Boats and trains take me through Greece, Italy, France, Switzerland, and Germany. The trip is one long adventure. I immerse myself in paintings, sculptures, historic sites, theater, and dance. I also climb the Swiss Alps, hike in Bavaria, and meet fascinating people along the way. I have the time of my life precisely because everything is so foreign. By contrast, landing in Israel feels like coming home.

A week later, I'm on another flight. This time I'm returning to the United States. I spend a few weeks with my family and then fly to Washington, DC. As with my trip to Europe, I learn a lot at American University and have a tremendous time, but a part of me is always anchored in Israel.

In December 1987, during my first semester at American University, the Palestinian Intifadah breaks out. As the Israeli military learns to manage the growing violence in the West Bank and Gaza, Arab and Jewish students on my campus wage a propaganda war. I've been here four months and help found a group that works to counter the accusations and misleading information being distributed by Arab students.

Two members of our group are Israeli; I am one of three Jewish American students. It's not an easy task. News coverage focuses on young men throwing stones at armed soldiers and jeeps. Our antagonists use the sympathy generated to accuse Israel of atrocities, defend the actions of terrorists, and undermine Israel's legitimacy.

School-sponsored events meant to promote cultural awareness among students and mark special occasions like Israel Independence Day and Palestinian Land Day, basically gave those who cared about the

Israel-Arab conflict about ten opportunities a year to try to out-argue each other, distribute pamphlets, and vent their frustrations. I doubt that either side convinces anyone of anything. Our interactions, I'm sure, only serve to deepen an onlooker's impression that the problems in the Middle East are unsolvable.

At the time, I have my own doubts about Israeli military actions. It's hard to understand why a soldier would ever shoot at a civilian. After all, they are only throwing rocks. I wonder if the army would do better just to ignore the rioters. But I know it's easy to judge when you don't have to live with the consequences. Although there is much posturing and loud debate when others are looking, I do form friendships with several members of the opposition. One of them, Kamal, is the grandson of Grand Mufti Haj Amin al-Husseini. His grandfather led the Palestinian community during the British mandate and became closely aligned with Hitler's Third Reich during World War II.

At a Lebanese restaurant near the university, Kamal and I meet regularly to discuss the situation in the Middle East. We refrain from oversimplifying the issues and use our time to gain a better understanding of each other's perspective. I learn a lot from him and enjoy our conversations immensely. He personally accepts Israel's right to exist and wants to live together in peace, but he is in the minority. He confirms that most people in his circle are anxious for more war and violence. They seem to think that the Intifadah is a battle they can win and that it presages a greater victory against Israel. A student from Syria says to me, "We need just one more war between Israel and Syria. We'll let that decide everything and we'll be done with it forever."

I've never run away from a fight, but I prefer talking my way out of tight spots. Yet I know I'll have to join the military when I move to Israel, and I'm a little concerned about my ability to function as a soldier.

It just doesn't fit my self-image.

I think of myself as a poet, not a warrior. I steer conversations away from my future military service, and I avoid thinking about it. When I am forced to talk about it, I deflect questions as best I can.

I'm not troubled by thoughts of my own death. I am still young enough to feel impervious to danger, but I'm concerned about being a failure. Soldiers need to be physically strong and mentally tough. I'm a nice, outgoing Jewish boy who has led a relatively privileged life. I don't think of myself as being very rough-and-tumble. I think of myself as an individualist who doesn't kowtow to authority figures just because they have a title. I doubt that I'll be able to march in step and I wonder if I'll be able to follow orders without question.

During the summer of 1989, I return to Israel to take a summer course at Hebrew University in Jerusalem. I study Hebrew and learn enough to formulate essential questions like "Does this bus go to Jerusalem?" and "I'd like to order two slices of pepperoni pizza." I can read road signs and menus, but I can't read the newspaper or write a love note. When I'm not studying Hebrew on campus with people from across the world, I am traveling in the country and visiting friends from Kibbutz Tzora. Karen, who has remained a close friend, is also traveling in the country. We meet up and travel to the Sinai Peninsula with a friend of mine from the course. When I leave the country after completing the course, I'm not sad at all. I know I'll be back soon.

Combining college credits earned in Israel with courses taken at American University enables me to graduate in December 1989 after only two years. I stay in Washington, DC, for another few months working as a waiter and planning my next step.

I formally start the process of moving to Israel. Before the establishment of the state, the British mandate limited the number of Jews who could move to Israel each year. This hardship, keenly felt during World War II, was reversed when the newly established state of Israel instituted the Law of Return, which automatically provides any Jew with Israeli citizenship.

Over the last fifty years, Israel has been providing protection, liberty, and opportunity to Jews who have come from the Americas, Europe, Africa, the Middle East, and India. Now, in 1990, hundreds of thousands of Jews from the former Soviet Union are streaming into the country. Unlike these other immigrants, I'm not running away from adversity, but the Law of Return does make me feel like I already belong.

And, due to the long-standing, good relations between the United States and Israel, I am able to retain my American citizenship and become a dual citizen.

Now that I've decided to go, I need to figure out where I'm going to live. Generally, young people who move to Israel from Western nations are part of a group associated with one of the many Zionist organizations. I don't want to join a group. I just want to move to the country. I write Kibbutz Tzora and ask them to let me live there while I acclimate to the country and serve in the military. I'm thrilled when they respond positively to my request.

I pack up the things I've accumulated after living in DC for three years and return to New Hampshire. Over the next two months, I spend a lot of time with my parents and sisters. I say good-bye to my grandparents, aunts, uncles, and many friends. Not once, either in jest or by way of side comment, does anyone suggest that I'm making a mistake or ask me to reconsider my decision. Everyone seems genuinely happy for me.

I come from a close family, and I'm going to miss them all very much. I remind myself and everyone else that I'm only a ten-hour flight away. Airlines, telephones, and letters will enable us to remain connected. But I know it won't be the same. The number of calls and visits each year will decrease. We all know it, but I tell myself this is just part of growing up. This is the time in my life to take a chance. Unlike most other immigrants, I know I can return to my country of origin and start over again whenever I like. If I'm unhappy, all I have to do is call my family and tell them I want to come home. They'd welcome me with open arms.

I will leave for Israel on June 26, 1990. It will be six years after my first trip to the country. During my last month in the United States, my parents and I speak often about my upcoming military service. Since I am my mother's only son, I can't serve in a combat unit unless she signs a waiver. The Israeli military also asks parents to sign a form like this if another member of the family has been killed while serving in the military.

Sitting in the den with my mother and father, we talk it over. I tell them that serving in a combat unit is the best way for me to establish common ground with Israelis. In America, when people my age first meet, someone always asks where you went to college. In Israel, someone always asks where you served in the military, and serving in an elite unit is as prestigious as going to an Ivy League school in America.

My parents understand this, though they can't help but voice their concerns for my safety. Couldn't I provide valuable service as part of an intelligence unit or with some other desk job? After all, I have a college degree. I concede that they are right, but I tell them that I need to experience Lebanon, the West Bank, and Gaza for myself if I really want to understand the central concerns of Israelis, feel a part of the country, and speak about current events with any credibility.

In an attempt to reassure them, I also say that I intend to serve with the very best. In an elite unit, I can count on receiving the best training and equipment. In addition, I'll be serving with Israel's best and brightest. They will keep me from harm. My parents remain worried, but they support my decision and sign the form.

Later, they pose a question that surprises me. They ask if my moving to Israel is in some way a rejection of the life they have lived in the United States. I am shocked by the suggestion. I view my upbringing as having been relatively idyllic. I have never wanted for material or emotional support. I make it clear to them that the stability and nurturing they provided have given me the strength to move away. I'm able to take this step only because I know that the distance will not impact our love and respect for each other. Before we move on to dinner, we embrace. I am proud to be their son.

On June 26, 1990, we drive to the airport together. My sisters and parents kiss me good-bye. They wish me well and tell me to call them as soon as I can. I have two large duffel bags. One is filled with T-shirts, shorts, sneakers, and a couple of pairs of pants. The other is packed with my favorite books.

I'm so filled with anticipation that the ten-hour El Al flight seems brief. When I land, I tell the girl at passport control that I'm a new immigrant. Since Israel is a nation of immigrants and their offspring, Israelis differentiate between immigrants who have been in the country for years and those like me who have just arrived.

I was told by Israeli representatives in the United States that a representative from the Jewish Agency meets every new immigrant, but no one is here to greet me. Perhaps it's because I'm here on my own. Maybe it's because everyone is too busy helping the thousands of new immigrants from the former Soviet Union who are landing each day. I find my way to a small office. The bureaucrat takes a quick look at my paperwork.

Moments later, I am given a light blue passbook that officially designates me an Israeli citizen. He also gives me a voucher for a taxi. The government will pay the taxi driver to take me wherever I want to go in the country. For a moment, I consider how much fun it would be to have him drive me two hundred miles to Eilat, but I rein myself in and direct him to Kibbutz Tzora, which is less than twenty miles away.

When I arrive, I drop my bags off at the cafeteria and walk to the kibbutz's administrative office. It feels like I never left. I am warmly welcomed and am told that I will be staying in one of the large apartments I used when I was on the College Academic Year program. They give me a key and remind me that dinner is between 6 and 7 PM.

Over the next few months, I work in the fields, renew acquaintances, run in the nearby hills, work to improve my Hebrew, and go to the military induction center in Jerusalem. I'm told that I can wait a year, perhaps more, and give myself additional time to acclimate to the country.

But I don't want to wait. I'm almost twenty-two years old. If I wait an additional year, I'll be five years older than the other soldiers and three years older than my commanders. I don't want any more time to pass. I'm anxious to get started. It takes convincing, but the commander of the office agrees to push my date forward. I'll be joining the military in November.

Over the next few months, I take a number of tests with high school graduates from Jerusalem. Since I'm in good health and have never broken any bones, I receive the highest physical profile. My score of ninety-seven means I've passed the first prerequisite for serving with an elite combat unit. In addition to the physical profile, the military uses intelligence tests, a psychological profile, and various socioeconomic criteria to attain a combined score that helps determine the types of units to which a recruit can apply. Those with the highest combined scores are invited to test for elite combat units, intelligence units, and air force pilot training.

I'm able to take some of the tests in English and that helps, but I lose a couple of points for being a new immigrant and for not having any family in the country: Assimilating to a new country and not having an extensive support system could affect my stability. On the other hand, I probably gained points for being highly motivated and having a college degree.

The military does not share the final combined score with me, but I couldn't have fared too poorly because I receive a request for additional testing in Tel Aviv. I take more intelligence tests and am interviewed by an officer. I don't know what I'm testing for, but I make it clear that I don't want a desk job of any kind.

To my relief, I'm asked to consider joining a combat unit called Nachal, which is connected to the kibbutz movement. The unit is mixed, with men and women serving together. It is an attractive option, but often these units are mainly comprised of new immigrants like me. Their mandate is to help soldiers assimilate. I didn't come all the way to Israel to serve with twenty people from France. I want to experience the same military service as the Israelis. Serving with Nachal would feel like I took the easy way out. Also, I'm concerned that my own assimilation into Israeli culture will be hampered if I'm mostly serving with new immigrants like myself. I thank the recruiter for his time, but decide against it.

Months pass and November approaches. As I complete the last of the paperwork, the commander at the induction center reminds me that I can still defer military service for another year, perhaps longer— and given my relatively advanced age, waiting might shorten my required service to less than a year. If I join the military now and serve in a combat unit, I'll have to serve at least two years. I don't hesitate for a moment. I thank her for all her help, hand her the signed forms, and return to the kibbutz.

I now know where I want to serve. The paratroopers have a reputation for rigorous training as well as a storied history. Also, I know several people on the kibbutz who have served in the unit. Everyone seems to think that the paratroopers are among the best. It's also the only combat unit to demand that recruits test into it. I don't know if I'm good enough, but I'm going to try.

Lonely Soldier

In August 1990, Iraq invades Kuwait. The United States establishes a naval blockade and works with the UN to demand an Iraqi withdrawal by January 15, 1991. Most people believe that war is imminent. No one knows how this will impact Israel. Palestinian terror attacks increase, killing twenty-three Israeli citizens. At the same time, hundreds of thousands of immigrants from the former Soviet Union move to Israel. This massive influx, as well as successful high-tech ventures, creates an economic boom for the country.

Chapter 1

Wanting the Red Beret

O ver the last five months, I've run on dirt paths to increase my stamina and made every effort to improve my ability to speak and understand Hebrew. I'm now well beyond being only able to ask where to find the bathroom, but I'm far from being able to communicate fully and completely understand what's being said.

Collectively, members of the kibbutz have spent hours describing military life while we're working in the fields or relaxing in the community's lounge, but I still don't have a clear idea of what to expect. At 5 AM on November 6, as ready as I'll ever be, I kiss my girlfriend good-bye. I hope I look more relaxed and less anxious than I feel.

I cut through the cow pasture and climb over an eight-foot-high fence, carrying a knapsack filled with socks, underwear, shorts, T-shirts, small notepads, pens, and a paperback novel. I reach the road that links the kibbutz to the wider world. After ten minutes, I cross the main road to the same bus stop that has taken me to Jerusalem many times in the past. Today I'm standing in the dark waiting for a bus to take me to Jerusalem. From the local induction center in Jerusalem, I'll be taken to a base near Tel Aviv, called Bakum, where everyone in Israel begins his or her military service.

While I'm waiting, a car approaches. I point my index finger at the ground as Israelis do when they want to hitch a ride. It's as if I'm asking the car to stop right where my finger is pointing. My bus should be coming along soon, but asking for a ride has become a reflex. I recognize the vehicle as being one of the twenty cars used by kibbutz members. As the car stops beside me, I see that it is Yaakov. I've worked with him in the almond fields. He rolls down his window and says, "Where are you going?"

"Jerusalem."

"I'm going to Tel Aviv, but I can drop you off at the next junction."

I gladly accept, because more buses stop at that junction.

I tell him I'm going to Bakum, and he wants to know where I am going to serve.

"I don't know yet. Where did you serve?"

"With the tanks."

The five-minute car ride is over. Yaakov pulls over to the side of the road. Before I open the door, he offers his hand and says, "Good luck."

"Thanks, Yaakov. Drive safe."

I'm already out of the car and shutting the door when I hear him say, "You're going to be all right."

"I hope so." I shut the door and wave good-bye. Ten minutes later, a bus stops and picks me up. Traveling on the modern highway connecting Tel Aviv and Jerusalem, I look out the window and see half a dozen rusted trucks on the edge of the road. I know them well. They've been resting here for more than forty years. During the Israeli War of Independence, Arab forces blockaded the road to Jerusalem. The Jewish citizens in Jerusalem were under siege, and the Palmach staved off starvation and capitulation by delivering vital supplies in convoys. These convoys came under attack; fierce battles were waged along this road. As a constant reminder of the sacrifices made by these men and women, several vehicles damaged in the fighting have been left to rust where they broke down. On the kibbutz there lives a woman who drove one of those trucks. She looks younger than her sixty years, and it's hard to imagine that this attractive blonde with a pixie-like stature, sweet disposition, and mischievous smile ever knew a moment of stress or anxiety in her life. As we pass by these vehicles, I wonder what I'll experience in the next two years and how I'll handle it.

When I arrive at the central bus station in Jerusalem, I walk to the local induction center. From there, a chartered bus is waiting to take me and a dozen other young men from Jerusalem to Bakum.

Soon after arriving, I climb onto the bus and find a seat. I'm one of only a few people on board; everyone else is outside mingling with their parents and siblings during their last moments as civilians. An hour later, as our packed bus leaves, a small crowd of people is still there to wish their children good luck. On the bus, several guys are talking easily among themselves. Others, like me, are sitting quietly and looking a bit anxious.

Once we arrive at Bakum, we all pour out of the vehicle. I follow everyone else. When we reach the main gate, I need to show the guard my paperwork. My hands aren't shaking and I don't feel queasy, but my jaw muscles are tight. The guard says something about taking a left, I think, but I can't be sure because he speaks too quickly for me.

Adjusting my knapsack, I follow the other young men who are already walking down the road. Despite that fact that I don't know where I'm going or what awaits past this gate, I am now less anxious and realize that these first steps are taking me to my next adventure.

There are thousands who have been arriving from communities

across Israel over the last couple of weeks. There may be several dozen like me who traveled halfway around the world just to stand in this long line. To start, a black-and-white picture of me is taken. The picture is quickly developed and stapled to a brown document that identifies me as number 5035379. The guy ahead of me was 5035378. I am officially an Israeli soldier now.

Like the hundreds in front of me, I slowly walk down a corridor filled with stalls. I'm reminded of a country fair, but instead of my trying to knock over milk bottles to win a prize, the proprietors at each station throw uniforms, belts, canteens, blankets, and many unidentifiable items at me. There is no yelling. In fact, the guys in the stalls are young men themselves. They are all smiling good-naturedly.

Thinking about my military identity number, I realize that more than five million men and women have experienced a day just like mine since the beginning of the nation. Some went on to be combat soldiers; others pushed paper. I know I want to serve with the infantry. I tell everyone I want to join a combat unit because it's the only way for me to really understand the Israeli–Arab conflict. I think that spending time in Lebanon, the Golan, the West Bank, and Gaza will make me more knowledgeable. And given the fact that I grew up in America, if I serve with a combat unit it will make it more difficult for Israelis to dismiss my viewpoint. That's what I tell everyone and that's what I tell myself.

Once I have all the gear the military has to offer, I follow the others toward a large cement quad that looks like the parking lot at a mall. The lot is packed with tents that are designed to house about twenty people.

Entering the tent to which I'm assigned, I immediately feel like a curiosity. At twenty-two, I am four years older than most. I'm also the only non-native in the tent. They all ask where I'm from and are enthusiastic when they learn that I'm from the United States, but the conversation ends soon after that discovery. I don't think much about the ways in which I am different from my new friends but my speech is halting. They must find me as difficult to understand as I find them.

A sergeant or officer—I can't tell the difference between them yet—walks into the tent and says something. I don't know what he's announced, but I follow the others as they leave the tent. As it turns out, we're on the way to a dining hall. My first meal in the army consists of eggs, cottage cheese, tomatoes, cucumbers, bread, and hot tea. It's a lot like kibbutz food. The chatter around me echoes in the large hall. It's like being in an aviary. The birds are restless and seem to have a lot to say. I wish I spoke their language.

That night, I take out my copy of Gabriel García Márquez's *Love in the Time of Cholera*. The lightbulb hanging in the tent is bright and I don't need a flashlight. Within an hour, I am asleep. At dawn, someone who feels entitled enters the tent and yells something. I pull on my olive-green uniform, lace up my black boots, and leave the tent with everyone else. The man who woke us calls my name and says, "You're a *chayal boded*,* right?"

I have heard that term often enough on the kibbutz and have seen it used on the many forms I have filled out since I've come to Israel. "Yes, I am."

"Follow me."

And like a good soldier, I do as I'm told.

In my previous lives I didn't care much for rules or authority figures. By almost any standard, I was probably considered a good kid and a solid citizen, but I had my share of disagreements with high school teachers, and signs that said KEEP OUT rarely worked on me. Now I move quickly and in lockstep with everyone else. Once I understand

---

* In Hebrew, the term means "lone soldier" and refers to someone without family in Israel.

what I'm being asked to do, I'm more than happy to oblige. I recognize the change in my behavior, but I'm too busy trying to understand what's going on around me to think much about it.

After following what seems like a circuitous route, the man whom I think is a sergeant stops near a small office space. He says something about returning to my tent when I'm done here, but I don't really know where I am, why I'm here, or what I'm about to do. I don't know if I'm supposed to wait for him to return or if he expects me to find my way back on my own. His job is done, though, because he turns around and leaves. I walk toward the office building and see about a dozen men sitting on the ground. I approach the office and am told by the attendant to sit with everyone else. As I walk toward the others, a member of a group sitting in a loose circle offers a friendly smile. I say, *"Ma'kneesh'ma?"* (How are you?)

His smile widens and in lilting English I recognize as South African, he introduces himself as Jonathan.

I'm invited to sit with them and I learn that Jonathan and his friend Nathan were both part of the Habonim (the Builders) youth movement. Like me, they moved to Israel soon after they graduated from college, but since they were part of a Zionist movement, they have been studying Hebrew for years and speak the language with near fluency. I also meet a twenty-six-year-old former British barrister and pharmacist named Martin. He has been living in the country for several years and is engaged to be married. Martin looks like he could carry Jonathan, Nathan, and me for several miles without breaking a sweat. I'm glad to see that I'm not the oldest person here.

They explain to me that every *chayal boded* is processed here before being sent to his individual unit. They've been here for almost a week already. For days, they have been sitting and waiting for the office workers to read their names off a list. When people are called, they sign papers and move on to the next stage.

By this day's end, none of us has been called. We find our way to the dining room and return to our tents.

Over the next few days, I get to know Jonathan, Nathan, and Martin fairly well. As it turns out, they all plan on joining the paratroopers as well. It is clear from our conversations that they are all much better informed than I am regarding what to expect. I learn that once we complete this initial step, we will meet with an officer, who is a psychologist by training. Even though the military has ample information to develop a personal profile, this thirty-minute discussion is another opportunity for them to evaluate my motivation level and fitness for duty.

Jonathan says, "They are going to ask you where you want to serve. You have to tell them paratroopers. You have to make clear that this is your first, second, and third choice."

Although people on the kibbutz also told me I needed to tell "them" that I only wanted to serve with the paratroopers, until now I didn't know who "they" were. I say, "Got it."

After nearly a week of returning to this same spot, my name is called. Jonathan and the others left a couple of days ago, but I'm hopeful that I'll see them again. Like everyone else, I complete my paperwork and soon find myself in a small office. The officer, looking at the thin file that probably contains almost everything the military knows about me, says, "What's your first choice?"

I say, "I only want to serve with the paratroopers."

He smiles at me as if I'm an amusing child and says, "What if they don't want you? Then where would you like to go?"

I say, "It's the only place I want to serve. I only want to be with the paratroopers."

After several rounds, he gets bored with my responses, makes a notation in my file, and says, "I wish you the best of luck."

I thank him and walk out the door, not really sure what is going to happen next.

Another day passes and after breakfast, out of the blue, a sergeant comes up to tell me that I will test for paratroopers. Today!

I say, "Thank you, sir. Where do I go? When does it start?"

I understand from his response that the testing will begin immediately, but I clearly look lost when he's giving me directions because he stops himself mid-sentence and says, "Never mind. I'll take you there. Give me a minute."

We arrive at a fenced-in area with a small opening that serves as an entrance. "Here you are. Good luck."

Walking through the entrance, I keep going until I run into several soldiers with clipboards. Their uniforms don't identify their rank, but it's clear from their age that they have been serving with the military for a number of years. As I approach, one of them says, "What's your name?"

"Adam Harmon."

"Personal ID number?"

Having memorized my number while hanging out with Jonathan and the others, I say, "5035379."

"Okay, Herman, join the others."

I make my way to the nearby field. There must be more than a hundred soldiers standing there. The atmosphere is relatively relaxed. For most, it probably is just like the high school physical education tests that they took just a few months ago. Over the next hour, we engage in a mixture of physical tasks ranging from short runs to push-ups, sit-ups, and similar group activities that seem geared toward measuring our ability to work together and think critically. Everything must be done quickly and is a race against the clock.

By the last exercise, I'm exhausted. The whistle blows and even though my legs burn, I take off running as fast as I can. It seems like I've only traveled for a few seconds when I hear the whistle blow again. The others quickly drop for push-ups. I immediately follow suit. I have time for ten push-ups when the whistle blows again. I get up and start running. I don't have the energy to know whether it's the heat, my exhaustion, or the fact that I drank water only moments ago, but I start feeling nauseous. When the whistle blows again, I fall to my knees and throw up. Fearful that I will be disqualified, I immediately throw out my feet and start performing push-ups. When the whistle blows, I run again until the whistle blows once more. Again, I throw up and immediately transition to push-ups. Running up and down a hill several times, I continue with my dry heaves every time I stop running. Just when I think I can't take any more, we are told to stop.

The man giving orders tells us we have completed the physical exam. He wishes us all good luck, tells us that we'll be interviewed by a panel of officers tomorrow, and walks away. On my way back to my tent, I dwell on the fact that I barely finished. I'm sure I was judged not physically strong enough and certainly having insufficient language skills. If they knew how close I was to quitting, I know they'd reject me. When I arrive at my tent, no one is there. I relish the time alone and the quiet. I wash up, lie down on my cot, and fall into a deep sleep.

The next morning, I am led to a row of administrative offices. More than a hundred men are milling about the open courtyard where I am told to wait until called upon. I had hoped to see Jonathan, Martin, and Nathan, but they aren't here. Every so often a name is called and the individual enters one of the many offices. Given the pace and the number of applicants, it's clear that I'm going to be here a long while. Eventually I sit down in the middle of the quad and make small talk with a couple of the guys next to me. If they are fascinated by my being from the United States, they are awestruck to learn that I've already graduated from college and am twenty-two years old. Either that or they find it ridiculous, because they both break out in laughter.

While we're waiting, a large soldier with wings on his breast and patches on his arm approaches us. He says, "Are you Herman?"

After I nod, he says, "Come with me for a moment."

I follow him to a quiet corner in the shade. "My name is Gal. I have an offer for you. Have you heard of the Chan unit?"

"No."

Gal continues talking, but I can't honestly say that I'm able to follow what he says. It's clear that he's trying to tell me that the Chan unit plays a vital role and comprises some of Israel's best soldiers. Everything else is lost on me, but I don't want to interrupt him and let him know how little I really understand. When he finishes, he says, "And I'm offering you a chance to join us. What do you say?"

I knew from people on the kibbutz that the paratroopers are divided into several different types of units and foremost among them is the elite paratrooper Sayerit. On the kibbutz, I had the opportunity to know a member of this unit—his name was Niv—and given the fact that I was being approached before I'd even been interviewed by the panel, I assumed that he had put in a good word for me. Of course I don't know if it's true, but just the thought reassures me that I might have a chance.

I don't quite know where the Chan falls on the spectrum, but I know that it must be below the Sayerit in terms of prestige. When Gal is finished, I say, "Thank you so much for this offer. I really appreciate it. When do I need to give you an answer?"

"You need to tell me before the test for the Sayerit. You can avoid the test and join the Chan immediately. But after that, it'll be too late."

I appreciate the offer, but it feels like taking the easy way out. It feels like cheating. I thank Gal once again and rejoin the two guys I just met in the quad. The moment I sit down, one of them asks what the soldier wanted.

"He said I could join the Chan if I wanted. I could just do it right now. What do you think?"

I see their eyes bulge. Full of emotion, one of them says, "Grab it. I'd grab it like a gift from heaven if I were you. That's fantastic!"

They are slapping my back, genuinely pleased for me. "What are you going to do?"

"I don't know. I had hoped to maybe get into the Sayerit."

"It's a gift. You should take it."

I'm not so sure. After another hour of waiting and debating, my name is finally called. I enter the office and am faced by two men and a woman sitting together at a long table. Opposite them is a small plastic chair. Hoping to appear friendly and hide my nervousness, I sit down and say, "Hello. How is your day going?"

They smile but do not answer. Then the man sitting in the middle starts the conversation. "Well. How did your day go yesterday?"

"Not as well as I'd hoped. It wasn't easy."

"Yes, but you finished and are here now."

Only then does it dawn on me that the people from my group who went missing may have actually quit. "That's true. I'm grateful for that."

The other man asks why I want to join the paratroopers.

"I understand that paratroopers are the best. I want to serve my country and learn from the best."

"Why did you move to Israel?"

I say, "I feel at home here more than anywhere else in the world. I don't know how to describe it. This is my home. I wasn't born here, but I deeply care about Israel and want to do my part to keep the country and its people safe."

The woman chimes in: "You're alone in the country. How does that affect you?"

I say, "Obviously, it's a little difficult not having my family here, but Kibbutz Tzora has given me a home, and I have many friends there."

So far the questions have been easy. Then the man in the middle says, "Being a paratrooper is dangerous business. Is there anything in your history that would indicate how you deal with danger?"

It takes me a few seconds to answer. I've certainly taken more than my share of risks over the years, but nothing really stands out in my mind as being dangerous. And then I remember an incident that occurred a few months ago during Succot, the holiday celebrating the receiving of the Ten Commandments.

"My girlfriend and I were returning from the Dead Sea. She was very sick with an infection and in a lot of pain. Because of the holiday, we couldn't find a doctor in the area and were on our way to a hospital in Jerusalem. Just before we entered East Jerusalem, our car was hit by two stones. I was concerned, but tried not to worry about it. More importantly, I didn't want her to worry.

"As we rounded a corner onto the road that takes you from the Mount of Olives to the old city's walls near Lion's Gate, I saw thousands of Palestinians on the street. I've never seen a riot before. I was troubled, but I knew that we couldn't turn around. If we did, it could take us hours to find another way into Jerusalem. I decided to push forward and hope for the best.

"There were no Israeli police, only a Palestinian standing in the middle of a sea of people who looked like he was trying to direct traffic through the crowd. There were only about six other cars with Israeli license plates. People were screaming and banging on the cars. Following the Palestinian's directions I drove toward Lion's Gate. I was hoping that there would be a way out and to the city.

"Once we had climbed up the narrow street leading up to the gate, I realized that I had made a mistake. The road was a dead end. At first, I waited, hoping that calm would be restored soon. Moments later, a Palestinian threw a cinder block through the windshield of the car ahead of us. Sandwiched between two cars and unable to maneuver, I reversed into the car behind me and drove into the car ahead of me until I created enough space to exit. My intentions became clear to the crowd, and dozens moved toward us. Up until now, I was very careful not to injure anyone.

"People were hitting our car with their fists and one guy jumped on the hood, but I continued to slowly press forward through the crowd. It took more than thirty minutes, but eventually I got past the Damascus Gate, where Israeli police were in the process of reining in the crowd."

"What does that experience say about you?" asked the woman.

"It says that I won't panic, even in difficult situations. I'll keep my head and stick to my task no matter what."

The questioning continued for another fifteen minutes. It was clear that they wanted to determine my level of commitment and to gain a sense of my personality. Even though Gal's offer should have made me feel confident, I couldn't help thinking that I didn't present myself very well during my interview.

Late that night, a sergeant or officer—I still don't know the difference between them—orders me out of my tent. Silently, I follow him for several minutes until we arrive at an open area. There are about fifteen young men standing at attention in rows that run three people deep. I don't need to be told what to do. I've been here long enough to know that I need to join one of the rows or start a new one. Luckily, the last row only has two guys in it. I prefer to be in the back because only those who stand in the front are ever asked to verbally respond to those who give orders. I stand there for several more minutes while a few more guys arrive. In the end, we are about twenty-seven men.

When we're all assembled, a man stands in front of us and says, "Of all those who have been accepted into paratrooper training, you are among the best." He continues speaking, but I don't fully understand what he's saying. All I know is that I am among those who have been personally invited to test for the paratrooper Sayerit. I also understand that we are not to mention this meeting to anyone. When I return to my tent, I'm so excited I find it hard to sleep. I spend much of the night alternating between reading and fantasizing about my new life as a member of the world's most elite commando unit.

Chapter 2

First Days

The next morning, I am taken to a bus that will bring me to one of the paratrooper training bases. Named for the Arab village nearby, it is called Sanur. Before I climb onto the bus, I see Jonathan, Nathan, and Martin. They are on their way to the base as well. I'm grateful to see friendly faces, glad to be able to communicate freely once again, and appreciative that I now have found some able translators.

In Sanur we will receive pre–basic training. This is the start of a fourteen-month journey. If I reach the end of it, I'll be a fully-trained paratrooper. We exchange our black boots for red ones, are given a large duffel bag full of equipment, and sign for a Galil assault rifle. We are instructed on the proper use of our equipment, learn how to clean our weapon, are taught how to shoot, and are introduced to basic military protocols.

At every stage, I am deeply indebted to Martin and my friends from South Africa. Not only do they kindly translate for me whenever they can, but they also seem to have a much clearer understanding of what needs to be done. It's almost as if they have already learned how to fire their weapons, waterproof bandages, keep water in canteens from making any noise—any of the many tasks we need to accomplish every day and often throughout the night. In every way, they are so much more self-assured and competent than me. They also take in all of our new experiences with an easy, almost cavalier attitude that I find very reassuring.

The two weeks at Sanur pass quickly, but the long days are filled with so much activity that it feels like I've been here for a month when we are told that those who want to test for the Sayerit must come forward. Over the last couple of weeks, I thought about Gal's offer, and finally thanked him for the opportunity, but told him I need to try out for the Sayerit.

He wished me the best of luck.

On the day testing begins, we ride in modified buses. These aren't the yellow school buses of my youth. Rather they are large, rugged vehicles that seem more comfortable on dirt paths than modern highways. All the windows are covered with wire mesh.

I ask Jonathan what we can expect. He tells me that the testing will last for about four or five days. He doesn't know specifically what we'll encounter, but he does know that the paratroopers are testing to see if we work well as a team, how we work under stress, and our level of commitment. I tell him that I barely finished the initial daylong test and know I'm not nearly in as good physical condition as most of these guys. He says, "Don't worry about it. By the third day, we'll *all* be broken. And only those who really want it will finish."

At once his words fill me with both hope and dread.

After a few hours' drive, we arrive at a large base named for the British officer Orde Wingate, who was critical in developing the Israeli military's esprit de corps. We are directed to a large field, where people are being divided up into groups of about twelve men. There may be more than five hundred men vying for about twenty-five spots.

As part of the process of placing us in groups, I am separated from my friends and join eleven others. Even though we are all in direct competition with one another to some extent, everyone is friendly and warm. We exchange names, discover that we are all from different parts of the country, and find out that two people among us are already serving in different military units, but have decided to try out for the Sayeret.

I am glad to discover that everyone on my team speaks a fair amount of English. I am given a large duffel bag with the same basic equipment I received at Bakum and later at Sanur. We all follow Yanev, one of the three men who will be testing us, to an open area on the field's perimeter. He gives us instructions that I don't understand, but I see everyone else digging into their duffel bags, so I follow suit. Luckily, one of the guys who speaks fluent English, Eyal, explains that we need to set up our two-man tents. He says, "I know how. You can help me."

By the time Eyal and I have put our tent together, Yanev returns. He's all business, but I can't help but be surprised that there isn't any overt hostility on the part of the commanders toward the recruits. Having been brought up on American movies, I was prepared for plenty of yelling and abuse. Instead, commanders are, at worst, simply brisk and matter-of-fact. In fact, over the last few weeks, they have acted like big brothers and caring teachers.

When we receive instructions or line up for inspection, we arrange ourselves in a shape that resembles the letter *U*. In Hebrew, the letter *Chet* resembles this shape.

Now, as we form up in a *Chet*, I know Yanev is going to make this the toughest week of my life, but I don't think he's looking forward to breaking us. When he orders us on a hike carrying stretchers laden with sandbags, his words are filled with empathy, not malice.

By late afternoon, the weight of the stretcher rests heavy on my shoulder, and despite our easy pace, the jostling grates against my skin. As we walk, Yanev asks each of us questions. He wants to know where we're from, and why we want to join the Sayerit. We may be a cross section of the country—from kibbutzim, from some of the wealthiest neighborhoods in Israel, and from some of the poorest—but our reasons for being here are all similar. We all want to serve our country and we all want to serve with the best. A few are looking to follow in a father's or brother's footsteps. The more I hear everyone respond similarly to this central question, the more I think that we all must have deeper, more personal reasons that we aren't quite willing to share just yet.

I don't need to check my watch to know that we've been out here for a while. The sun is beginning to set. We've been walking at an easy pace, but I am discovering that even this is difficult when you are carrying a loaded stretcher. When we stop to drink water, I feel a great sense of relief. It is clear that some of us are suffering more than others. Eyal seems to be taking it in stride.

After a two-minute break, we take up the stretchers again. Yanev picks up the pace and says, "We don't want to miss dinner."

None of us has eaten in hours, and we are all anxious to return to camp for a meal. We press on for another hour, weaving our way through dirt paths until we arrive at the field. We see several men already milling about, but as we arrive near our area Yanev says, "Just another hour until we're done."

His little trick works. All of a sudden, my energy and enthusiasm are wiped away. The stretcher feels heavier and my shoulder begins to ache. Yanev, speaking nonchalantly, says, "Come on, we don't want to be the last ones to finish, do we?"

We continue along another dirt path that slowly rises on an incline. At the top, we can see that we are on a high cliff facing the Mediterranean Sea below. Yanev says, "Lovely view, isn't it? Anyone up for a swim?"

Dror, a tall guy from Ashkelon, says, "Yes sir. Looking forward to it."

His overeager tone is dripping with sarcasm. Yanev shows his appreciation by saying, "Good. You all were going to have twenty minutes to get there and come back, but since you're so enthusiastic, I'd like to see you do it in fifteen. Move."

I don't know our distance to the water's edge, but it looks far. I don't know if we could have done it in twenty minutes. I doubt anyone is angry with Dror. If I understand that this is all part of the game, I'm sure they do as well. One by one, our stretchers make it down the steep, sandy hill that leads to the beach. The angle of descent and the deep sand cause the stretchers to feel heavier, and our attempt at speed makes our footing unsure. When we make it to the bottom of the hill, Eyal says, "Eleven minutes," and our three stretchers move as fast as our legs will carry them to the shore. When we arrive, Eyal says, "Nine minutes." As we run back to the hill, I no longer feel my shoulder's pain or my leg muscles' burn. We don't stop running when we reach the hill. No one has to call time or encourage us; we keep moving as fast as we can up the hill. When the last stretcher reaches the top, Yanev quietly asks, "Are you on time?"

Eyal answers, "No sir."

"And what did I say about being on time?"

Udi, who stands next to me in the front of one of the stretchers, says, "Being on time is holy."

Yanev shakes his head. "That's right. What am I going to do with you?"

We stand there silently for several minutes, the stretchers on our shoulders, as dusk is fast becoming night. Even Dror doesn't have anything to say. Yanev says, "Okay. I'll give you another chance. Twenty minutes to the shore and back again. Move."

Instead of being despondent or upset, I am exhilarated and full of energy. On the way down the hill, I notice that I'm not alone. The second time up the hill seems easier than the first and when Yanev asks if we've made it on time, I am filled with pride when Eyal says, "Yes sir."

After we trudge back to camp and are allowed to put the stretchers down, Yanev brings us tonight's dinner. Among the twelve of us, we are given a loaf of bread, two tomatoes, a cucumber, some jam, and a can of the Israeli version of Spam, which is made out of chicken. Handing the food to us, Yanev says, "This food is for dinner and breakfast. Save some for tomorrow morning. After you're done eating, set up a guard and get some sleep. You'll need it. Be up at six AM."

We carefully divide up the food and organize a list for guard duty. Each of us will stand guard outside our tents for only fifteen minutes tonight, because Eyal and the others doubt that we'll be sleeping until six. Unfortunately, they will be proven correct.

I greedily eat my slice of bread, a sliver of cucumber, a tomato wedge, and a piece of meat. The meal is far from satisfying, but I am more thirsty and tired than hungry.

Since I'll be the third person to stand guard, I make my way to my small tent. I lie on top of my sleeping bag with my boots on. Thirty minutes later, one of the guys taps my foot and I rise. He hands me the list and tells me that the next person on the list, Fur, can be found on the left-hand side of the third tent. I thank him and wish him good night.

When I finish my guard duty, Eyal is sound asleep. I close my eyes and pass out. We are awakened by loud shouts and explosions. Eyal jumps out of the tent while I put my boots on. I assemble with the rest of the team. Yanev is standing in front of us. He says, "I hope everyone had enough rest. We have a very busy day ahead of us."

As subtly as I can, I angle my arm so that I can see my watch. It's 12:30 AM. I've been asleep for less than an hour. Yanev says, "As you know, in the Israeli military we have a tradition. What we do during the day, we also do at night. Stretchers up."

We all run to the stretchers. Having learned from earlier in the day, I make sure that I am next to someone of equal height.

I'm beginning to get used to the stretcher. The next morning Yanev starts off at an easy pace. After a relatively short walk, we are given permission to lower our stretchers. Yanev says something very quickly, which I completely miss. Usually, one of the guys will take a moment to answer my inevitable questions. In this instance, everyone sprints into the forest without saying a word. At first, I'm left standing with Yanev and the other commanders, slightly bewildered. I don't know what I'm supposed to be doing, but I know enough to follow everyone else. They all have a few seconds' head start, but I'm surprised to discover that I've run for several minutes without seeing anyone.

While standing in the middle of the forest trying to figure out what to do next, I notice one of the guys covering himself with leaves behind a small bush. It doesn't take more than a moment for me to understand that we've been ordered to hide in the forest. I don't know when they're going to arrive, but I expect that Yanev and the others will be combing the forest soon and that my objective is not to be found.

Assuming I don't have much time, I run ahead a little until I find a large tree with lots of leaves at its base. The trunk is too narrow and without enough heavy branches for me to climb, so I gather as many leaves as I can find and use them as cover. As expected, when the commanders walk by, I'm immediately discovered. I'm pleased to see that almost everyone else was also caught fairly easily.

As a group, we all walk back to the main path, take a few swigs of water, lift the stretchers, and start walking. The route is circuitous. There are many lefts and rights. I'm not really sure where we are. I'm just glad that my feet are still moving. Nonchalantly, Yanev says, "Who can bring us back to the place we began?"

At first, no one answers. He says, "What, none of you was paying attention?"

Eyal says, "I'll try."

"Okay, Eyal, take your stretcher out front and lead away."

Despite many pauses, Eyal succeeds in bringing us back to the place where we ran into the forest. I don't know if Yanev notices, but I'm impressed.

From here, we continue walking toward a large dune with plenty of sand. From the smell of the air, it's clear that we're near the water. I am relieved to learn that we can drop our stretchers. One of the commanders says something about a circle. I don't know what he's talking about, but two members of my team do. Walking in opposite directions, they create a small trench with their feet that forms a large circle. When they are finished, we are told to drink some more water. As we form a *Chet,* Yanev stands in front of us and says something about staying in the circle. I don't know exactly what he means, but I enter the circle with everyone else.

I ask Eyal what's going on. "You've got to stay in the circle. If someone pushes you out, you lose."

Everyone is grinning boyishly, but underneath the embarrassed smiles I see the competitive spirit. I wonder if there are any rules, but there isn't time to ask. Yanev yells, "Now!"

I have just enough time to gain my senses as one of my teammates approaches. Stabilizing myself like a sumo wrestler, I dig my heels into the soft sand, lean forward, grab my adversary by his uniform, and start pushing him backward by keeping my arms locked and my feet moving forward. When he's near the edge, I give one quick shove and he's on the outside. I turn for a moment and see the mêlée. The single combat has changed into a free-for-all.

I push the person next to me, who is engaged in a tug-of-war with Dror, out of the circle. Dror has just enough time to smile before I throw him out as well. Instantly I'm attacked by two people. They successfully move me toward the circle's edge, so I drop to the ground. They try to lift me up, but they don't have much chance. While they try to work on me, they are attacked themselves by others. I'm tired and winded, but I quickly rise and am looking for my next challenge when someone grabs my collar from behind and starts pushing. He's smaller and leaner than me, but he is very strong and equally aggressive. We push and pull at each other without gaining any advantage until we find ourselves wrestling on the ground.

Eventually, several hands reach out to separate us. I see that my shirt is ripped; he looks fairly disheveled as well. As Yanev approaches, he and I both stand up. "Well, we're going to call this one as even. Is that okay with you two?"

I say it's okay with me.

We are given thirty minutes to eat and relax on the beach. It feels like a lifetime. When our time is up, Yanev approaches us.

"It is important to properly execute *scheela*.* For this reason, we are going to practice *scheela* until you get it right. Everybody up and form a line."

* Hebrew term for the method used by a soldier to lie flat on the ground and pull himself forward with his arms and feet.

I make my way to the end of the line, which seems to be turning into my usual tactic. If I'm close to the end, I'll have plenty of opportunity to watch what the others are doing and time to understand what I must do.

Once we have formed a line, we march toward the steep hill that leads back to the dunes above the beach. When we reach the very bottom of the hill, Yanev says to the first person in line, "Drop now. *Scheela* to the top and then back down again. Understood?"

I don't know what we are doing, but I respond with everyone else: "Yes sir."

I watch as the first person flattens his body against the ground, bending his arms at the elbows so that his hands are just above his head. He starts pulling his body forward with his bent arms and gaining added leverage by pushing with his legs. Yanev watches him inch forward, lifts his leg, lightly pushes the recruit's butt closer to the ground, and says, "Keep your butts low to the ground. Otherwise they'll be shot off."

One by one, we all become a dark green, panting, grumbling chain writhing up and down the steep sandy hill. I can't count the number of times I climb and descend. Very quickly, I become entirely focused on finding the strength to force my body forward. I ignore the thirst, the eyes stung by sweat I can't wipe away because I'm covered in sand, and the exhaustion. I remember the fear that I won't be good enough and let that make up for the lack of sleep, nutrients, and conditioning. While I climb, there are hundreds of small victories and seeming defeats. Eventually Yanev says, "Just one more. Let's see you do it."

Once we're finished, we all stand in our four rows of three men. I had hoped that standing would feel good after all the time on the ground, but I see that it's early in the afternoon and that the day has barely begun. Looking at the faces that surround me, I take little comfort in knowing that I'm not the only one having a difficult time. As ordered, we pick up the stretchers and climb a dirt track that leads to the top of a hill. We continue under Yanev's direction, but the monitors follow behind as we walk at a moderate pace. When we reach the top, we are given permission to lower the stretchers.

Yanev motions us to follow him, and we all walk toward a steep ledge that is covered in foliage and continues straight down to the bottom of the hill. Yanev says something about running to the bottom of the hill and returning to this spot, adding that he is watching out for us, but I don't understand the nature of the task. Once again, everyone takes off and I follow. I'm feeling frustrated about not being able to understand, and as we jog to the bottom of the hill, I ask Eyal what we need to do. "Climb to the top of the hill without them seeing us," he says. "If they see you, they will call your name. The person who reaches them without being caught wins."

While everyone races toward the bottom of the hill, Eyal pauses. "Adam, I have an idea. Follow me."

"Where?"

"I know how to get around Yanev and the others. Come with me."

Torn between my desire to trust Eyal and an increasingly reflexive need to mimic the actions taken by everyone else, I say, "No, I'm not sure. We should go with the others."

"I think you're all going to get caught. You choose what you want. I'm going this way."

As I watch him take off in the opposite direction, in an apparent attempt to find another way, I sprint to the bottom of the hill, lie flat on my stomach, and begin a slow, determined, climb to the top. One by one, Yanev and the others call our names. I am pleased to be one of the last people caught, but I am only a little more than halfway up the hill when I hear my name. While Yanev and the others are looking for the last two people along the edge of the hill, Eyal appears from behind us. Pretending to shoot us with live ammunition, he shouts, *"Aish! Aish! Aish!"* Fire!

Yanev and the monitors turn around in surprise. They are all smiles and congratulate him. While the rest of us are speaking with Eyal and feeling glad that at least one of us got the better of the commanders, Yanev says, "Tal, I see you. Come on out."

After another night of running around in the darkness interrupted only by *scheela,* we return to our tents. A small pool of water has formed in the slight decline where I stowed my sleeping bag. It is soaked.

I lie down on top of my bag with my boots on, listen to the rain strike the tent, watch the pool of water by my face grow, fall asleep, and then wake up abruptly when I hear shouts. Once again, they aren't going to let us sleep. I gulp down water from my canteen and walk toward the stretchers.

I am surprised to see that we are no longer twelve people. There are only ten of us. I assume that the others are in the bathroom or still sleeping, but Yanev sets me straight. "As you can see, two members of this team have decided to leave. If anyone here wants to be warm, dry, or eat a decent meal, just step forward right now. There is no shame in it."

No one steps forward.

Between the endless walking with the stretchers, the *scheela,* and all the other small tasks we're asked to accomplish until nearly dawn, I arrive at a point where I no longer feel the pain emanating from the torn skin on my bruised shoulders and don't seem to be bothered by my rubbery legs. I'm light-headed and a little dizzy, but I assume that this is because of my exhaustion and the food rationing. When we return to our tents, I fall asleep immediately. Forty-five minutes later, I am awakened for guard duty.

In the night, it seems that we lost another. We don't talk much about the fact that people are leaving, except to say that it is a shame. We take the stretchers back to the beach, run with them in the water, and make our way back to the forested section of the training ground.

After lunch we all sit in a circle. For the fourth or fifth time, we engage in a discussion that Yanev initiates and moderates while the monitors take notes. For the first time, we are all given sheets of paper and pencils. We are asked to answer the questions on the paper. I ask Eyal to translate for me. He lets me know that the purpose of the questionnaire is for us to grade each other. The questions ask me to identify who has demonstrated leadership abilities and other desirable attributes, but the ones I bet matter more than the others are the questions asking me to write the names of those on my team I think should be allowed to join the Sayerit and those who should not.

During a brief interlude, one of the guys confides that he is thinking of quitting. As I do my best to convince him to stay, I realize that my own resolve has stiffened as a consequence. When we rise again, I take up the stretcher and confidently indicate that I'm able to take the lead and navigate our way back through the forest to our starting point. No one is more surprised than me when we find ourselves on the trail that runs parallel to the field where our tents are pitched.

By the next dawn, we are down to seven. There are more stretchers, *scheela,* discussions, opportunities to rate one another's performance, and tasks. In addition, individual runs are timed, as are the number of sit-ups and push-ups we can complete in a set amount of time. We are even given thirty minutes to write a poem or a song to express how we're feeling about our experience. Although I'm given the option of writing something in English, I stubbornly cling to the belief that using English would be an admission of defeat. I'm sure I make little sense, but everyone is supportive. As always, monitors with clipboards make marks on paper every step of the way.

It's finally over. We have put the stretcher down for the last time. The sandbags are emptied, our tents are taken down, and our equipment is packed. Yanev personally wishes each of us good luck and thanks us for our perseverance. We are served hot tea for the first time since we arrived here five days ago. Before we leave, we are called up individually for an interview that is similar to the panel discussion we experienced when we were first selected for paratrooper training.

I am asked why I want to join the Sayerit. They ask about my age and if I think that will impact my ability to work well with my teammates. They want to know if I'm willing to sign on for an additional year. I answer these questions and others. Even though I again choose to speak Hebrew despite their giving me the opportunity to speak in English, this time I feel I have done an adequate job presenting myself.

Those of us who completed the testing period are taken back to Sanur by bus. I am greeted enthusiastically by Jonathan and the others. Each tells me about the moment when he decided to quit and seems very impressed that I lasted until the end. They are all confident that I will be chosen for the Sayerit, but I know that everyone on my team showed the same level of determination and ability. I am surprised to discover that many teams finished with only three or four people; in one instance, a team was reduced to two. Five hundred people started the testing and fewer than seventy of us finished.

A couple of days pass. We all wait anxiously because we are going to be divided into four paratrooper companies. Three of the companies will be trained for fourteen months. When the training is complete, each company will disband and the soldiers will either join one of the three paratrooper battalions or be sent to officer training school. The fourth company will be comprised of the Sayerit, the Chan, and the Orev platoons. They will train for nearly eighteen months. Those who complete that training will belong to one of three units that directly support missions planned by the commander of the paratrooper brigade. I still can't differentiate among the various units, but I know that I want to be asked to join them. Finally, we are all called into a large auditorium. I sit on the floor next to Jonathan, Martin, and Nathan.

One of the commanders starts calling out names of the twenty or so people who are being selected for the Sayerit. As each person rises and walks to the center of the auditorium, we all clap in acknowledgment of the achievement. Several members of my training team are called. I'm not surprised to hear Eyal's name. My name is not called. Jonathan and the others are quick to tell me not to worry. The names for the Chan are read and again my name is not among them. I do my best to hide my disappointment but I doubt that I'm doing a very good job of it.

The only consolation is that I am sent to the same battalion as Jonathan and Nathan. It hurts that they didn't consider me good enough for the Sayerit, but I must have done very poorly because I wasn't even asked to join the Chan.

The company I join is divided into three platoons. Jonathan and Nathan are in the first platoon; I'm in the third. When I enter the long barracks that houses the approximately seventy-five members of my platoon, I feel alone. I'm the only foreign-born national in the company. The guys seem standoffish, but I realize that this may just be an expression of my own anxiety and a reflection of my current disposition.

Stashing my gear on an available cot, I ask if we have any orders for tonight. I am told that we are free to sleep until five in the morning. My name is added to the guard list. Not ready to sleep and needing to see familiar and friendly faces, I visit Jonathan and Nathan. We speak for a bit before I wish them *Liela tov*—good night. While walking back to my barracks, I decide to try talking to the commander from the Chan. It can't hurt and it might help.

I climb up the hill to where the Chan is stationed and ask for Gal. "Herman. What can I do for you?"

"I understand that it may be too late, but is there any way for me to join the Chan?"

Taken slightly aback, as if this is the last thing he expects to hear from me, he says he's sorry. It is too late. There's nothing he can do for me.

Seeing the disappointment in my face, he says, "Don't worry. You're with a very good unit. You'll see. It's going to be okay."

I thank him and turn around quickly because I am so filled with emotion that I feel near tears. I walk slowly back to my barracks wishing I had just gone to bed.

Chapter 3

The Basics

I am still deeply disappointed not to be selected for any of the specialized units, but I'm going to do my best to keep a positive attitude.

Luckily, several guys in my platoon speak a sufficient amount of English to help explain orders. I feel like an outsider, but everyone in the platoon tries to make me feel like a part of the group.

For the first few days, our three platoon sergeants instruct us in basic military discipline. The sergeants start with the importance of always being on time. For instance, if we don't arrange our heavy assault vests in neat rows of three within the time set by a sergeant, we are ordered to put them on. Then the sergeant points to a pole or some other object in the distance and says, "You see that pole? From right to left. Thirty seconds. Move."

In a mad dash, we all run toward the pole, scurry around it, and sprint back to the sergeant, who watches our every move. Planting ourselves right in front of the sergeant, we tumble ourselves into rows that are three recruits deep. We never make it back in thirty seconds on the first try. The sergeant says, "That's horrible. That took you over a minute. You have thirty seconds. Move."

The platoon runs back and forth literally dozens of times before finally completing the task in thirty seconds. As one of the faster runners, I am among the first to reach the sergeant. Instead of being appreciative, he says, "Being fast does you no good. Why aren't you helping the others?"

The fast and strong learn that our fate is tied to the success of the entire group. As a result, we start pushing and pulling the slower members of the platoon forward. In this way, our roles and responsibilities are defined. The strong learn to help the weak, and the weak push their own limits so as not to hinder the progress of the group.

Since childhood I have watched movies and TV series that depict US military training, and I spoke with Israelis prior to my induction, but Israeli military training is nothing like I expected. Israeli commanders don't invade my personal space and scream insults at me. They calmly and quietly run us into the ground. It is more grueling than I ever imagined, but it is far more hospitable and fair than I thought possible.

The first officer who speaks to us is the commander of the paratrooper brigade. When this high-ranking officer, known as Boogie, arrives, all four companies are assembled together.

We aren't ordered to arrange ourselves into a military formation. We all stand relaxed as if we are being addressed by a principal at a school rally, but his speech isn't designed to rouse us with good cheer. Instead, he says that many of us will not complete our paratrooper training. He speaks about the complex nature of today's battlefield and the dangers it poses. Although he lauds our commanders and us for being specially selected, he mostly forewarns us of the dangers and difficulties that lie ahead.

I don't understand everything he says, but it is clearly meant to be sobering. As we all walk back to our barracks, a lanky youth from the north, Yiron, says, "Makes you wish you'd stayed in the United States, doesn't it?"

"Was the speech that bad?"

"Well, he said many of us will quit, be injured, or be killed."

I say to him, "I'm not going to quit, but I can't say I like the alternatives, either. What about you?"

"I still don't know how I got accepted here in the first place. I'm sure they'll figure it out soon enough and find me a place in the kitchen."

I understand exactly how he feels.

That night, at about 1 AM, our sergeants storm into the barracks shouting.

Reacting as quickly as we can, we pull on our boots, grab our weapons, take a magazine full of bullets, and scramble into formation in front of our barracks. When we're assembled, the recruit who is standing in front of the first row shouts, "Ready for attention."

And we all shout in unison, "Attention."

The sergeants look us over. They don't look particularly happy, and I expect that we're going to be running all night long. As if to confirm my fears, the first sergeant, Aran, says, "After me at a run."

We follow him at a steady clip in the dark. Climbing one of the steep hills that border the base, we eventually crawl through a hole in the fence and continue running into the hills. Finally, we stop in a small clearing shrouded by surrounding trees, and I see that we are not alone. The two other platoons of our company are already assembled. Each platoon forms one side of the U-shaped formation that is typically used to create a forum for discussion. It is a dark night, but the area is dimly illuminated by several torches.

While my platoon forms up opposite the second platoon, I watch the light from the flames reflect in the faces of the men standing in front of me. The sergeants stand in front of each platoon, with their backs to us. I wait silently and immobile like the others. Before I have a chance to start imagining the purpose of our being here, someone shouts, "Attention for the company commander!"

In the last couple of weeks, I have had only glimpses of the officer who commands my platoon. Waking us in the middle of the night, having us run in the darkness, and arriving to find the rest of the company bathed in firelight is dramatic, but none of it was necessary. This is the company commander. He's a captain with the Israeli paratroopers. He's been serving for four or five years. We've been in the military for about a month. To be a company commander, he must be an exemplary leader in the field, demonstrate the highest levels of skill in combat, and be trusted to transform us into some of the best soldiers in the world. Before we even see him or hear his voice, we feel we're about to meet a god.

When this tall, dark-haired, sharp-featured figure strides forth, he seems as if he were born for the role. All eyes are trained on him, and our bodies remain taut as we listen. Following the cultural norm of identifying soldiers by the month and year of their induction, he addresses us.

"November Zero, you have the good fortune to have joined the best company in the military. Your officers and sergeants have been specially selected from the best units in the military. You all volunteered to be paratroopers, and to be a paratrooper means to be the best. You are going to work harder and achieve more than you ever thought possible. You were all chosen to join this company because you are among the nation's best. Your officers, sergeants, and I are going to demand nothing less than one hundred and ten percent from you at all times. That's how you become the best and I tell you now that we are going to be the best paratrooper unit in the entire brigade."

And without another word, he stands silently as if he's looking right through us. To the side of him, I can see the company's three officers. I am pretty sure I can make out my platoon's officer. He's the tall, muscular one with a square jaw and a look of smoldering anger. Someone shouts, "Attention, the company commander departs."

About one hundred men shout in unison, "Attention!"

One by one, each platoon makes its own way to the barracks. We are all too excited to go directly to bed. Everyone is chattering away, describing their reactions and impressions. Some provide snippets of gossip regarding the things they've heard about our company commander. It is said that he came to the company after having commanded a team in the Sayerit. It's clear that he made quite an impression on all of us.

Since literally every waking moment is filled with training and eating with members of my platoon, I rarely see Jonathan and Nathan. Given the language barrier and the lack of even a moment's respite, I don't know much about the people with whom I serve. When we communicate, it is to clarify our orders, ask to borrow someone's cleaning equipment, or make an offer to help, but I don't think any of us knows much about the interests or thoughts of the other members of the platoon. The important thing is that we all learn quickly who works hard and who doesn't.

Of the thirty or so members of my platoon, there are five of us who consistently volunteer for additional duties and actively work toward making sure that the platoon completes tasks on time. The others claim that they are too busy preparing their personal equipment to help, or simply disappear for short periods of time to catch up on much-needed sleep. But there isn't time for resentment.

Most days begin the same. The last soldier on guard duty wakes us all at a time designated by one of the sergeants, which is usually around 5 AM. We all quickly climb out of our cots, put on our gym clothes, sling our Galil rifles around our necks, grab a magazine full of bullets, and assemble outside. Someone always lags behind the rest of us or someone forgets his magazine and needs to run back inside the barracks. Either way, it seems like we are often in danger of not being ready on time.

On those mornings when we're not ready, the sergeant who has arrived to take us on our morning exercise must first discipline us. The punishments vary, but invariably the sergeant says, "Time is holy. When you are given a time, you will meet it. Is this clear?"

We all shout, "Yes sir."

He says, "Okay. Position Number 2."

The entire platoon drops to the ground, we all place our guns by our side, and look as if we are going to perform push-ups, but we're not that lucky. Instead, the sergeants will keep us locked in midair until our arms shake. Those who collapse from fatigue are immediately reprimanded. The punishment lasts until we are all left exhausted.

I am amazed that a task that would be easy for one person to complete becomes nearly impossible when more than thirty people try to do it together. It doesn't take us long to realize that the key to success is for the thirty of us to work together as if we were one unit. To accomplish this, some of us push the slower people forward during runs, keep track of time when we're trying to complete a task, and establish order out of chaos by giving commands to our peers.

I'm beginning to worry about my language skills. Yes, it is nice to know that whenever I try to give a command, I unintentionally elevate morale by amusing everyone with my butchered Hebrew, but the downside of this situation is becoming more and more apparent.

When we learn basic field medical techniques, I watch the instructor closely and mimic the others as they work. Although everyone makes mistakes, mine are due to misunderstanding the sergeant's instructions.

For instance, I create a tourniquet *below* Roni's imaginary leg wound. If this were real, he would bleed to death. Errors at this stage are without consequence, but I start wondering if I should have taken a year to learn more Hebrew before I entered the military. My lack of understanding is a source of constant frustration, and now I worry that I'm going to get someone killed.

As a result, I create a list of the commands we use each day. Often, when I can't remember how the command is pronounced, I ask someone to help me before I write the phrase phonetically in English on a notepad. I study my list every night before I sleep. When I master a word, I put a check next to it. Every day the list grows, but my progress is slow.

One afternoon, our sergeant, Yotam, takes us to the outdoor gun range just beyond the base and orders us to plant fifteen green cardboard cutouts shaped like soldiers twenty-five meters from where we'll be shooting.

After two yellow bull's-eye targets are stapled to the top and bottom of each cardboard cutout, we divide into two groups. I always choose to be in the second group, giving myself the opportunity to understand the commands as well as make a connection between the orders given and the actions taken by the members of the first group.

This is the third time I've ever fired my weapon, and it is still a nerve-racking experience. While the actual shot doesn't rattle me, I become flustered every time I have to repeat and follow a series of commands I don't understand. Now that it's my group's turn, I step forward with the others and wait for the first command. "Magazines in!"

Along with everyone else, I repeat "Magazines in" as I place the magazine inside the opening at the bottom of the weapon. The commander says, "Everyone in prone position," and as I lie down with the others, I mumble something that sounds similar to the command given.

For the sixth time, I hear a description of how to aim and shoot the weapon. Unfortunately, I only understand enough to know how to load and fire the gun. I'm not clear on whether I'm supposed to pull the trigger when I exhale or when I hold my breath. Every time I hear it explained, I seem to miss a critical word that would make the instructions clear. The commander then says something else I don't understand before ordering, "Load your weapons."

Once again, I mumble the first part and then say, "Load your weapons," as I slide the bolt back to put a bullet into the chamber.

The commander says, "Fire when ready."

Despite the white plastic earplugs the military has provided and the fact that we are all shooting a single bullet at a time, it's an unsettling experience. Instead of concentrating on the target, I focus on the noise of the bullets being fired, the sight of the shells falling on the ground, and the smell that accompanies the shooting. I try to hold my weapon steadily, look through the sights, and focus on my target. I try firing while holding my breath and firing as I exhale. I'm not sure which one works better. I also do my best to keep my eyes open when I pull the trigger. After my third shot, the sergeant kicks my legs and says, "Herman, keep your legs open."

I don't understand the commands any better by the end of my third round of firing, but I realize that I feel more comfortable and get better results when I shoot during my exhalation. I certainly won't be winning any awards for marksmanship today, but as I help lug the targets back to the base, I notice that my shooting is on par with many of my peers.

The rest of the day is spent practicing waterproofing our bandages and learning other techniques to prepare our equipment for the field. One thing is clear: Good soldiers pay close attention to detail. At the very least, it seems as if the only chance of avoiding punishment is to be a perfectionist. Since the sergeants can always find fault with something we've done, much of our day is spent performing push-ups or running to point B and returning to point A in under thirty seconds.

I don't resent the punishments; I am aware that these are as essential to our training as learning to shoot and carrying a stretcher. They are meant to train us to follow commands, understand the value of time, take our work seriously, and appreciate the value of teamwork, to say nothing of instilling an understanding of the hierarchy and our place in it. And all that running around has to be good for our conditioning.

Even while being run ragged, I keep all this in mind. I see how exasperated many members of my team become. I don't know that my insight would reassure them—in fact, I'm sure they all know it themselves—but I still find it frustrating that I can't share my thoughts with the others. I do the only thing I can do—I push the weaker people from behind, keep time, and encourage everyone with smiles. During training, the sergeants often urge us to be more intense by saying that we must have *"retsach bi'anigh"*—murder in our eye. Sometimes while we are being punished, I shout the phrase with my strong American accent that they all find so amusing. I hope by introducing some levity, I'll help distract those who feel overwhelmed. For myself, making a joke of it all lightens my own load and serves as a reminder that these sprints will eventually end and we'll move on to the next thing.

Following standard Israeli Defense Forces procedure, the training exercise undertaken during the day is repeated at night. After dinner, I find myself back at the shooting range, repeating commands and shooting as best I can. Unfortunately, I learn that my night vision isn't nearly as good as the others'.

Night shooting begins by standing next to our targets and slowly walking backward. We are told to shout when we can no longer see our target. Several paces after walking back, I don't see my target, but fail to raise my voice, embarrassed.

Once we've reached the point where someone had the courage to acknowledge his weakness, we fire three sets of rounds. Though my target is invisible, I have a good guess where it is. At the end of each set, we check our results. Mine aren't terribly impressive, but they aren't discernibly worse than anyone else's. I am grateful for this small favor.

Once we're done shooting, we run back to our barracks. It's just past 10:30 PM. We have thirty minutes to clean our weapons and provide the sergeants with tonight's guard duty list. Every night we need to create a list that designates when and where each of us will be on guard duty. At 11 PM, one of our platoon sergeants, Tzvi, arrives to check our weapons. He checks each weapon, tells each of us how our work can be improved, and gives us another thirty minutes to get it right. On his second visit, Tzvi relents. We are free from group activity until the morning.

Before basic training, we were responsible for guarding only our barracks. Now each platoon takes an active part in guarding the base as well. Two patrols walk along different sections of the base's perimeter; several stationary areas need to be guarded as well. Most nights, each of us guards at least an additional hour. Given the limited opportunity to rest, every minute counts. For this reason, failure to replace a guard on time is considered a great affront.

In this instance, we don't need the sergeants to tell us that being on time is holy. For every minute that someone is late, the person being replaced loses a minute of sleep. People who are repeat offenders are labeled "sociomats."

In the military, to be called a sociomat—a person who only cares about himself—is the worst kind of insult. Only after being left waiting at various stations for thirty minutes, an hour, and once for two hours, do I understand why the Sayerit placed such importance on the questionnaires that asked us to rate the personalities of the members of the team. Especially for a small, close-knit unit like the Sayerit, it's vital to exclude any potential sociomats.

Even though we are in the middle of the West Bank and close to the nearby Arab village of Sanur, none of us is really concerned about infiltrators. We are told that Palestinians have attempted infiltrations in the past to steal weapons and ammunition, and have even attacked recruits. It's not that we don't believe this to be true, but it does seem rather unlikely that someone would consider a base filled with hundreds of paratroopers a vulnerable target. Our only real concern is that one of the sergeants or an officer will catch us being negligent in our duties.

Catching a nap while on guard duty is a relatively common offense, and the punishment often means having to forfeit a weekend leave. At the very least, the punishment will involve quite a bit of running.

Besides the physical training and the focus on discipline, we endure a seemingly endless succession of inspections. Although our cots and the barracks need to be neat, the sergeants aren't interested in the way we've made our beds, and even *their* uniforms are a wrinkled mess. They *do* pay very close attention to whether we have prepared our assault vests correctly or if our bandages have been properly sealed so as to remain sterile in the worst weather. Also, almost every other day we need to open one of our wool blankets and place all our equipment on it. We need to show that we have two canteens, nine magazines, one assault vest, one helmet, three sets of uniforms, two pairs of socks, the underwear no one uses, one sleeping bag, canvas for a two-man tent, several short metal spikes for the tents, a medium-sized bag, a shovel, two wool blankets, a polyester jacket, knee pads that we aren't allowed to use, a plastic cup, a spoon, a fork, a knife, and several other items that fill the large duffel bag called the kitbag.

It seems as if every time we are inspected I am missing one item or another. At first, I assume I'm being careless. Throughout my life, I've lost wallets, cameras, plane tickets—it's not unusual for me to be for-getful. But losing equipment is a serious and punishable offense, and as the days pass, I start paying closer attention to mine. I place smaller items on or in larger items so as not to let them slip away. Before I fin-ish a task and leave an area, I take an extra moment to make sure I have everything I brought with me. There is some improvement, but I'm still usually missing one item or another. It's inexplicable until I mention my frustration to David, a member of my platoon who speaks English. "Well, you know, some people may be helping themselves."

It is as if he just told me the world is flat. "Why would they do that?"

A roguish smile emerges on his face. "You know, people lose things and they need them. So maybe some of them help themselves."

It sounds to me like he is speaking from personal experience. I start placing my duffel bag under my cot at night. When I leave for guard duty, I place it in the nook between my cot and the wall. I use my sleep-ing bag to cover it up and keep it hidden. I stop losing items and won-der if it's because of my precautions or if David has asked the others to take pity on me. Either way is fine by me.

All days are hard, but Thursday night is the longest. Thursdays are called White Nights. I don't know where the idiom came from, but it refers to the tradition of keeping recruits awake all night long. No one sleeps on Thursday. At first, we are kept up practicing various tech-niques for the preparation of our equipment. Of course, it's a perfect night to dole out punishing runs as well. The tasks and training for each Thursday have all been different, except for the fact that we never get to sleep.

Tonight, I discover, marks an important milestone in our evolution as soldiers. Tonight there will be a forced march. David tells me that we will have a forced march every Thursday until the end of basic training, which is three months from now. In military time, three months is a lifetime. Each time, the forced marches will be longer. Since this will be our first one, tonight's will be short and relatively easy. Before the end of basic training, we'll work up to a ninety-kilometer march.

After dinner, Yotam enters our barracks and gives us orders to prepare the stretchers. Although many of the guys look anxious, the testing for the Sayerit taught me that I can carry stretchers as well as most.

Most of the night is spent preparing our equipment for the march. Around 2 AM, Yotam makes a fifth and final check of our equipment. He gives us five minutes to assemble outside. Our platoon is quickly divided into three groups. In each group, someone carries a stretcher. I take the stretcher for my group. Given my unimpressive height and the way the stretcher is tied to my pack, its handles constantly hit the back of my head as we walk. Each group walks in two columns toward the base's main gate. The first group leaves with Tzvi at its head, the second with Nitzan. Yotam talks to us for several minutes. It's clear that he's just killing time so they can create space between our groups.

When Yotam believes enough time has passed, he says, "Third platoon. This is your first march. Work together and you can accomplish anything. Two columns after me, let's go."

In two short lines behind him, we follow as he marches at a near run ahead of us along the main road parallel to the base. With a straight back and his hand gripping his M-16, he looks like he is ready for anything. While we all struggle to keep up, he seems to move effortlessly.

Sooner than I would have expected, the lights from our base are swallowed up by the night. There aren't any streetlights and there's no moon out. I focus on sustaining my pace and trusting Yotam. The march is much longer than I thought it would be. We've been out for a while and I'm exhausted, but this isn't unusual. To buttress myself, I remind myself that I endured a longer, more difficult march with heavy stretchers when I tested for the Sayerit. Looking at those around me, I know I'm not the only one who is tiring.

Along the side of the road, I notice silhouettes of large houses. Yotam marches us forward. The road gradually narrows, and we climb a rolling, curvy hill. Concentrating on each step, my head is mostly lowered and my eyes are focused on the road. Suddenly, Yotam stops and I look up to see a dense neighborhood of homes. We also see another group from the second platoon. They are marching toward us.

I don't need to be told that this isn't part of the plan. No one would take a group of untrained recruits into an Arab village.

Yotam and the sergeant from the other platoon, Aviad, talk to each other for a few minutes. I notice that Aviad is carrying a radio; Yotam isn't. Since this was meant to be a short hike along the main road, it was probably decided that Yotam didn't need one. Aviad speaks briefly into his radio and he and Yotam confer again.

Yotam returns and says, "We've made a mistake. Obviously, we shouldn't be here. We're going to join Sergeant Aviad and his group and return together. We'll take the lead, and Sergeant Aviad will follow. Any questions?"

When no one responds, he says, "Stay in two columns. Let's move quickly and quietly."

He doesn't appear nervous or anxious, but it's clear that he is taking our situation seriously. Exhaustion is immediately forgotten and adrenaline takes over. It's around 3 AM. I know we're not going to run into a mob at this hour, but my body recognizes the difference between training in a controlled environment and a real-world experience.

Either Yotam knows a quicker way back to the main road or he makes a mistake. I'm certain we're on a different path than the one we marched up, but I keep this thought to myself. After several minutes of running along the road, Yotam climbs over a three-foot-high stone wall that hugs the length of the road. We follow him into an orchard parallel to the road. My guess is that he wants to keep us out of sight.

In the orchard, our pace slows. We haven't been in here for more than ten minutes when I hear a noise. Yotam drops to the ground instantly. Turning to us and speaking in a low whisper, he says, "Down. Down. Everyone down." Like everyone else, I drop, mimicking Yotam by dropping to one knee, but everyone interprets Yotam's command differently. I notice that the noise's rhythm has picked up, but it isn't until I see Aviad run toward Yotam with his body bent that my brain finally translates the noise and I understand that someone is shooting.

Yotam and Aviad engage in a quick conversation before Aviad points his arm toward the road and says, "Stay low and move toward the road. Sit beneath the stone wall." No one runs. We do as we're told. We make our way to the road and stretch ourselves out in single file against the stone wall. I see Aviad speaking on the radio and watch Yotam pace along the side of the road as the bullets continue to bang away. Luckily, the snipers shoot worse than me. Yotam says, "Place your magazines inside your weapons. But do not load your guns. Keep your safeties on."

Before today, I've probably placed a magazine in my weapon fewer than twenty times. This is the first time I've had to do it because I may need to shoot someone. Sitting against the wall, I wonder how I'm going to react. With the sound of the bullets in the background, I realize that I am not overcome by fear. I'm anxious and nervous, but I'm ready and willing to stand up if necessary.

Yotam jumps over the rock wall and enters the orchard alone. I watch as he stands and shouts, "Put your weapons down. We are soldiers of the red beret. Paratroopers. Stop firing now and come out."

I don't know whether his actions are brave, stupid, or useless. I've been in the military for only a month and barely know how to use my rifle. I certainly don't know anything about tactics, but when he says the words *red beret* his pride in himself and his unit is evident. The words reverberate in my ears, and an echo of that feeling takes root in me.

Time passes and I eventually notice that the weapons fire has stopped. Aviad, who has been on the radio, signals Yotam with his hand. Yotam says, "Take your magazines out and prepare to be checked."

We follow the order as if we were at a gun range and not on the edge of an Arab village. With his flashlight, Yotam makes sure that there aren't any bullets in the chambers of our weapons.

After he has checked our rifles, he says, "Raise your weapons to ninety degrees and clear your weapons. Then return your safety."

After our weapons quietly click, indicating empty chambers, Yotam says, "Two columns after me."

It is still night, but it is decidedly lighter out now. A few minutes later, we round a corner and I see two trucks, several jeeps, about ten soldiers talking among themselves, a few Israelis in civilian clothing, and two blindfolded Arab men sitting on the road.

Yotam greets the soldiers with a wide smile. I've never seen them before, but he obviously knows them. After he and Aviad speak with them for several moments, Yotam takes the group aside and says, "If you want, you can take the trucks back to base. It's been a long night and I understand that. But if you're willing, we can finish this evening like paratroopers. What do you say?"

None of us hesitates. We all readily agree to return to base the same way we left it, on foot. I don't know if Aviad's group decided to take a ride or not, but we don't see them as we run back to the main road. Whether it's the fact that we've had some rest or the excitement of the night, we all seem to have plenty of energy.

When we arrive at the barracks, Yotam asks us to stand in a *Chet*. Once we have assembled ourselves, he says, "You did well tonight. All of you. Now tell me, how did you feel?"

None of us knows quite how to respond.

"Were you afraid? It's okay to be afraid. I just want to know how you're feeling."

Again, no one knows how to answer. A few awkward phrases are expressed, but none of us seems capable of describing his reaction to tonight's events. Yotam looks at me. "What about you, Herman?"

I say, "I'm fine. I wasn't worried really. But I don't understand what happened."

Yotam explains. I don't catch everything, but a few things are clear. We ended up on the outskirts of the Arab village of Sanur by mistake. A couple of Arabs saw us and thought we were coming to kill them. Aviad contacted the base, and they sent soldiers to apprehend them. It seems that the Shin Bet—the Israeli equivalent of the FBI, which is primarily charged with counterterror activities—was there as well.

Before releasing us, Yotam says, "You were meant to go three kilometers tonight. In the end, you went almost thirteen. You did well. Good night."

In the next couple of days, I learn that Yotam wasn't at fault. A sergeant from the Sayerit was supposed to be waiting on the side of the road to provide Yotam with a signal that would lead us back to the base. When Aviad's group and later our group passed by, the sergeant was relieving himself in the woods.

Because they never received the signal to stop, Yotam and Aviad marched much farther than planned. They should have realized that they had missed their turning point long before we reached Sanur, but they were just being hardheaded, by-the-book soldiers. Although I expect more thoughtfulness and initiative from my commanders, I can't help but hope to emulate the calm and professional manner with which these two nineteen-year-olds handled our situation.

Chapter 4

Field Training

A little more than a week after my first forced march, the four paratrooper companies pick up and move to the main basic training camp, Cha'mam. Since both Sanur and Cha'mam are in the West Bank, we are again driven in fortified buses. Wire mesh frames the windows to keep stones and Molotov cocktails from penetrating the Plexiglas.

When we arrive, the first thing I notice is that Cha'mam is more compact than Sanur. It is nearly devoid of buildings. At Sanur, we slept in barracks and ate in a small cafeteria; even though we spent most of our waking hours training outside, we were surrounded by physical structures that gave shape to the base. By comparison, Cha'mam seems vacant and is given shape by the shrubs and not-so-distant hills.

As I help unload our platoon's gear, I see a concrete rectangle the size of a basketball court. On either side of the rectangle is a row of small cement squares that are used as floors for tents. The only structure appears to be a small lavatory. From the size of it, it's hard to believe that it is meant to meet the needs of the two hundred men from the two companies who will be based here.

One thing's for sure: I'm going to be living in and eating out of tents for the next several months. I've led a fairly cushy life, but I've always enjoyed camping. I'm not concerned about the living conditions.

We raise the tents and stow the company's equipment. It's late at night by the time we're done. Settling into our platoon's tent, I select a cot in the middle because it is near a lightbulb. This will make it easier for me to read at night. Also, I've learned from bitter experience that the wind and rain creep through the corners. I'll be warmer and drier if I stay in the middle.

It's been a long day and night, but the sergeants decide that our equipment must be thoroughly inspected before we go to bed. My ability to clean and organize my gear has improved, and it pays off. Tonight Yotam needs to look deep into my weapon before he finds something wrong. I expect that it'll take hours before they let us pass inspection, but I'm delighted that it took him more than a cursory look to discover an area that required improvement.

Our first days at Cha'mam are similar to Sanur. The days begin with a morning run, pull-ups, push-ups, brief inspections followed by punishments, and a quick breakfast. Our experience is different from Sanur, though, in two significant ways. First, since the base is much smaller, guard duty is less of an issue. Second, the training is far more intense and lasts much further into the night.

We are now ruled by the clock. Even the amount of time given for bathroom breaks is allotted by our sergeants.

Our sergeants and commander remain psychologically distant, but they are still more like demanding teachers than the tyrants I imagined. They encourage questions and provide instruction in a calm, professional manner. Not only do our commanders fail to bark at us, but I am keenly aware that the men with whom I serve are also very quiet.

There's no chanting of military cadence or singing of bawdy tunes while we run. People shout commands, but other than a few furtive glances while training, there is only silence and concentration on the assigned task.

The commanders first focus on developing our ability to move and fire our weapons. We line a hill with multiple cardboard targets, each about the size and shape of a person's head. To each target we attach a balloon. Then we return to our starting point and line up to drill. As always, I place myself near the end of the line in order to watch and learn from the others.

When it's my turn, Yotam says, "Begin your search," and continues with the overly complicated command that is used to start us off. I repeat the command as best I can and, with Yotam walking behind me, look straight ahead, move forward, and rely on my peripheral vision to find the targets.

I don't know exactly where they are because we distributed them an hour ago and many of them have been repositioned during the exercise. Yotam shouts, "You're under attack!" and I see my first target on my left. I notice that it blends easily with the stones and brush. Quickly, I slam the weapon into the nook between my left pectoral muscle and my shoulder. While lowering my head to look through the sights, my right forefinger reaches for the safety, and I shout, "Fire. Fire. Fire."

I continue moving up the hill, shouting "Fire" every time I see a target. As always, every exercise begins with a dry run. I run up the hill and continue along for a few minutes more, pretending to fire my weapon several times along the way. Finally, Yotam shouts, *"Sofe targeel"* (End exercise). On the way back down, he says, "You did okay, Herman. Remember you're being fired at. You need to hit the ground every three seconds. Is this understood?"

"Yes sir. Thank you, sir."

I've just completed the easy part. Next it's with live bullets. Yotam begins this exercise, "Raise your gun ninety degrees."

I have protected my hearing with makeshift earplugs made of toilet paper. Repeating and acting on each of Yotam's orders, I insert a magazine in the receiver, pull back the bolt, and flick the safety back on. "Begin your search."

I start walking and muddle the command I'm supposed to repeat. I think it refers to looking for the enemy, but I don't know for sure. Yotam ignores the fact that I'm talking gibberish. He and the other sergeants are used to it by now.

With a bullet in the chamber, my tension level increases tenfold. This is exactly the same exercise I completed moments ago, but my weapon is no longer a piece of metal, it's a deadly force and I'm going to pull the trigger. Will I pull the trigger accidentally while running or when I hit the ground? I might hurt or even kill someone.

With Yotam walking behind me, I move forward trying to remember where I saw the targets during the dry run. Suddenly Yotam smacks me on the shoulder and shouts, "You're under attack!"

I'm not moving any faster than I did during the dry run, but the excitement and anxiety cause me to breathe more heavily. The toilet paper in my ears amplifies the sound of my own breath and the clenching of my jaw.

I see my first target on my left, slam the weapon into my shoulder, and flick the safety off and on to semiautomatic with my right forefinger. I fire two short bursts into the target and surge forward up the hill.

I know Yotam is behind me, but I am completely focused on my search for new targets and my need to count. When I reach three, I fling my body to the ground. With my left hand holding my gun straight, my right hand eases the rest of my body to the ground in a controlled fall. This movement is known as a *pazatsdah*. By now I've done this hundreds if not thousands of times, but this is the first time I've done it with bullets in my gun.

Holding my rifle with both hands, I yank my body into a spin and twirl in a circle toward my left. I stand up quickly and race forward counting to three. All the while, I'm looking for the next target and searching for a bush or rock that I can use for cover in the next second. Every time I find a target, I flick off my safety, lean my body forward slightly, look through my sights, and fire two rounds into the target. When I see a second target close by, I quickly kneel and fire again. Then I rise, run for three more seconds, dive to the ground, and repeat the process until I reach the top of the hill. There I see several more targets in front of me.

I fire at the one closest to me, flick my safety on, run to a small group of rocks on my right, hurl my body toward the ground, flick my safety off, fire at two more targets, flick my safety on, and start running forward. I halt only when I hear a voice say, "Stop. Gun at ninety degrees."

It's not Yotam.

After I take my magazine out, remove the remaining bullet in the chamber, and tilt my weapon so that a commander can check to make sure it is empty, I see that my weapon is being examined by the company commander, Yoav. He speaks with a calm, easygoing tone, but it does little to relieve my anxiety. While he's making sure my gun doesn't have a bullet in it, I am remembering all the mistakes I made during the exercise. I am embarrassed. I'm also concerned because I know that people are removed from combat units if they are deemed incapable or unfit to perform their duties. "Herman, how do you think it went?"

"Not very well. I was standing when I should have kneeled after my third target. I'm not even sure I hit any of the targets."

He says, "Well, we'll see how you did on the way back. You moved well to me." He points toward the small rock pile. "Tell me, why did you lie down and shoot from there?"

"I was close to the target and I thought it would provide me some cover."

He says, "Good thinking. Now go back and lie down how you did before."

We walk back. After I lie down behind the rocks, he says, "Take a look at your legs."

I stretch my head back and see that my legs are spread out a bit more than shoulder length apart, just as I was trained at the gun range. He says, "Your legs aren't protected at all. They need to be on the other side of the rocks. You need to think of your body placement. Now, show me how your body should be."

I adjust my legs so that they are more aligned with the rock. He says, "I know you've been taught to position your body this way while shooting on the range, but when you're in the field, you always need to think about what you're doing. The enemy isn't going to give you any second chances. Understood?"

"Yes sir. Thank you, sir."

"Okay. Now go count your hits and return to the group."

On my way back down the hill, I count the number of bullet holes in each target. I mark off the new ones I made with a black Magic Marker. When I reach my platoon, a couple of the guys ask me how it went. Everyone saw Yoav walk down the hill after me. For the most part, they all want to know about my conversation with him. They want to know what he said and how he acted. In matters of style, they want to know how he slung his weapon and whether he carried a handgun. To anyone listening, the questions asked and the responses given would do more to expose our adulation of Yoav than to explore his character.

And as always, the training undertaken during the day is repeated at night.

Even though it takes us less than twenty minutes to walk from our main tent to the training ground, our commanders decide that we should sleep where we train. We learn very soon that sleeping in our cots will become a luxury. We pitch our two-man tents in a clearing at the bottom of a hill. For some unfathomable reason, it's been decided that three people should sleep in each two-man tent. Even with two people, these tents are fairly cramped.

I quickly discover that I'm slightly claustrophobic. Many nights I lie awake feeling like I'm suffocating. Sometimes my loose-fitting uniform feels too constricting. Other times, it's simply an undefined panic related to being wedged between another person and our duffel bags. When it hits, I can occasionally calm myself using meditation techniques learned from my father when I was in high school. Other nights, I just get up and relieve whoever is on guard. If I can't sleep, someone else should.

Once our commanders determine that we have sufficient training attacking cardboard cutouts, they start teaching us how to work together as a group. The Israeli army loves the number three, and we begin our training using a three-man formation.

This triangle-like formation, the *choolia,* has one person in front and two people positioned behind the leader at equal distance. The people who choose to be in front are those most comfortable taking positions of leadership. Still not comfortable with the commands, and being left-handed, I usually stand on the left side of the formation.

When Yotam sends us off, Yiron, who is in the lead position, starts walking. David and I, who are standing several feet behind him, follow. Forming a triangle, the three of us start making our way up the hill when Yotam shouts, "You're under attack!"

The three of us shout nearly in unison, "Straight line! Straight line!" David and I run forward. Yiron kneels, points his rifle at the small target just ahead, and says, "Fire. Fire. Fire. Fire."

By the time Yiron is pretending to fire at the target, David and I are standing on either side of him, pointing our guns at the same target, and shouting, "Fire. Fire." Yiron then shouts out another command. It's about finding cover and looking for targets up ahead, but I can't seem to grasp the individual words to remember them. David repeats the command and I mumble it as best I can. We all run forward for three seconds before we each dive to the ground, roll to one side, and find cover behind a rock or bush. I prefer the rocks.

We all take the dry run very seriously, but there are often shared smirks at the silliness of grown men shouting "Fire. Fire." Since I first learned the word in the context of the military, it is automatically linked with my current usage. I understand why it makes Israelis think of childhood games, but for me the word is still serious because it presages the use of live ammunition.

The tension and anxiety caused by the use of live rounds is multiplied by the number of people involved in an exercise. When I'm on my own, I can really only hurt myself, but now there are two others I can injure or kill. Gone are my concerns about losing a chance to return home for the weekend. These thoughts are replaced with worry that I'll accidentally shoot David or Yiron in the back.

Before we start, we stand in a miniature *Chet* with Yotam. He asks us how we thought it went. We each give an analysis of our successes and failures. Yotam provides his feedback as well. One of the few suggestions he makes is that we spread out farther while we run. He also wants us to mix up the way we're firing our weapons. He wants to see the front person kneeling more to provide cover while the people behind him catch up.

When we return down the hill, Yotam orders us to put our helmets back on, insert our earplugs, and load our weapons. This time, there are no shared smirks. We're all business. We run, drop, leapfrog, and shoot our way up the hill. When Yotam orders us to stop and remove our magazines, and checks to make sure that our weapons are clear of bullets, we stand once again in formation for a debriefing. We give our comments, Yotam provides his input, and the three of us walk back down the hill together. While counting how many bullets hit targets, we're all smiles and sharing our own memorable moments of the experience. Yiron tells us how his gun jammed. David seeks our pity. He shows us his hand and describes how he dropped directly on a thorny bush. His hand still hurts. I mention how it felt like it took me an hour to change my magazine.

As infantrymen, knowing how to fire and maneuver with our rifles is a basic and essential skill. After a few days, it's clear that it will take months, if not years, to master these rudimentary exercises. But the military doesn't wait for us. The goal, for this stage in our training, seems to be for us to receive a minimal level of competence in a wide range of specialties.

We've received instruction on all the equipment, from the machine gun and mortar to the RPG and radio, but now we are going to start using the equipment on a daily basis. The members of my platoon are quick to point out that the kind of equipment given reflects a commander's opinion of a recruit. For instance, those who are assigned the radio have shown promise as future commanders. Those who are assigned the machine gun or mortar are considered strong and reliable. Those who are asked to switch their heavier Galil rifles for the lighter M-16 are being tapped as sharpshooters because they shoot well and have demonstrated a willingness to take care of their equipment. For a sharpshooter, the latter attribute is almost as important as the first because the M-16 is a temperamental weapon. The Galil can be thrown in the mud and still function. For the RPG, size matters. Due to the weapon's length, it hits short soldiers on the head as they move. Tall soldiers tend to end up with the RPG.

Yotam tells me that I will have the privilege of carrying the mortar. The mortar, along with its smoke, illumination, and high-explosive rounds, is the heaviest weapon in the platoon. Chanan and Barak, our two machine gunners, may disagree, but I quickly learn that this is a common argument. In a culture that celebrates the person who suffers the most, I feel particularly proud.

Between exercises, we review each of these weapons in detail. I don't understand much of what I'm taught. I don't know at what rate our Galils fire, I don't know the effective range of the mortar, I don't quite understand what the sergeant means by the RPG exploding twice, but watching Yotam work the mortar, I understand that I need to twist the valve on the side three times to launch the shell and it's obvious that by raising and lowering the narrow pipe, I can shorten or lengthen the shell's distance. I also know that the gray rounds are explosives, the yellow ones create illumination, and the green ones are used to generate a smoke screen.

When it's time to practice with the mortar, I'm very excited. Pointing at the burned-out vehicle in the distance, our officer, Menachem, says, "I will lead the attack team to the target. We'll flank it from the left and use the wadi as cover."

Menachem points to the place where the wadi bends slightly and says, "When we reach the bend, the firing team will begin to hit the target with the machine gun and the mortar. Any questions?"

I don't know about the others, but I'm too nervous and excited to think of any. This is the most complicated exercise we've done. I can't wait to finally use the mortar. We all return to the starting point of the exercise at the bottom of the hill. We begin with the usual daytime formation we use in an open area. Menachem is at the head. There is a three-man *choolia* on his left and another on his right. Behind him, the rest of the platoon arranges itself into several other three-man teams. I'm in the back, trudging along with the mortar.

When we reach the hill, almost everyone forms up in two columns after Menachem. Barak and I follow the platoon's first sergeant, Aran, up the hill. Before we reach the top, Aran has us get down to a low crawl. The three of us slither our way to the top. Once there, he says, "Barak, move over slightly to the right, start laying out your ammunition. Herman, plant yourself right here, lay out and arrange your mortar shells. Both of you get ready to fire on the target on my command."

I can see Menachem and his team make their way in the wadi. Aran checks the way Barak has positioned his machine gun and laid out his ammunition. He looks me over as well and asks me questions about the mortar. He obviously wants to make sure I know what I'm doing. He doesn't correct me, so I must have provided the right answers. When Menachem's team reaches the bend in the wadi, Aran instructs Barak to start firing at the target and tells me to start firing the mortar. While Menachem and the others advance, Barak shouts, "Fire! Fire! Fire!"

I know I'm mangling the command, but after I pick up one of the gray shells, pretend to rip off its safety cap, and mime placing the round in the tube, I say something close to, "Mortar shot."

I continue pretending to shoot mortar shells until Aran, who sees Menachem's team close in on the target, says, "Okay, that's enough."

Barak and I rejoin the others at the bottom of the hill fifteen minutes later for a debriefing. Menachem's team does most of the talking. They provide their input on how well it went and ask questions. After Menachem and the sergeants have responded, we ready ourselves to try it with live ammunition.

This time, when Aran gives the order, I rip the small wire from the top of the mortar shell, slip the shell in the tube, angle the tube at about sixty degrees, brace myself for the launch, and turn the firing screw slowly. On the third twist, there is a loud, baritone *thomp* sound completely unlike gunfire.

The mortar tube tries to jump out of my hand, but I'm applying enough pressure to keep it steady. When I look up, I can't see the mortar round in the air. It's moving too fast, but I am happily surprised to see it actually strike the target moments later. Both Barak and Aran give a supportive shout of congratulations before Aran says, "Come on, Herman. I don't want any of those rounds left at the end of this exercise. Let's see if you can hit it again."

While Barak pours bullets on the target, I continue to launch mortar shell after mortar shell. I'm filled with excitement. Between the machine gun, the mortar, my stuffed ears, and the adrenaline, I can't distinguish a single distinct sound. It all combines into one deafening thrill.

I see Menachem and the others run out of the wadi and begin leapfrogging toward the target. I'm not concerned about hitting them. Aran is going to tell me to stop before they are in range. Aran watches Barak closely and provides small tips that help Barak work more efficiently and effectively. Barak continues to unload on the target and I keep launching mortar shells. Aran says something I can't quite make out. Since he's still standing next to Barak, I assume he's talking to him and rip the safety off another shell, slide it in the tube, turn the screw, and launch it.

I see Menachem and the others continue moving toward the target. Aran is speaking louder, because I can hear him more clearly. He's saying something that sounds like, *"Chadal. Chadal. Ya'diot."* He must be mad at Barak—it sounds like he just called him an idiot. I stay focused on my task and grab another mortar shell. Before I have a chance to wrap my fingers around it, Aran slaps me hard on my helmet. The shock and the force of the strike rattle me. I look up. Pointing at Menachem he says, *"Chadal. Chadal.* What are you thinking?"

I say that I don't understand.

Barak looks bemused, but Aran's face is all tension when he says, "What do you mean you don't understand? I said *Chadal*. Don't you know what that means?"

I say no.

"Herman, if you don't know something, you need to ask."

"Yes sir. But I've never heard that word before. I didn't know to ask."

Aran must see the logic in my argument because his face relaxes into a broad smile of understanding. He says, "Herman, *chadal* means 'stop.' Menachem and the others were very close. If you had launched another shell, they could have been killed or wounded."

Some days I feel like I'm moving forward in understanding the language and making strides in my training, but they are often followed by days like these. I feel like I'll never be of any use.

Later that day, Menachem hears David explaining an exercise to me in English while he walks by our tent. He enters our tent, possibly for the first time. Speaking gruffly, he says, "David, no more English. He's never going to learn if you guys speak to him in English. Tell the others. Herman, it's for the best. You'll see."

He walks out as quickly as he entered. David shrugs and says in Hebrew, "I'm sorry. But don't worry, it'll be okay."

I pull guard duty for the first time at the base's entrance two days later. It's an easy task, since no one ever wants to enter our area. I expect to stand in front of the gate and look at the hills. When I relieve the person guarding before me, I notice the radio leaning against a nearby rock.

Speaking with people is one thing, but communicating over the radio is something entirely different. The radio literally has a language of its own. I'm able to get by with ordinary Hebrew, barely, but I'm completely befuddled by the idioms used on the radio.

The radio is probably silent forty-seven out of every forty-eight hours, but as luck has it, someone calls in. After listening to the person repeat himself several times without anyone responding, I start thinking that I need to pick up the handle. I try communicating with him. I have no idea what he wants. I see another soldier walking nearby and I run to grab him and coax him back to the gate with me. He speaks with the voice over the radio for a minute. I ask him what the man wanted. He says, "It was nothing. He wanted to let us know that we can expect a supply truck to arrive. He also said to not let that American on the radio again."

Chapter 5

Field-Tested

After another day of exercise is complete, Yotam enters our tent while we're cleaning our weapons. He says, "The platoon has been asked to lead several patrols in Nablus tomorrow. The city will be under a curfew. We will patrol the streets. You'll receive more information after tonight's training. Any questions?"

This will be our first deployment in the West Bank. The Intifadah has been going on now for about three years. Large-scale mobs of Palestinian protesters hurling stones, concrete blocks, and Molotov cocktails from roofs are a concern, but soldiers are increasingly confronted by militants with guns and knives. When Yotam leaves, the tent is filled with nervous excitement. We are at once confident in our abilities and aware of our lack of experience. We recognize that we may face, for the first time, real danger.

Breakfast is served early this morning to give us time for an additional inspection of our weapons and gear before we head for Nablus.

We line up, and Menachem checks our equipment and asks each of us different questions. To my mind, even when he's asking us whether we have fresh water in our canteens, he's really gauging our mental attitude and readiness for today's task.

Last year at this time, I was sitting at a Lebanese restaurant in Washington, DC, having a conversation with Kamal. I remember our discussions vividly. Today, gearing up to patrol the streets in Nablus, I wonder if I'm going to run into any of my former classmates. I certainly hope not. I'm feeling very ambivalent about our assignment. On the one hand, as long as Israel remains in control of the West Bank and Gaza, we need to rein in the violence. On the other, I sympathize with the Palestinians' frustration and desire to live in a state of their own. I just wish that they accepted my right to live freely and securely within my own state. I also wish, for their own good as well as ours, that they had chosen the Gandhi and Martin Luther King model of protest as opposed to stones, Molotov cocktails, knives, guns, and bombs.

Most of my trepidation today has to do with concerns that this kind of mission will change me somehow into somebody I won't like or recognize. I console myself by recalling something our commanders have said countless times. In the Israeli military, soldiers are obligated to disobey any order they feel is immoral. German soldiers used the fact that they were just following orders as an excuse for their crimes against humanity. Israeli soldiers don't have this luxury. If an Israeli soldier believes that an order is immoral, he or she is required by military law to disobey. A soldier doesn't need to articulate the reason or cite a regulation. All that matters is the personal belief that you are being asked to do something that is wrong. I hope I won't be placed in this position, but I fully intend to use my own best judgment as a guide.

Before we even leave, Menachem sits with us and reiterates, once again, our moral obligation as Israeli soldiers. He describes what we can expect to see while we're in Nablus and repeats the rules of engagement. He says, "You are only allowed to fire your weapon if you believe that your life, or the life of another soldier, is in danger. If a person is approaching you and endangering your life, tell him to stop. Always speak in Arabic because he may not understand Hebrew. If he continues, tell him to stop or you'll shoot. If he keeps coming, fire a warning shot in the air. If he still moves toward you, fire at his legs. If he continues despite all of this and is getting close, then shoot at the center of his body. Is that understood? Any questions?"

This time, there are many questions. We discuss more than a dozen different scenarios. Menachem provides clear direction, demonstrates a sincere appreciation for our concerns, displays a breadth of knowledge, and exudes confidence. As a result, he gains our trust, and when he leaves we are eager for the day to begin.

When we arrive, our buses stop at the outskirts of the city. The entire company settles in an orchard to listen to Michal, an attractive twenty-year-old education officer. Every so often, she provides us with a tutorial on the history, politics, demographics, geography, and recent events relating to the places we train. I enjoy these discussions because they offer thirty whole minutes of rest and because they provide context to our efforts. I like knowing the significance of the places selected for our forced marches. The lessons create a connection between the biblical past and the present. This is a tremendous way to get to know the country.

Sitting down, I realize that history lessons will extend beyond training. Michal talks about the ancient history of this area. She tells us that the Romans named it Neo Polis and the Arab difficulty with the *P* sound led to the city being known as Nablus. To Israelis, the town is known as Schechem. Thousands of years before the Romans called it "New City," Isaac settled here. There still exists a grave that is recognized by many as the site where Jacob's son Joseph is buried. Religious Jews have established a small synagogue at the grave site and engage in Torah study here.

While the officers and sergeants engage in a last-minute conference presumably to finalize their plans, the rest of us try to engage Michal in conversation under the guise of interest in ancient history.

As usual, our company will divide up into three platoons. When Menachem returns, he tells us that our platoon will divide into three groups, each led by one of the sergeants. Each group will patrol a different part of Nablus. He explains the rules of engagement once again and wishes us luck.

Ten of us follow the platoon's first sergeant, Aran. Since a curfew is in place, the streets are empty of cars and people. Just as we've practiced at Cha'mam, we divide ourselves into two columns, with Aran at the head. I've been to East Jerusalem before, where most of the city's Arab population lives, and several villages up north, but this is the first Arab city I've been to that isn't considered a part of Israel.

It isn't luxurious by any measure, but it's not a slum, either. I've seen worse neighborhoods in Washington, DC. There are many large detached homes, three-level apartment complexes, cars parked along every street, and shops. I don't expect many here would thank Israel for their relatively high level of personal and political freedom compared with that of other Arabs in the Middle East, or their standard of living. I am under no illusions. First and foremost, they consider us an enemy.

Much of the day passes without incident. We walk the streets and the residents stay indoors. While our company patrols, units with more training and experience are conducting raids on suspected terrorists. Our job is to help catch anyone who slips away and to ensure that the other units won't be interrupted by throngs of city residents. Every so often, several stones fall nearby, usually thrown by someone between the ages of fifteen and twenty. They are all probably trying to prove something to a sibling, parent, or girlfriend.

They know our rules of engagement as well as we do. They annoy us enough to cause us to chase them, but not enough to cause us to consider using our weapons. When we do run after them, it reminds me of the sergeants running us around for punishment. As with the sergeants, this is much like a game. We're cowboys, they're Indians. We're cops and they are robbers. As long as everyone sticks to the rules, no one gets hurt and everyone walks away tired enough to feel like they've completed a hard day's work.

While walking in the middle of a neighborhood, four stones that would fit snugly in a teenager's hand whiz past us. One of them strikes Aran in the leg. He gives chase in the direction he presumes is the stone's origin, and we follow him. We climb over a low wall just in time to see someone round the corner on his way to the adjoining street. Aran sprints forward. Aran is big and bulky, but he can run very fast. I find it difficult to keep up. One minute later, I see Aran clutching the shirt collar of a boy who is about fourteen or fifteen years old.

Speaking with a harsh tone I've heard only a few times before, Aran says, "There's a curfew. What are you doing outside?"

The boy says nothing. Aran doesn't seem surprised. He says, "Give me your identity card."

The demeanor of the boy changes slightly. I see his face become slightly less defiant. He says, "I'm sorry, sir. I just wanted to go visit my friend."

Aran, still holding him by the collar and pressing him against the stone wall, says, "You and your friend like throwing stones at soldiers, right?"

The boy says nothing. Aran says, "Go back home now. God forbid I see you again. Do you understand?"

The boy nods. Aran releases him and the boy walks away. He doesn't exactly strut, but I like to think he enjoys showing that he doesn't feel the need to run.

By the time the day ends, we have run after six or seven different kids. In one instance, we join Yoav on a chase up a long hill after a teenager. The kid loses us in the woods, and Yoav doesn't seem to mind. I think he was more interested in seeing how far he could push us than he was in catching the teenager. When we return that evening to Cha'mam, I don't feel any less ambivalent about the day. I know our patrols serve a purpose and realize that capturing wanted terrorists saves lives, yet I can't help but understand the other side's point of view.

While on guard duty at about two in the morning, I'm still thinking about my day. I remind myself that the curfews and patrols are a small but necessary piece of a security system that is designed to keep Israeli citizens safe from terrorism, but I'd much rather be on a raid capturing a terrorist. I don't enjoy patrolling, but if someone has to do it, then it might as well be me. Besides, given the increased activity of Hezbollah up north, the upcoming US war against Iraq, and Syrian saber rattling, I know that we won't be patrolling streets for long. Whether I meet someone I know while patrolling the streets or raiding a house doesn't really matter. It's irrelevant. I'll treat every Palestinian I encounter with the respect, decency, and humanity he or she deserves.

It's now the middle of January 1991. The United States is poised to strike Iraq, and Israel is bracing itself. Iraq has threatened to rain Scud missiles on Israel, and it is widely believed that they have chemical warheads. We've been training with gas masks for weeks now. Gas masks have already been distributed to Israeli citizens. Every day, we discuss Israel's precarious position.

President Bush has requested that Israel not retaliate to an Iraqi attack because he is afraid that an Israeli response will undermine the alliance he has built. Israel wants to acquiesce, but there is concern that

Israeli inaction will weaken a deterrence critical to the national defense. Most recognize America's overwhelming power, but many wonder if America will be willing to do what it takes to rid the world of the tyrant. Often, it is argued that the United States will not allow pilots and soldiers to take the risks that are necessary to topple Saddam Hussein. In the end, most agree that Israel should rely on itself alone for protection against the bullies in the neighborhood.

While the rest of the country listens to news reports and waits, we continue to train. In fact, I think Yoav is using the upcoming conflict as an excuse to train us even harder. As always, other units are in their cots long before we return to base and we're already on our way to the field before anyone else is up.

On January 15, with the US attack imminent, the three platoons that make up my company are sent to perform various tasks. My platoon is sent back to Sanur. Primarily, we are here to guard the base, but Menachem uses the time to move us forward in our training. On our first day back, those who aren't already guarding learn how to throw grenades for the first time. Before we try it, Menachem shows us how simple it is to remove the pin, count to three, and throw.

When it's my turn, I join Menachem in a small trench. He's crouching low, as if snipers are shooting those who stand up. He hands me the small gray grenade and says, "Are you ready, Herman?"

"Yes sir."

"Remember, as long as you hold the safety clip in place, the grenade will not explode. Once you release the safety clip, the grenade will explode in four seconds. Understood?"

"Yes sir."

"Good. Now remove the pin."

While I crouch next to him, Menachem says, "Herman, you went to college in the United States, right?"

In 1984, collecting sand and shards by the Western Wall

Photo: Karen Berman

Saying good-bye to
my sister Deborah
before moving to
Israel in 1990

Photo: Carol Wilks

Photo: Author's collection

The Kibbutz Tzorah apartments, where I lived in
1986–87 and 1990–92

Photo: Elizabeth Macklin

The swearing-in ceremony
for paratroopers at the
Western Wall in 1991

In the kibbutz apartment
next to a poster from the
anti-occupation museum exhibit

Photo: Elizabeth Macklin

Menachem placing the red beret on my head after the 90-kilometer march

Smiling with Avner but barely able to stand after the 90-kilometer march

After we receive our berets, the platoon gathers to celebrate.

Photo: Author's collection

Practicing method for clearing a room while at Yerocham base

Photo: Carol Wilks

Gilead and Nilly Barelli making me feel
at home and part of the family

The Ronens—my adopted family at Kibbutz Tzorah

Lecturing about Ammunition Hill to fellow attendees of Hebrew School

On Mount Herman with other members of the
Alpine Special Operations Unit

Members of Uri's
reconnaissance unit
relaxing between exercises

With Uri next to
training ground
during Operation
Defensive Shield

Uri, Daboosh, Nadav, and me after nighttime surveillance in the rain

Photo: Oren Gabay

Returning after a successful capture of an Islamic Jihad leader

Photo: Author's collection

Photo: Author's collection

Group picture of reconnaissance unit after arrest of suicide bomber

Photo: Author's collection

Guarding a captured suicide bomber while
waiting for Shin Bet to arrive

Photo: Author's collection

Relaxing with Uri and happy that we won't be using our Barrett rifles

I don't know what distracts me more, the fact that he's speaking to me informally or that I have a live grenade in my hand. I say, "Yes sir."

He says, "What did you study?"

"International relations." I understand that he's trying to make me more comfortable with holding a live grenade, but I'm not feeling at ease.

"That must have been interesting. Do you have brothers?"

"I have three sisters."

"And they don't want to live here in Israel?"

"No. They enjoy visiting here, but they have their own lives in America."

"And what of your parents?"

I feel like telling him that enough time has passed. I've learned the lesson. Instead, I say, "They live on a tropical island. It's a paradise. They love Israel, but they have a great home and a wonderful life."

"A tropical paradise? Now throw the grenade!"

Peeking out from the trench for only an instant, I throw the grenade at the target. Seconds later, it explodes. Menachem and I stand. I can see the smoke clearing by the target. He says, "Good job, Herman."

After another day filled with an unusual number of punishing runs and a night of drills, I find myself guarding the base's ammunition depot with Dror. We stand together engaging in aimless chatter designed to pass the time. While we're talking, Dror notices a light moving across the sky. It is too high to be an airplane, too low to be a satellite, and too slow to be a shooting star. Dror suggests that it might be a Scud missile. I tell him that it's unlikely. Three seconds later, I hear an air raid siren for the first time in my life. I recognize it immediately because it sounds just like the sirens I've heard in war movies.

We have indeed just seen a Scud missile flying to Tel Aviv. In line with our training, we both reach for our gas masks, which are in the brown satchels snugly tied to our legs. Dror struggles with his; he is having trouble tightening the straps. We've been told to keep the mask tightly sealed around our faces. The missile is long gone. I'm nervous and don't know how many other missiles may be on the way, but I don't feel like I'm in immediate danger.

Dror, with his hands still pulling at the straps on his mask, says, "I've ripped my straps. I can't tighten it around my face. What should I do?"

I don't know how long it will take for the missile to strike and don't know whether the impact will affect us, but I know Dror doesn't need to be here. No one is going to raid this place tonight. I'm sure I can handle it on my own. Dror is still pulling on his straps. "Dror, run back down to the platoon now. They'll have another mask for you."

He says, "No. I can't leave my post. I can't."

I understand Dror's conflict. He's been conditioned to fulfill his responsibility without fail. I'm watching his hands move more quickly and watch his agitation approach panic. I make my decision. I grab him by his shirt collar and say, "Come now. We're going back down now."

He says, "No. We can't."

Literally dragging him down the hill and toward our platoon, I say, "None of that matters now."

When we arrive, the others have the biohazard gear out and ready for use. I tell Menachem about the mask, and he has both of us join the administrative staff who are in a sealed room.

Here my gas mask is unnecessary. I take it off and listen to the civilian radio along with everyone else in the room, and almost everyone else in the country. We're all tense and waiting. Menachem hasn't been gone long when we hear the first reports. In all, seven missiles strike Israel. Luckily, it is apparent that they do not contain chemical warheads. In fact, it doesn't appear as if there have been any serious injuries.

We hear the siren again. All clear. I walk with Dror back to the platoon. In the barracks, we spend several hours relating our experiences, but like good soldiers, we do not completely squander the opportunity to sleep.

Over the last couple of months, several members of the company have left. For the most part, they leave because the discipline or the life of a soldier doesn't suit them. One person, though, joined our group just two days ago. His name is Alon. He just left the Sayerit. Alon doesn't tell us why he left or mention whether he was dismissed, but he makes it clear from the outset that our platoon is merely a way station: It seems he has an uncle who is a high-ranking commander. He tells us that he just needs to stay with us for a couple of months, prove himself again, and he'll be off to a better place.

He's strong, young, and no fool. I can certainly understand why he may have been chosen for the Sayerit, but I can't help but make the comparison between the two of us and wonder what it was about him that made him a preferable candidate. I'm sure his uncle's position didn't hurt, because his attitude couldn't have helped him.

Alon is asked to carry the machine gun. He tells us that he carried one in the Sayerit and talks about all the additional ammunition he would take. It was a great way to prepare for Lebanon, maybe even Iraq, he tells us.

In preparation for the march, Yoav orders us to form two columns—the first platoon up front, the second in the middle, our platoon taking up the rear—and wishes us luck. Within a couple of minutes, we're moving at a quick pace. I'm at the end of our column, marching next to Alon. One of our sergeants, Tzvi, is right behind us. We haven't been moving for more than ten minutes when Alon, who is breathing heavily, says, "I've got to stop. I need to pee."

Alon steps out of the line, and I watch Tzvi run up to him. "What are you doing?"

"I have to stop. I have to pee. Just a minute."

Tzvi, who started out training to be an air force pilot and is generally regarded as the most conciliatory and smartest of all the sergeants, speaks roughly for the first time in my memory. "Are you kidding? There is no stopping. This is a forced march. Get back in line and hurry up."

Alon fumbles with his pants and runs forward to join the advancing column. We're on a flat, straight, sandy section, and Yoav must think that this is a good opportunity to make some time because our speed increases dramatically. We're practically running. Another ten minutes pass and Alon is again breathing heavily and weaving slightly. He's having a tough time of it. He trips over his own feet and falls. Both Tzvi and I run to him immediately. Alon is entangled in the machine gun and its straps. While Tzvi helps take the gun off him, Alon says, "I can't. I can't."

Tzvi looks at me. I say, "I can take it."

He says, "No. Get Barak. Now."

Barak, who carried the machine gun until he lost the right to do so when he faltered during a forced march several weeks ago, is eager to prove that he has the strength and determination to regain the privilege. Alon is still on the ground.

Yoav attacks the kilometers, and the company combats the fatigue. After the first few kilometers, my feet, which our medic said weren't fit for the march, become numb to the small needle pricks I feel with every step. I focus on the mountain range on our right. I know I'm going to discover where the range begins before the night is over.

A little more than an hour passes, and Barak has slipped back through the ranks until he is beside me. He isn't completely steady on his feet and looks a bit disoriented. Unfortunately, he looks a little like Alon did several kilometers ago. Tzvi says, "Barak, I told you to stay close to the platoon commander."

Without showing any evidence that he's about to run forward, Barak says, "Yes sir. I know, sir. I'll try, sir."

I don't know why—perhaps out of guilt for not having a pack on my own back, or maybe I just want to see Barak succeed—but I tell him to grab on to the back of my vest.

With Barak's massive hand gripping me, I run between the two columns at full speed toward Menachem. When we are right behind our officer, I stop looking at the beautiful desert scenery and look directly at his feet. Matching steps with Menachem, Barak and I keep pace.

I can tell when Barak needs encouragement. When he's engaged and determined, he stands straight and his grip slightly slackens, but when he starts giving in to his exhaustion, I can feel him pull harder at my vest and feel the additional weight as he leans back. At these moments, I try to provide encouraging words. I don't say much. I certainly don't know him well enough to know what motivates him. I tell him he's doing great. I tell him he can do it. I tell him that we're going to do it together. I tell him that I believe in him. I tell him that we're not going to fail and that we will stay close behind our platoon leader until the end.

As I've already discovered, encouraging Barak and helping him strengthens me. I will not fail him. The hours pass and the initial climb is torturous, but our up-and-down progress from one hill to another is much worse. Barak hangs in there and I continue to provide encouragement. A few more hours pass without any end in sight. Dawn arrives and we're still clearly very far from our endpoint. At one point, I see

Menachem turn around for the first time and look at us. I'm sure my attempts to encourage Barak sound idiotic, but I don't care because we've come this far and we're going to make it to the end.

Another hour passes and we are now marching on a wide unpaved road. The platoon is no longer divided into two columns. We are now bunched together into several small groups. Up front and near Menachem are those of us who are feeling strong. Most are in the middle; some are in the back. They are doing their best to just make it to the end. Barak slackens his grip and lets go of my vest. I turn around and see him smiling. He says, "Herman, I'm okay. Really."

Moving alongside him, I say, "Good."

Menachem says, "Barak, come here."

They exchange a few words and I see Barak smiling broadly as he runs beside our commander. I am almost moved to tears. Barak comes from the closest thing Israel has to a slum, Kiryat Melachi. Ironically, it literally means "city of angels" and was, in fact, named for Los Angeles.

Built in the Negev desert in 1950, Kiryat Melachi is one of many development towns built to absorb the large influx of Jewish refugees from North Africa and Middle Eastern countries such as Morocco, Egypt, Iran, and Iraq. After Israel became a nation, Jews in these countries were no longer safe and fled to Israel. At the time, the Israeli population mostly comprised Ashkenazi Jews who had spent generations living in Western and Eastern Europe. As a result, they were well educated and emulated Europeans in most ways. By contrast, most of the arriving refugees hadn't had the same opportunities. Since the Ashkenazi Jews valued Western ways, they belittled and patronized these Eastern Jews. For years there was friction between these two groups, the Ashkenazi seen as elitist and the Eastern Jews undervalued. Over time, the gaps have closed, but there remain several small towns like Kiryat Melachi that suffer from high unemployment and inadequate social services.

According to the platoon gossip, two of Barak's brothers have served time in prison. He has found it difficult to adjust to the paratrooper discipline. He is a bit rough around the edges and isn't one to volunteer for additional duties, but he's never been a bully and I believe that he is a good person at heart. Watching him over the last few months, I've already seen how the military has helped him mature.

I know that carrying the machine gun gave him a great deal of pride. Given his performance tonight, I'm sure he has won the right to carry it again.

Finally, we arrive at the end of our march. A morning meal of sweet blintzes, tea, and water is greedily enjoyed. Yoav makes a short speech to the entire company. Afterward Menachem addresses our platoon. He tells us that he's very proud of us, but the only comment that really means anything to me is when Barak comes over to me, slaps me hard on the back, and says, "I never would have finished if it weren't for you. You carried me the whole way."

Chapter 6

The Search

In February 1991, we return to Nablus. I don't know how long we'll be here. Our commanders haven't told us. The entire company is now squatting in a massive building in the middle of the city. Our first few days consisted of patrols, but I think the main purpose of those was to familiarize us with the area and to let the local population know that we're here.

When we walk the streets, we wear flak jackets underneath our assault vests. These will protect our torsos from knives and stones, but not bullets or Molotov cocktails. We wear our helmets as well.

We soon know why we are here. The Shin Bet has us search several homes. It's unlikely that we'll uncover any weapons, wanted terrorists, or useful intelligence, but we could get lucky. Even if we don't come across anything interesting, regular visits by the military to the homes of those who are known to be supporters of the PLO and other terror organizations is probably useful. Intruding on the lives of these supporters of terror and the families of known terrorists may disrupt their activities and deter some from action. I'm uncomfortable with the idea of entering a stranger's home at gunpoint and concerned that we are going to provoke further hatred, but then again I don't claim to fully understand the dynamics of the situation.

As we drive to our objective, Aran points to an abandoned but relatively modern apartment complex. He tells us that Israel built the complex nearly a decade ago to help alleviate housing shortages, but PLO leaders forbade Palestinians to occupy the buildings.

Magazine clips are in our weapons and bullets are chambered, but our purpose is not to harm the Palestinians. We don't want to create martyrs for the people to rally around. And the Shin Bet wants to be able to question these men. Israeli intelligence can't learn about methods or develop personality profiles from the dead. Over the last couple of months, we have been taught to use our arms, legs, heads, and rifle stocks first and foremost. It's possible that we may have to fire on Palestinians, but only as a last resort.

After driving a short distance, our truck stops. The first of us to climb down from the vehicle quickly spread out to establish a perimeter.

Menachem divides the platoon into three groups.

I am with Menachem's team. We knock on the door of the first house on our list. No one answers. Speaking in Arabic, Menachem says, "Open the door. This is the IDF. Open your door right now."

While Menachem and two others wait by the large, rusted metal door, the rest of us spread out around the house. The home's entrance has a large tile patio with more than enough room for the round table and six chairs that overlook their neighbor's home.

As Menachem knocks on the door, we focus on the nearby windows and streets. No one seems to be interested in us, but I continue to look in earnest. Menachem bangs on the door again. He says, "Open the door. I don't want to break it. Open it now."

A few more moments pass and then a lock turns. A heavyset woman in her sixties opens the door slowly. Menachem says, "Come out. You and anyone else in there. Now."

Leaning on the door, she turns her head back toward the room behind her and shouts something in Arabic. Moments later, she pushes the door wide open. A young teenage boy exits the house, wearing jeans and a T-shirt. Avichai, whose family is originally from Morocco, speaks Arabic fluently. He tells the boy and the woman to stand by a table in the corner of the patio. As the boy walks past, he seems to evaluate our weapons, equipment, and demeanor. We're obviously not the first soldiers he's ever seen. I can't help but think about how different our lives have been. My worst fear as a teenager was being caught speeding. I never had to worry about soldiers or police searching my home. I can't imagine how all this impacts him, emotionally and otherwise.

Two older brothers, a sister, and a man in his forties exit the house. The brothers are in their twenties. They are dressed in jeans and polo shirts. The girl, who is in her late teens, is dressed in jeans and a blouse. As the three of them walk toward the table, they appear more amused than belligerent. I'm sure they see this as a futile exercise.

The middle-aged man, whom I assume is their father and perhaps the son of the older woman, is dressed in a nice pair of slacks and a button-down shirt. If he were to put on a jacket, he'd look like a salesman. In fact, except for the old woman who is dressed more traditionally, they all wear modern, Western clothes little different from the garb of Israelis or Americans. The only difference is that the quality is lower and the styles are less fashionable. The clothes also look like they are worn most every day.

While everyone else guards the periphery and watches the family, Menachem, Yiron, and I enter the house with our weapons raised and at the ready. Menachem is first in the door. He moves to the right and I follow immediately behind, moving to the left. Yiron waits by the door. While walking to the left and toward the corner wall, I look closely at the room in front of me. I'm searching for someone waiting in ambush or anything out of the ordinary that might indicate that the room has been booby-trapped. It's unusual, but it is happening more often as Palestinian terrorists improve their bomb-making skills.

Neither Menachem nor I find anything to be concerned about. Unlike training, we move slowly and don't yell. Speaking just a little above his normal voice and with a bit more urgency, Menachem says, "Clean."

I acknowledge that I've heard him and respond, "Clean."

A door that leads to the rest of the house is on my left. Yiron sees this and moves behind me. The door is open. That helps. Following the training we received at Cha'mam, I enter the room by pressing my back against the wall closest to me. As I move along the wall on the left, Yiron moves along the opposite wall. Skirting the furnishings, we make sure the room is empty and safe. When each of us is sure, we shout, "Clean!"

Menachem joins us, and the three of us quickly search the rest of the house. Only when we're convinced the place is empty and without booby traps do we exit. Menachem motions with his hands and asks the father to join us. Using Avichai as an interpreter, Menachem says, "We need to search your place. I'd like you to come in and help."

He nods.

With our guns lowered, six of us follow the man inside his house. Menachem has him open the pantry door, cabinets, and bureaus. While Menachem, Yiron, and the man look through the furniture, the rest of us take a close look at the basement, the kitchen, the living room, the bedrooms, and the backyard. We find Jordanian passports for the entire family, which is not all that uncommon. Palestinians don't have a state of their own, so they need passports from a recognized country to travel abroad.

Menachem reviews these documents and makes sure their information matches that on the family's Israeli ID cards. It does. In the closet, one of the guys finds about fifty brochures in English. Menachem calls me over and asks me to tell him what they say. It's fairly typical PLO propaganda.

"Anything you'd consider dangerous?"

I tell him the writing is boring, but other than that, it's just propaganda. It's all about Israeli human-rights violations.

Menachem sneers, but he doesn't say anything. I put the pamphlets down.

We're done. Menachem thanks the man and tells him that we're leaving.

Once the family is back inside the house, Menachem turns to me and says, "Human rights violations? If this were Syria, he'd be dead right now."

Over the next few hours, we search several other homes. We don't find anything of interest, but the first platoon came across a wanted individual. He just happened to be home when they searched the house. When checking documents, the officers reference a sheet of paper known as the Bingo list that identifies the people the Shin Bet is looking for, using ID numbers. None of us knows why the Shin Bet is looking for him. He may be a terrorist, but he looks like a university student to me. It's hard not to wonder if the list is accurate. There are about a hundred ID numbers on it. Has the Shin Bet identified one hundred key terrorists that need to be arrested in the region? I'm not convinced. That's a lot of terrorists.

The man is blindfolded and handcuffed. For a blindfold, a soft cotton strip that is usually used to clean our weapons is wrapped around his eyes. His hands are bound by a white plastic band that is folded in our weapons' handgrips. Three guys from first platoon stand next to him. When the Shin Bet arrives in a command car, two men in civilian clothes exit the vehicle and speak briefly with the man before helping him to the back of their vehicle. They drive off, and I wonder what's next for him. Is he a victim of circumstance or is he going to lead our security services to other terrorists?

As we walk to the next home, I wonder if members of the first platoon have just saved innocent lives or ruined the life of an innocent man. I'll never know. I look up at the windows nearby and tell myself to stay focused on the task at hand. Right now, I need to make sure that no one gets shot or pummeled with stones because I failed to pay attention.

After searching and patrolling the streets for most of the day, we return to the abandoned building that serves as our temporary base. Following a quick debrief, we place our assault vests neatly under our cots and take off our flak jackets. My shirt is soaked through from sweat. I take a moment to drink from my canteen. Afterward, I grab a package of salami and several slices of bread. I join the others. We eat our dinner standing and talk about our day. I'm encouraged to see that I'm not the only one asking questions about the value of our work here.

After an hour's rest, my platoon gathers in an area set aside for briefing. It has maps of Nablus, a listing of the radio frequencies used by the various units working in the area, and a number of plastic benches. Once we settle in, Menachem says, "We have been tasked with an important mission tonight. The Shin Bet believes that a wanted terrorist will be at his parents' home tonight. I need eight volunteers."

I raise my hand immediately but I'm not alone. I am among those selected. I would have volunteered in any case, but knowing that the Shin Bet has been tracking this individual makes me think he's a real enemy. I return to my cot, pull my flak jacket over my shirt, slip on my assault vest, and check my ammunition. The eight of us assemble, and Menachem and Aran join us moments later.

Menachem tells us that we will be driven by truck to the far edge of the village. From there we will walk to the target's home. He checks our equipment and chats with each of us briefly.

We've practiced raids like this many times before and entered several homes since we arrived here. As a result, even though I don't understand all the particulars discussed during the briefings, I can follow the commands and know what needs to be done. After all, it's not rocket science.

By the time we reach our target's home, it's about two in the morning. We are divided into two teams. One team of six will protect us from attack and make sure that no one leaves the house. Menachem, Eyal, Yiron, and I are going to enter the house. Just like this afternoon, Menachem bangs on the door and tells the people inside to open up. After two more attempts, the door opens and we herd the two adults and four children together. They tell us that no one else is in the house and claim their oldest son is not home.

Menachem enters the house first. Yiron follows. At the entrance, a small light is on, but the rest of the house is dark. My eyes quickly adjust. Flashlights would give away our positions as we move through the house, so we leave them on our vests. After a quick sweep, the house appears empty. Menachem orders us to take a closer look. We divide up. While Menachem and Yiron take the two rooms on the left, Eyal and I search the rooms on the right side of the house more thoroughly.

Using a flashlight with a red lens, we search the kitchen pantry, the dining room, and a bedroom closet. Checking underneath the bed, I notice a crack in the wall that extends almost all the way up to the headboard. I point my light steadily at the area for a moment, stand up, and motion for Eyal to take a look. He takes my flashlight and leans down. When he stands up, he nods. We don't need to say a word.

I move to the other side of the bed and we slide it several feet, scraping the legs against the tile floor. I wince because I know we've just lost the element of surprise. Pointing the light at the wall, we see the outline of a small door and a small hole that must function as a latch. I put my flashlight away, look at Eyal for a moment, tighten my hold on my rifle's handgrip, and open the door. I see stairs leading to what looks like a basement.

Eyal is right behind me. The stairs creak. There are only seven steps. Now I can see that we're entering a very small bedroom. There are cardboard boxes, crates, and books on the floor, with a poster on the far wall. The bed takes up most of the floor. By the time I reach the last step, my gun is raised and pointing at the tall, lanky man who is still in bed.

He's awake, but looks tired and disheveled. The safety of my gun is still on, but there is a bullet in the chamber and my finger is very near the trigger. If he tries to attack either of us, I am well positioned to respond. Eyal moves behind me and to my right. Looking nervous but ready for anything, he says, "Hands in the air. Stand up."

The man gazes at us sleepily and calmly. He doesn't seem all that concerned. My body is tense, but steady. My heart is beating quickly. I know that he's not going to hurt me but I'm scared that I'll be forced to shoot him if he tries anything. The irony doesn't escape me: We are pointing loaded weapons at him, but we're the ones who are anxious. Eyal says, "Get up. Now."

With his hands in the air, he slowly stands. He points at and reaches for his pants. I nod. While he puts his pants on, Eyal shouts, "Menachem! Menachem, we've got him. Down here."

Moments later, Menachem makes his way down the steps. He takes a white plastic band from his gun, placing it around the hands of our captive. We radio that we've found our target and usher the family back into the house. A command car takes the man away, and thirty minutes later we walk back to a truck waiting to return us to the base.

* * *

It's about 11 PM and I'm on guard duty. I'm on the rooftop alone. I have a radio next to me but I try to ignore it and hope it returns the favor. I've been up here for about an hour. Since this building is one of the tallest in the city, I can see most of Nablus. I'm enjoying the view and the solitude when a siren begins to wail. Iraq has been firing Scud missiles at Israel since the outbreak of the Gulf War, so I'm used to it by now and not terribly concerned. Besides, we're in the West Bank; missiles simply fly overhead on their way to Tel Aviv. I put on my mask as required, but I'm not in any hurry.

To my surprise, I see lights come on in several homes. Within a minute, both hills and the valley in between that make up this city are flooded with lights. Our building butts against nearby apartments. I can see the dressing gowns and bathrobes of people standing on their balconies. I hear the chanting, but can't make it out at first. Quickly, as the entire city chants in unison, I hear they are saying, "Saddam! Saddam! Saddam!"

They seem euphoric. Now they start a chant I've heard many times on television, "With our blood and with our soul, we sacrifice for you." Jumping up and down, the people join the next chant, "Death to the Jews."

The hatred of two hundred thousand people has an impact. I know there are millions more like them in cities, towns, and villages across the West Bank and Gaza. About 250 million others spread across the rest of the Arab world feel pretty much the same. Standing here alone on the roof, I feel a little ridiculous with the gas mask on my face. While they are shouting for my death and wishing for my people's destruction, I don't want them to see that the missile is having its intended effect.

I'm not afraid for my personal safety. I don't think this is going to turn into a riot—and even if it did, I'm sure we can handle it—but I'm now seeing for the first time how passionately I am hated. Experiencing it is much different from watching it on TV. For them, it's personal.

They don't just reject the idea of me, they hate me. Standing on the roof, witnessing the extent of their hatred, I'm not sure that a political accommodation between leaders will actually lead to real peace. This kind of hate isn't turned off like a faucet or with a signed document.

Two days later, we complete our brief duty in Nablus. It's time for us to become more than infantry soldiers—to earn our wings. We are ordered to an air force base located near Tel Aviv. Before we leave, I learn that the Scud that caused the town of Nablus to scream and shout with joy fell short of its objective. It fell outside a Palestinian village in the West Bank. Up until now, the Palestinians have refused Israeli offers to provide gas masks. Now, I understand, they are clamoring for them, and the Israeli military is setting up distribution centers across the West Bank.

Chapter 7

Wings

As our buses pull into the Tel Nof air force base, all eyes are glued to the windows. We are excited because this is where we will be taught to jump out of planes. The many large buildings, manicured lawns, and signs all point to the fact that this base serves a variety of functions beyond our paratrooper training. Indeed, it more closely resembles a small city than any military base I've seen.

Like young children excited on our first day at school, we point and jabber about all the sights that claim our interest. Our playground doesn't have swings and monkey bars, but there are parachute-packing facilities, female sleeping quarters, and large planes parked on well-tended grass lawns. As we drive by, I'm probably not the only one who is wondering if these planes resemble the ones we'll be jumping from during the next few weeks.

From this day forward, we no longer have to call our sergeants or officers "Commander"; we are all on a first-name basis.

While we settle in our tents, Yotam informs us that we will meet with the jump school's commander in an hour. He doesn't give us a task to accomplish before the meeting. That means we have nearly an hour to ourselves. Although we are about to start our first day at jump school, Tel Nof feels like summer vacation.

When I was young, standing near the edge of cliffs or looking at the ground below from a hotel window made me anxious. Unwilling to give in to my fears, I tried to overcome them by climbing trees, scaling hills, walking on a friend's roof, and jumping from the garage onto the back lawn. As I grew older, I continued to make myself comfortable with heights by hiking. I like pushing myself beyond what feels comfortable. By the time I reach Tel Nof, I think I've overcome my fears to a great extent.

On the first day, the instructors tell us that we may break our legs or dislocate our shoulders during the training. I assume that they are talking about someone else.

After nearly two weeks of training on a series of machines that are meant to mimic the experience of parachuting, we must endure a contraption that is named for the Nazi leader who is the only man ever put to death in Israel for a capital crime, Adolf Eichmann.

He was hanged.

The "Eichmann" demands a long climb up a ladder several stories high. At the top, there is a narrow platform that resembles a plank. The platform is just wide enough for two people to stand on.

For the first time since we started our training, my fear awakens. I do not want to climb that ladder, but I'm not going to let anyone know it. Neither will I let my fear determine what I can and cannot do. Feigning eagerness and ignoring the rumbling in my stomach, I volunteer to climb up first. I slowly make my way to the top. It seems to take forever.

I make the classic mistake of looking down when I'm less than halfway up. I don't want to continue, but it's too late now. I focus on moving each hand and foot to the next rung. I imagine what will happen if I lose my footing now. I hope that I will have the wits, strength, and luck to grab one of the rungs if I fall. When I make it to the platform, it doesn't feel much like a sanctuary. It's way too small, and I feel a slight breeze.

The instructor says, "Herman. You're going to love this one."

"I wouldn't be too sure of that."

While he straps me into the harness and checks the lines, he says, "You're going to be just fine. Trust me."

Looking at the short plank that ends a couple of feet away and trying to ignore the fact that I can see far into the distance at this height, I ask him, "What should I do? Do I jump off?"

"No. Just step off the platform whenever you're ready."

I take two steps forward and line up my toes along the edge as if this is a diving board, and a pool full of water waits a few feet below. I look out at the horizon before me and close my eyes. For the first time since I arrived here, I am truly afraid. I imagine what will happen to me if the ropes aren't properly attached. Then I take one bunny hop forward and plunge toward the ground. I'm falling straight down. I keep my eyes closed until I feel a slight yank that slows my descent. I open my eyes. I'm momentarily halted two feet from the ground before they let me fall the rest of the way. I don't land perfectly, but I'm unhurt.

We're ready for our first real jump. It's the middle of the afternoon. We're told that the sand at the drop zone is deep and soft. Landing should be easy, but we still need to worry about making it out of the plane without incident and hope that our parachutes open correctly.

Perhaps it's willful ignorance and self-deception, but I'm excited and re-laxed. Over the last couple of weeks, I've come to trust the instructors. If something goes wrong, they'll know how to handle it.

Once we have our equipment, we're transported to an airstrip. We are divided into several groups. David and I will be the last two people in our group. Waiting to be told that we can enter the planes, we sit down on the tarmac and lean back on our parachutes. David tells me that his father served with Ariel Sharon's famous paratrooper unit. "You know, I joined the paratroopers because of him. I wanted him to be proud."

The sun is shining brightly, but we end up waiting on the tarmac for hours. We are told that the wind velocity is too strong for us to jump. Most of us use the time to nap. When the engines start up, my stomach ties itself up into knots while I force a smile and feign excite-ment.

A ramp on the back of the plane drops down, and we climb aboard. Two groups of men sit across from each other. We strap ourselves in as the back of the plane closes. When we take off, I search the faces of the men beside and across from me. I see the tension and am glad to know I'm not alone.

When it's time, we all stand and check the parachute of the person in front of us. David slaps my back and shouts, "Nine okay."

I slap the back of Doron, who's standing in front of me. "Eight okay."

We continue until everyone in the plane has been checked. While we wait for the light near the door to turn green, I hold on to the strap that connects my parachute to a metal line running the length of the plane. When I jump out, it will pull the parachute out of its packing. A member of the parachute team that has been instructing us opens the door. It's bright and sunny outside. I look back at David and smile. I'm anxious and nervous, but I'm also excited.

The light turns green. Everyone shouts the cheer that we learned during training. I still don't know exactly what it means and I doubt that I'm pronouncing it right. Let that be my big worry today. The guys in front start moving toward the door. Some of them place their hands for a second on the edge of the doors before pushing themselves out. Others just walk out the door. All of them simply disappear. In seconds, I'm approaching the door. It's only a few feet away. Our altitude is nine hundred meters—about half a mile. It looks it.

I concentrate on the task at hand. I need to be holding my strap correctly and throw it forward just before I jump. I'm ready. Doron jumps out. I move forward and start throwing my strap. Suddenly the instructor jumps up, pushes me back into David, and shouts, "No! Herman, stop!"

I'm confused and scared. "What, what did I do wrong? I'm sorry."

I turn my head back at David. "I'm sorry. I must have done something wrong."

He says, "What happened?"

I turn toward the instructor. "What did I do wrong?"

He ignores me, talking into his headset. I turn back to David. I'm embarrassed. "I was ready. Really. I was ready to go."

David says, "So was I. I was ready, too. What happened?"

I look back at the instructor. "What did I do wrong?"

Laughing, he says, "Nothing. You didn't do anything wrong. We wanted to do something special for you. Move forward. Stand by the door."

I do as he says. I place my toes by the edge of the floor and press my hands into the sides of the door. I can feel and hear the wind. The plane's large turbine engines are roaring close by. I see the land below. The instructor says, "We thought you'd enjoy this. Just stand here. We're going to turn the plane around."

After the first moment, anxiety is overwhelmed by adrenaline. I look back at David for a moment. He's smiling. I wonder if he's just glad that it's not him standing here. As the plane makes a wide circle, I spend the next several minutes absorbing everything in sight. I can't wait to jump. When we're above the training ground again, the instructor shouts, "Herman, jump like a panther!"

I don't think panthers are indigenous to Israel, but for some reason Israelis associate the cats with great strength. Over the last few months, commanders have exhorted me to fight like a panther and run like a panther. Today, I'm to jump like one.

With all the force I can muster, I leap into the air. I feel the thrust of the wind push me away from the plane and I start counting. By the time I say "two," my body has started changing position. My feet begin to lift up toward the sky. If my parachute doesn't open, my body will probably become inverted, but I'm not worried. I say "three" and feel a slight tug. My feet drop back down. I look up and see the large, green silk canopy spread out above me. I look down. My body is correctly aligned. It's an odd sensation. I don't feel like I'm falling. There is a slight breeze, but it's as if I'm hovering in the air and the earth is rushing up toward me.

All that's left for me to do is enjoy the ride. I admire all the other parachutes floating in the distance. I can hear a few random shouts, but for the most part I enjoy the quiet. I take a small piece of chocolate from one of my pockets and place it in my mouth. It tastes delicious. I start singing "Jeremiah Was a Bullfrog," one of the few songs I know by heart. Having properly savored the moment, I prepare for the landing. The earth has nearly reached me. I press my arms against my head and bend my knees slightly. My landing is less than perfect, but I roll adequately and am able to stand without injury moments later. As promised, the landing site's deep sand makes for a soft touchdown. I release myself from my harness, pack my parachute in a bag, and walk back to the waiting buses.

We repeat the experience during the night. If possible, the night jump is even more beautiful and enjoyable. The moon is bright. I can see the silhouettes of the others as I fall. In the dark, we maintain operational silence. The silence is breathtaking. Afterward, we try a daytime jump with the sack that contains our equipment. Thinking about the instructor's warning that we'll break our legs if we land with it still attached to our harness, I don't relax until I watch it fall away from me. It's still connected to me by a twenty-foot-long rope, but it dangles safely underneath me.

Families are invited to witness our last jump. This is another one of those awkward moments. I wish my parents were here to share my joy and success. I don't begrudge the others, of course, and I'm not exactly sad; I just don't know what to do with myself. Where do I go? I don't want to insert myself into some other family's special moment, but I can't exactly hide, either. I thank those who invite me to join them and their families, but I float along the periphery. Near the parking lot, there is a small van selling pita, falafel, and soda. I purchase something to eat and can't help but notice two soldiers standing to the side wearing uniforms from the US military.

One of them says he's from Detroit.

I ask them if they are training here as well, but they tell me they are not permitted to say.

It doesn't take me long to figure it out. They are probably part of a team manning a Patriot missile battery. I tell them, "Thanks for all your work."

Having completed the course successfully, we are given our wings and a two-day vacation. We are far from completing our paratrooper training, but this is an important milestone.

Since Cha'mam is in the West Bank, I've been returning to the kibbutz via Jerusalem. Today is the first time since the outbreak of the Gulf War that I'm taking a bus from Tel Aviv. The Tel Aviv bus station is generally a madhouse. Hundreds of buses pass through every day. The thousands of people catching buses here attract hundreds of vendors selling food, drinks, clothing, music, and other items. It's as much a marketplace as a bus station.

But when I arrive, I am surprised to see that the streets are deserted. None of the vendors are around; most of the shops are boarded up. Aside from a few soldiers like me, no one is here. It's a bit of a shock. I've had to don a gas mask countless times since the beginning of the Gulf War, but I've always been deep in the West Bank where the chance of a Scud attack was remote. For the first time, I'm seeing how the war has impacted the rest of the country. It seems wrong that being a soldier makes me feel safer than the average citizen.

Chapter 8

Earning the Red Beret

To earn the coveted red beret of the paratroopers, we must first complete a ninety-kilometer forced march from Tel Aviv to Jerusalem. Over the first thirty kilometers, we'll carry full packs and all our weapons. For the next thirty we will pick up the pace, but we'll off-load our mortars and RPGs. Of course stretchers and personal equipment will still need to be carried, and I'm sure that there's a twenty-liter water container with my name on it. For the final stretch up to Jerusalem, we'll have "wounded" to carry on the stretchers. We'll keep going until we reach Ammunition Hill.

It's sunny and warm. We're gathered at a memorial for paratroopers. I missed the first part of the explanation and I'm not quite sure, once again, why this place matters and was chosen as our starting point. The memorial site is close to a main road, and many cars honk in support of us. Yiron tells me that one of the radio stations is playing commercial-free music all night in support of our march, but Yoav has forbidden us to carry a radio. A radio during a forced march seems out of place to me as well, but Yiron tells me that it's not unusual for commanders to permit them. Yoav is just being Yoav.

When it's time, Yoav addresses us briefly. He reminds us that we have proven ourselves many times over the last few months. He says that he expects nothing less than our maximum effort tonight. With Yoav taking the lead, our company's three platoons follow him by the numbers. My third platoon takes up the rear.

Those of us carrying heavy equipment, like the large-caliber machine gun and the mortar, are up front and right behind Menachem. When we start, it's more like a fast walk as we make our way to a nearby field. Within minutes, the sounds from the road completely disappear. All I hear is the labored breathing of the six other men who gather right behind our commander. When I turn my head, I see the rest of the platoon stretching out in several small groups. The sergeants are running up and down the line, giving encouragement. Like the others around me, I take the coming trial very seriously. I know it's going to be difficult, but at the same time I feel euphoric.

After three hours, our pace is set. Two more hours pass and I realize that we are marching near my kibbutz. I mention it to Yiron and David, who are both next to me. They both nod in acknowledgment, but we're not going to waste our energy talking. We're picking up the pace. As the fields of my kibbutz approach, we're practically at a run. Seeing the place that has become my home motivates me. I'm not going to fall behind at my own doorstep. I keep up with Menachem.

At thirty kilometers, we have half an hour to rest. My shirt is soaking wet and I'm slightly dehydrated. I have no interest in food. I put my mortar in the truck but I've volunteered to carry a twenty-liter water container. After fitting the container's straps so that it fits snugly against my back, I spend the next twenty minutes drinking. I exchange a few quick hellos, but I'm focused on hydrating.

It's dusk. Since most of the soldiers are weighed down only by an assault vest, Yoav feels empowered to quicken the pace. After another two hours, it is pitch dark out and I'm trudging right behind Yiron. He's carrying the platoon's radio. I watch his footfalls and force my feet to match his. Two ammunition magazines in my assault vest have been hitting my left side since the march began, and it's starting to hurt. I tell myself to ignore it and focus on the path ahead.

Another two hours pass. Yoav keeps up the punishing pace. My legs are tired, and the water weighs on me. I can hear it lightly slosh around, and it's leaking. Water drops strike the back of my right leg. I tell myself that I'm not going to give up or give in.

I look at Menachem trudge confidently forward and twist my head to see the rest of the platoon behind me. Their faces are tight with concentration as well. If they can do it, I can, too. Besides, there is no choice. If I give up now, my friends are going to have to carry me the rest of the way. I won't have that.

When you visit Jerusalem, you can't help but notice that cars and buses labor to reach the top of the steep incline that leads to the city's entrance. I know Jerusalem is situated in the mountains, but I don't really understand what that means until tonight. One hour later, we reach another rest area near the Castel.

The Castel has been a strategic gateway to Jerusalem for thousands of years. From here, I know that we will have a steep descent before we start our final climb. A gasoline-powered generator and headlights from several vehicles light up the area. Menachem doesn't take up much of our time. He tells us we have twenty minutes. This will be our last stop before reaching Ammunition Hill.

The water container that had been my misery for the last thirty kilometers is quickly emptied by my thirsty comrades. Now I have only my assault vest. It's a relief, although my left side aches from the magazines banging against it.

Alon, the platoon's comedian, approaches me. He does a good job of adding levity during tense moments, but he always has a ready excuse to avoid work and consistently fails to arrive for guard duty on time. Almost everyone forgives him because he makes up for it by being funny. Although I understand the real value he brings to our group, I can't seem to forget what a slacker he is.

He says to me, "Herman, Menachem asked me to carry the stretcher. I can't do it. Can you take it?"

I stand there for a moment considering my answer. If it were anyone else, I wouldn't hesitate, but it is Alon and I'm exhausted. While I pause, Alon starts handing me the stretcher. I want to refuse it and tell him that he should carry it, but I can't. The same personality quirk that makes Alon so irritating compels me to acquiesce. The kibbutz movement was built on the founding principle that everyone should perform according to their ability and receive according to their needs. I don't know if I'll continue living on the kibbutz after I complete my military service, but I've always found this to be a wonderful ideal. I have to assume that Alon is doing all he can. The stretcher is a little cumbersome, but it only weighs about ten pounds.

"All right. I'll take it. How are you doing?"

He says, "Doing? I hear Yoav is trying to break a record. He's crazy. If he wants to break a record, we should have taken a bus. We'd have finished in thirty minutes."

I adjust the straps of the stretcher and swing it onto my back. It's not going to be too bad. I join up with the rest of the platoon. To warm up our legs, Yoav starts off at a relatively leisurely speed. Minutes later, our pace quickens. I begin to wonder if Alon was right and Yoav is trying to break some kind of record. Of course, I have nothing to compare it with. For all I know, our pace is relatively slow next to those of other units.

I stay focused on keeping up with Menachem. Over the next two hours, we march up and down forested hills. Thankfully, the pace slows dramatically. Five minutes later, I see why: We have arrived at a shallow river that we need to ford. Once we're across, we stop. Menachem says, "Open the stretchers."

Each platoon has three stretchers. In a perfect world, we'd be able to place the smallest, lightest members of our platoon on them. Instead, we need to place the three people our sergeants judge need a respite. Two minutes later, we lift the stretchers to our shoulders and march on. Moments later, we begin our main ascent.

Although four people typically carry a stretcher, we have ten people available for each. As we move, each of us, in turn, replaces a person who is carrying the stretcher. During the first two hours, most of us carry the stretcher for several minutes before being relieved, but as the kilometers pass, several members of the platoon grow noticeably less eager. Raviv, who is lying on the stretcher, tries to encourage us, but we ask him to be quiet. We're not upset with him, but we don't want the guy resting on the stretcher to tell us to keep pushing ourselves.

The next two hours are torturous. We are mostly climbing steep slopes. I'm exhausted. I know that I'm slightly dehydrated, but I don't have the energy or desire to start fiddling with my canteen. My side aches from the magazines banging against me, and my shoulders are raw from chafing against the stretcher. I know that we're near the end. I tell myself to hold on. I look at the top of the current hill and focus on reaching it. When we arrive, I select another point nearby and make that my next goal.

It is nearly dawn. The night sky lightens, presaging the coming sun and the end of our journey. As we enter a valley, I see high cliffs on our right and know exactly where we are. I've seen this spot from a bus hundreds of times. Jerusalem is just above those cliffs. As we pass an electricity grid, I can guess the rest of the route. We're going to climb these cliffs and end up in a neighborhood called Rommena. The *Jerusalem Post* offices are near here. This is the edge of the city. From here, it's a straight shot up Yirmiyahu, down Bar Ilan, and finally to Levi Eshkol Street.

This last climb is particularly tough, but I can see that we're almost done. I am determined not to fail. At the top of the hill we are, for the first time since we started this march, on pavement. Dawn is around the corner; the streets are still deserted. The sergeants and Menachem urge us on. They encourage everyone to help carry the stretchers. Now that we're on a road, Yoav asks us to quicken our pace. With surer footing, the help of the entire platoon, and the knowledge that we're less than two miles from our goal, we do. Now none of us is under the stretcher for more than a few seconds before being relieved. By the time we reach Levi Eshkol, we're sprinting.

When we reach the top of Ammunition Hill, we are asked to wait for Yoav to address us. In typical fashion, the entire company stands at attention with the stretchers on our shoulders until Yoav approaches. For a moment, he stands in front of us and just looks us over. I don't feel the weight of the stretcher or the pain in my side any longer. I stand upright and feel strong. I'm exhausted, but if Yoav were to ask us to keep marching, I'd be willing and able. Instead, he gives us permission to lower the stretchers. He tells us that he has commanded many units in the past, but he is particularly impressed with our determination. He reminds us that we've worked especially hard over the last few months and accomplished much. We completed the march in less than fifteen hours. This, he says, is a record.

We divide up into our respective platoons, and Menachem speaks to us as a group. I can see the emotion in his eyes. Unlike the sixty-kilometer march, I don't feel elated or particularly proud. I am just relieved that I completed the task. Speaking with the others, I learn that several people from other platoons and one from our own stopped along the way.

Before the red berets are distributed, we are given a few minutes to drink and eat. I drink water, but I'm not hungry. Finally able to relax, I feel my body ache. I take a look at my left side and see the swelling. It's blood red and the size of a baseball. I sit on one of the park benches and I don't know if I'm ever going to stand up again.

When we are called to line up, I don't feel completely steady on my feet. I look around at the nearly one hundred members of our company. The officers and sergeants from each platoon start handing out the berets. When Menachem places my beret through the loop on my shoulder, gives me a friendly shove, and extends his hand, I can't help but feel proud and lucky to have him as my commander. As if he has read my mind, he looks at me with a mischievous smirk and says, "Herman, are you ready to keep going?"

With an exaggerated look of seriousness, I say, "Yes sir. I'm ready."

He pats me on the shoulder and says, "You'll do, Herman. You'll do."

After the obligatory throwing of the berets in the air, a man in his late fifties who fought here during the Six Day War takes us for a tour of Ammunition Hill. This battle was essential to Israel's gaining control over Jerusalem in 1967. I don't know if it's my exhaustion, my Hebrew, or his communication skills, but I fail to grasp what he's saying. It's unfortunate. I am honored by his willingness to speak with us and would have valued hearing what it was like to engage in a battle that was decided by grit and determination. This will just have to be one of those missed opportunities.

I stop straining to understand the words and study him instead. I notice that he's smiling a lot. He's talking about a horrific fight and what must have been a terrifying experience, but his eyes almost dance with joy.

He reminds me of the pixie-like woman from Kibbutz Tzora who drove in the convoys during 1948. Like her, he is full of life. They both experienced harsh fighting and probably watched helplessly while close friends died around them, but they seem so full of joy and vitality.

By contrast, I have met several people my own age who seem emotionally damaged by their experiences in the military. It makes me wonder how my military service will impact me.

After our tour, we are released for a whole week. Right now, I don't have any plans beyond sleep. I arrive at the kibbutz around noon. When I wake, it's dark. I assume that it's Friday night, but I discover that it's already Saturday. I've slept about eighteen hours. I'm told that while I slept, my feet kept moving up and down as if I were still marching.

The kibbutz members ask me about the military, but I'm brief with my responses. I tell them that I find it difficult, but I reassure them that I'm doing okay. I tell them that I like my commanders and the people with whom I serve, but I don't give them any specifics. They briefly reminisce about their own experiences, but they are in their late thirties and early forties. Their own compulsory service is in their distant past. They don't press me for more details because they've seen and heard it all hundreds of times before. My experiences are new and exciting to me, but they are merely versions of the same story told by hundreds of thousands of soldiers before me.

The next morning, I wake up early and make my way to the cafeteria before dawn. If I'm going to be staying on the kibbutz over the next few days, I want to pay my way through work. I know that no one expects me to work—the army is paying the kibbutz a modest amount to offset the expense of housing me—but I feel I owe this community more than minimal effort.

I spend the next several days cultivating the fields in the vineyard and reconnecting with people on the kibbutz. Here, I'm reminded why we must always train hard. People are depending on us. I don't want to let them down.

By March 1991 the Gulf War is over, but Palestinian terror attacks are on the increase. During the next two years, sixty-five Israelis are killed by terrorists. At the same time, Hezbollah continues to gain strength in Lebanon. Roadside bombs and attacks on Israeli soldiers in the Security Zone are on the increase. And in retaliation for the targeted killing of Hezbollah leader Abbas al-Musawi, the Israeli embassy in Argentina is bombed. Twenty-nine are killed. Two hundred forty-two are wounded.

Chapter 9

The Jordanian Border

It is June 1991, and over the past few months we have alternated between training in the sand near Yerocham and actual missions on West Bank and Gaza streets. One week we train to attack Syrian positions alongside tank units, the next week we patrol Palestinian streets, man checkpoints, and sometimes make arrests. Because terrorism is Israel's primary security concern, our activities in the West Bank and Gaza are as essential as our learning how to coordinate missions with the air force, capture vital territory, or perform long-distance reconnaissance. Such patrols also provide an opportunity to gauge how well soldiers and commanders cope with the anxiety and complications that arise during actual missions.

After completing our last training exercise at Yerocham, the entire company joins together for a barbecue in a small grove near the base's perimeter. Gathered around a small bonfire, we eat hundreds of meat skewers, drink liters of Coca-Cola, mix, mingle, and reminisce. Soldiers and commanders lightheartedly mock each other. It's a completely en-joyable party that lasts deep into the night. We've known one another only eight months, but it feels like eight years.

As the red embers begin to cool, Yoav tells us what's next for our company. Over the last week, there have been rumors. Now it's confirmed that the company is going to be temporarily split up into two groups. For three weeks, first and second platoons will join the 202nd Battalion in Nablus. They will conduct patrols and make arrests. Third platoon, my platoon, will patrol the Jordanian border. We will work with a special operations unit called Duchifatt. The guys in the platoon call them Duchifarsh. The slight modification, a sign of deri-sion, is meant to indicate that the unit performs a useless function. They may be specially selected and have amazing gadgets, but the area they patrol isn't considered very dangerous.

I'm excited to experience something new, and curious to see what it's like to guard the border, but a part of me feels like I'll be missing out on the real show: the war against the terrorists.

And now Palestinian terror groups are kidnapping Israeli soldiers. Over the last few months, terrorists have passed themselves off as Is-raelis, offered rides to soldiers, and killed them. Since many Israelis are the children of people who fled Morocco, Iraq, Egypt, Iran, Yemen, and other Arab countries after 1948, it's not always easy to know the origin of someone offering you a ride. Clothing, type of car, accent, and visi-ble objects found in a car can help, but they aren't definitive. I don't think it would be hard to be deceived, especially if you're a tired soldier eager for a ride home.

Soldiers have been told not to hitchhike, but few pay attention. Often, it's the only way to reach a base on time. I follow a few simple rules. If I have a bad feeling, I make an excuse and let them go. I never enter the front seat because I could be easily attacked from someone in back. I always check the car out before entering. I never enter a car with more than two men. I also hold a magazine clip in my hand as a weapon. Until I'm safely out the door, I remain ready to react.

Before hooking up with Duchifatt, my unit was granted a 36-hour pass. Making my way back to the unit from Kibbutz Tzora, I'm hitching a ride. It's early morning and I'm alone in an isolated area. I don't think regulations permit this but I'm keeping a bullet chambered in my rifle. I'm not taking any chances with my life. If I'm a target, one second could make all the difference.

I can't confidently identify the driver who stops, but he's alone, time is short, and I need to travel north to Beit Lid. The man leans over to open the front door. I tell him that I prefer the back. I can't see the inside of the car very well until I'm in. As he pulls away, I try to imagine the ways in which I could be attacked from within the car and from without. Hoping that the two of us are alone, I focus on the possibility that he'll suddenly drive onto one of the many side roads. If that happens, I'll raise my weapon and tell him to stop immediately or I'll shoot. I've thought about this quite a lot. I've decided that it is better to be in prison for a failure in judgment than dead because I failed to act.

As it turns out, of course, he's just another kindly soul who wants to help out a soldier. He's one of the hundreds I've met since I joined the army. I love hitchhiking because it reminds me that my hard work and lack of sleep benefit real people. I may not personally do much to stop terrorism; still, just by showing up and doing my part I am contributing to the safety of this nation.

Once I arrive at Beit Lid, I walk past hundreds of other soldiers from various units until I come across members of my platoon. After briefly discussing our weekends, I say, "What's our timetable?"

Oren says, "We've got plenty of time. They just told us we have two more hours, but the bus isn't even here. My bet is we've got a while. Get comfortable."

Oren, as usual, can be counted on to provide solid information.

We were required to be here by 9 AM, but we don't actually leave until 2 PM.

If there's one thing I've learned, it's that much of military life is spent waiting. By 3 PM we're on the main road that leads to Tiberias and the Sea of Galilee. I'm looking out my window. I know that the Jordan River, which separates Israel and Jordan, runs parallel to this road. It's close by, perhaps less than two hundred meters. If it weren't for all the brush and tall grass, I think I'd see it from the road.

The bus slows and takes a right onto a short dirt path. In a matter of seconds, we reach the main gate of our base. A soldier waves us in. The base, about fifteen minutes from the Sea of Galilee, is called Dalameyah. As we unload our equipment, I see that the base consists of one small, single-story building. Half of the rooms are already occupied by Duchifatt. They've been here for three months. They are completing their three-year compulsory service, and we are just beginning ours.

Six of us squeeze into a room that is smaller than my dorm room at American University. We're not living in the lap of luxury, but it seems lavish compared with a thirty-man tent in the middle of the desert. We're even sleeping on actual beds.

Once we settle in, we all meet in a room that contains a map of the area, a list of radio frequencies used by units operating here, several radios that are probably always active, and a sign that reads MISSION: PROTECTING THE COMMUNITIES OF THE NORTH.

Adi, the commander of Duchifatt, welcomes us. Using the map, he describes our mission and the extent of the border we will patrol, which looks to be about twenty kilometers. Adi explains that two large open vehicles will drive along the border at all times. In each vehicle, there will be a driver, a commander, one of the four Bedouin officers who are based here, two soldiers manning heavy machine guns, a medic, and an additional soldier.

The Bedouin, like the Druze, are an Arabic-speaking community that encourages its men to serve in the Israeli military. Bedouin, a nomadic people, migrated to Israel, Egypt, and Jordan between the fourteenth and eighteenth centuries. Like the Druze, the Bedouin living in Israel have forged a strong relationship with the Jewish community. Since before the founding of the state, Bedouin have served with distinction in the military. Unlike the Druze, they are under no obligation to serve. Many of their young men volunteer every year. I am told that they are among the world's best trackers.

Considering the fact that the Jordanian border runs practically the entire length of the country, I welcome their help. Yet Israel doesn't rely on trackers or soldiers like me as its first line of defense. The country has built a sophisticated system of sensors and physical barriers to guard the border. Our job is to respond when necessary.

Buried sensors alert patrols when a person or animal approaches the fence. These amazing devices can distinguish between a rabbit, a bird, a wild boar, and a human. As a result, there are several different alerts. We will investigate each, but for the most part we can expect to respond to low-level alerts caused by animals or glitches. If a person tries to dig under, jump over, or cut through the fence, a major alarm will go off. When this happens, the alert is called *parash turki,* which literally means "turkey on the loose."

When Adi provides us with a history of the area, I am surprised to learn that there have been several infiltrations from Jordan this year. Usually, the border is quiet, but the Gulf War has incited Palestinian terror groups that seem to operate freely in Jordan. The Jordanians have military forces on their side of the border dedicated to stopping these would-be infiltrators, but these have not been very effective lately.

When Adi finishes, Menachem tells us that there will be a shift change in an hour. Members of our platoon will mingle with and learn from members of Duchifatt. He needs eight volunteers. The usual suspects raise their hands and are selected. We are told to bring plenty of water and some food if we want. We'll be driving along the border for the next six hours.

Before we leave, several of us study the map closely. We also write down the various radio frequencies and the code names for the units patrolling other sections of the border as well as the units that monitor border activity with sophisticated equipment. We'll provide some of these units with regular status reports while on patrol. Others will be contacted only if there's an infiltration.

Menachem sits up front and next to the driver. On either side of the vehicle, behind the driver's and passenger's seats, there is a slightly elevated chair. Rafik, one of the Bedouin trackers, jumps into the one behind the driver. He has a weapon and an assault vest, but like the driver, he shoves both in a corner the moment he arrives. That seems almost sacrilegious to me, but I realize that these two aren't here to fight. That's our job.

In the middle of the vehicle, there are two benches; a machine gun is attached to each side. I take one of the machine guns and Yiron takes the other. The guys from Duchifatt sit in the back with us. We cannot hide our excitement, but they don't mock us for behaving like children in a candy store. Instead, they answer our questions and treat us like peers.

The driver makes for a dirt path that takes us closer to the Jordanian border. Within minutes, we arrive at the fence.

Between the fence and the road lies a narrow swath of deep sand about five feet wide. As we drive on the road, Rafik looks closely at the sandy patch and the area on the other side of the fence. He's looking for an "impression" in the sand. Tamir, one of the guys from Duchifatt, tells us that they drag a tarp behind the vehicle every morning to smooth this area. It makes me think of an Etch A Sketch. In the morning, we'll wipe away all the squiggles made by creatures large and small.

While we travel up and down the road, the driver, Rafik, and Tamir point to areas of interest. I learn that the fence is divided up into many segments. At segment 244, we turn around. Another unit is responsible for the area beyond that.

It's quickly apparent that there isn't much to patrolling the border. For the most part, we simply drive around. Rafik is the only one who is doing anything of consequence, although it's hard for me to believe that he can actually see anything significant while we're driving about forty kilometers per hour.

At night, Rafik and Menachem use the small but powerful search-light to inspect the sandy patch and the area beyond the fence. Every so often, we park the vehicle and stretch our legs. Whenever we stop or pass preselected segments of the fence, we call in our position over the radio. Someone confirms receipt of the information. I don't know where exactly, but there are military staffers somewhere in the area monitoring vehicle positions and incidents. Throughout our patrol, we also communicate directly with the other vehicle from Dalameyah. It is patrolling a ten-kilometer area in the opposite direction. Also, we check in with several stationary lookout positions that are manned by reserve soldiers.

Within the first four hours, there are four low-level alerts. After each, we speed toward the fence segment in question. As we approach, we scan the area for movement. Every time, Rafik has an explanation. The first time, he blames a wild boar. The second time a rabbit. The third time it's another boar. The last one is described to me as a type of hedgehog. I'm looking at the same area and I don't see anything. I've traveled with the Bedouin in the Sinai. I realize that they are more in tune with their environment than someone like me, who grew up in American suburbs, but it's hard to accept that he sees anything at all. I can't even see any prints and he's identifying them.

The patrol is enjoyable; we spend much of our time talking. We haven't even been here a day, but this is the most time I've spent sitting down since I joined the military. Perhaps I should be more grateful that we've been sent here.

When the time for our patrol ends, we return to base and the next shift replaces us. We tell them that they are going to enjoy themselves and head for bed. I read for about an hour and fall asleep. I'm dreaming about the almond groves on the kibbutz when I'm awakened by the door opening. Menachem yells, *"Parash turki!"* (Everybody up!)

He leaves without another word, off to wake the others. Since I'm on the standby team, I'm still dressed and my boots are on. I jump down from my bunk, swing on my assault vest, grab my rifle from underneath my mattress, and make for the door. In less than a minute, the team is ready and most of the others have assembled as well. Menachem announces that a strong alert signal was generated and that a patrol found a ladder and some equipment. Teams with trackers are already searching for him. The standby team will provide support; we're just waiting for the driver.

We stand there silently. No one likes the idea that a terrorist may have infiltrated the fence, but we're eager to participate in the chase. When the driver arrives moments later looking like he could use a few more hours of sleep, we climb into the vehicle. We speed along wide dirt paths that run parallel to the main road and listen as the incident unfolds over the radio.

Bedouin trackers have examined the site and are confident that only a single person has gotten across. One patrol vehicle, another from a neighboring section, and the area's commander are giving chase. Since they believe the infiltrator is making his way to the main road, the area commander has sent us to head him off. Another vehicle is racing from the south, and the police are patrolling the main road.

As we drive, our intercept point shifts as the trackers gain a better understanding of the infiltrator's trajectory. When we arrive at our appointed station, Menachem has us fan out and conduct a search. It's a dark night. I'd have to trip over the infiltrator to find him. While we conduct our search, we hear over the radio that the infiltrator has made it to the main road and it's believed that he's hijacked a car. We continue patrolling the area, just in case. Two hours later, we learn that the police have found the car abandoned on a side road. Three hours later, we learn that he's been captured. I'm sure he's in for a long conversation with the Shin Bet.

It's nearly dawn, but it's now our turn to patrol the fence. We return to the base, grab something to eat, and exchange places with the night crew. The next few days are tough. Besides patrolling, we guard the base, keep the place clean enough to eat off the floors, learn about various weapons and equipment from our commanders and members of Duchifatt twice a day, take part in unplanned missions, conduct ambushes along the fence, and continue our exercise regimen. We barely sleep, and for some people their fatigue interferes with the fulfillment of their duties. The discipline required in showing up for guard duty on time is getting lax, which robs others of sleep. Petty arguments and tension between platoon members increase.

Menachem doesn't need to be told that everyone is becoming testy. Acting decisively, he asks members of Duchifatt to replace several of us who are guarding and calls us together for a discussion. We don't know what to expect, but we figure he's going to lay into us. Once we're all seated, he says, "It's clear that this is not working. Let's talk about it. What's going on?"

After several moments of silence, individuals speak up. We tell him that the patrol schedule itself is tough, but the additional work—the daily inspections of our rooms, the mandatory lessons, and all the guard duty—are too much. He listens to our complaints and says, "Okay. Obviously, there's nothing we can do about the patrol schedule. That's set in stone. I can't do much about the amount of guard duty, either, but starting today your sergeants and I will pitch in. That should help."

Over the last few months, our commanders have endured the rain, the cold, the lack of sleep, and the difficult training alongside us, but they do not participate in guard duty. In all fairness, we know that they plan the next day's training while we stand guard. It's not as if they rest more than the soldiers they command. When Menachem says that he and the sergeants will guard with us, he has already won us all over. We've never seen an officer stand guard before. It seems like an incredibly generous act and we respond to it. He also says, "As for the daily inspections, if you promise to keep your rooms and the common areas clean, we can just have inspections on Friday mornings. The additional training is important, but we can reduce the amount a bit. What's reasonable?"

We talk it over and agree to four lessons a week. We also agree to provide him with topics for discussion and to lead training ourselves. Those of us who have gained expertise with machine guns, mortars, RPGs, grenade launchers, and medical care will share this knowledge.

Menachem has talked to us as if we were peers. We are grateful to him and there is an instant change in everyone's attitude.

Life at Dalameyah remains difficult, but our early-morning runs aren't obligatory training anymore. Running becomes an opportunity to deepen our bonds, and it feels like a welcome respite. We run to a nearby kibbutz, swim in the pool, and run back refreshed. Within a week, we are running farther and faster than before. For all of us, the goal is to beat Menachem to the base's main gate. David and Omri each beat him once.

Not only are we working more as a team, but we're becoming more comfortable with Menachem as well. During late-night patrols, people occasionally fall asleep. The most enjoyable method for waking those who succumb to the monotony is to spill water on them. Now we even douse Menachem when he deserves it. Our impromptu meeting is the moment when our platoon becomes a real unit and Menachem becomes our commander.

On our second to last night at Dalameyah, we take part in an exercise to test the effectiveness of the fence's sensors and our ability to respond to infiltrators. As part of a team protecting the Bedouin trackers and the area commander, I carry the machine gun. Members of a special unit will infiltrate the fence and pretend to be terrorists on their way either to kill members of a nearby kibbutz or to hijack a car on the main road. We don't know when they are going to strike or what they are going to do. They have a six-hour window, and we are meant to go about our normal duties until the alarms are sounded.

Three hours later we get the call. I jump into a jeep with David, Yiron, and two Bedouin, and we follow the command car to the spot where the infiltration took place. When we arrive, the Bedouin inspect the area while the three of us spread out to guard the perimeter. The fence has been cut and the Bedouin have found tracks. They say that there are two infiltrators and mention that one of them is carrying a heavy bag. They believe that the infiltrators have a ten-minute head start. For once I think that I could be a tracker, too, as even I know that the alarm went off ten minutes ago. I'm watching our perimeter, so I don't see what they are looking at. My guess is that there are four footprints and one is much deeper than the other. From that they probably deduced the bag.

With the two Bedouin taking the lead, the rest of us guard the flank. They inspect the ground using flashlights muted by a red screen. I'm about ten meters away from them. Every so often, they stop and peer closely at the ground. They walk left and then right. We change direction a couple of times. After twenty minutes, we enter an orchard.

No longer on a dirt path, we walk along a paved road. One of the Bedouin says, "They stopped here. He changed the bag from one shoulder to the other."

I want to laugh. There is no way they can see that. Perhaps they can see something on dirt paths or in the brush, but on a paved road? Even though I should keep my distance and stay focused on the perimeter, I step closer and take a look at the spot they're examining. I can't see a thing. There are a few particles of dirt that the wind or a tractor has swept up from the fields, but there is no discernible pattern. I'm wondering if it's all a farce when he says, "They took a right into this row. Not long ago."

Playing along, we spread out, keep our weapons at the ready, and move into the field. As we walk, a tracker bends down to look at the field every few meters. We've walked about forty meters into the orchard when we hear two men shout, "Fire. Fire. Fire."

The exercise is over. The infiltrators come out of the trees and I see that one of them is carrying a rucksack on his left shoulder. I congratulate the trackers on their work. I'm a believer now.

Several days later, we meet up with the rest of the company in Beit Lid. We learn that their time in Nablus was at least as difficult as our own in Dalameyah, and they didn't have the benefit of a nearby swimming pool. They seem a lot more fatigued than us and far more fractious.

Menachem transformed our stress into an even stronger bond, but that does not seem to have happened with the other platoons.

Chapter 10

Raids

The situation in the West Bank and Gaza continues to deteriorate. The large-scale protests by thousands of youths and students in the late 1980s have been replaced by small gangs of terrorists affiliated with and funded by established organizations like Hamas, Islamic Jihad, and PLO groups that include Fatah, PFLP (Popular Front for the Liberation of Palestine), and the DFLP (Democratic Front for the Liberation of Palestine). The gangs receive training, weapons, and direction from these terrorist organizations. Much of the funding comes from Arab countries such as Syria, Iran, Iraq, and Saudi Arabia.

Over the last year, the frequency of terror attacks against Israeli citizens has increased, as have attacks against the Israeli military in the West Bank and Gaza Strip. Once soldiers only had to worry about blocks of cement, a Molotov cocktail, or a knife, but recent days have seen an increase in shootings.

In response, the Israeli military has redoubled its efforts to find and capture members of the terrorist gangs. Our commanders are provided names and locations by their commanders or directly from the Shin Bet. They work out a plan and then we walk several kilometers to the target's home, late at night. When we're lucky, we catch them. Other times, the information is wrong, or the terrorists are tipped off and escape.

I find the raids far more satisfying than the patrols. It's not because they are more dangerous; it's because there is far more clarity of purpose. When I'm patrolling a street, searching homes, or staffing a checkpoint, I see only that performing my duty impacts the lives of many civilians who are not directly involved in terrorism. Most of them are probably proud that Palestinian terrorists are killing Israelis, but I'm sure that few, if any, of those I meet are supporting terrorists in a material way. When we conduct a raid, however, we're going after a specific person who is directly involved in terrorism or has information that could save Israeli lives. I know that they are going to be interrogated by the Shin Bet and that this will be unpleasant for them, but I feel no internal conflict about these missions. We are told about the terrorists, their names, the group they belong to, and the actions they have taken, but I forget all of it soon after. It's not relevant. I understand that they are my enemy and that they seek to murder women and children. I'm not all that interested in their résumé. I want to know where they are and when we're going to get them.

For the last two days, we've been outside Ramallah, which—unlike other places in the West Bank and Gaza—is not overpopulated, and many inhabitants are doctors, lawyers, and other members of the professional class. In general, Ramallah is less volatile than other Palestinian cities, but many organizers of terrorism call this place their home.

Yoav is meeting with his superiors to discuss the upcoming missions and decide which units will carry them out. When he returns, he asks the entire company to meet in our makeshift cafeteria. Several members of the company are either taking training courses elsewhere or are on leave. As a result, only about fifty of the company's ninety or so members are here today.

We arrive a few minutes ahead of schedule so that we'll all be seated and settled before he arrives. When he walks through the door, a part of me wants to rise and salute him, but that is no longer necessary.

"Intelligence suggests that unusual activity is taking place at an unfinished complex in the industrial zone. We are going to investigate it tonight."

Yoav removes the large sheet of orange construction paper that has been covering a drawing that outlines his plan. Using both the map and the drawing, he points to our target. It is isolated on the east side of the city and is multilevel. To the west, on the opposite side of the street, is a small concrete plant. To the north, there is another, partially constructed building. To reach the target undetected, we will walk several kilometers to the east of it and climb this hill. At this point, we will divide ourselves into three teams. Third platoon will position itself on the west side of the building. First platoon will take the north, and second platoon will enter from the east. We will attack from three sides simultaneously, climbing rapidly to the top and working our way down. This place is supposed to be empty. Yoav tells us that anyone found inside is to be treated as an enemy, but to open fire only if our lives are in danger. "We don't want to create any martyrs, and a dead terrorist is of no use to us. Understood?"

Not quite in unison, almost everyone says, "Understood."

He turns to leave, then stops. "This mission was slated for Duvedan, but I told my superiors that we could handle it. Prove me right."

Duvedan is a relatively new special operations unit established after the outbreak of the Intifadah. Its members operate only in the West Bank, where they are tasked with the more complicated missions, including the capture of the high-profile terrorists. While we're happy to receive clean uniforms every couple of weeks, makeup and wardrobe experts help them blend in with their surroundings. A guy I know from the kibbutz serves with a similar unit, called Shimshon (Samson), which performs similar missions in Gaza. He has blond hair and blue eyes, but somehow they make him look like an average Arab.

They are an elite organization and therefore receive specialized training and the best equipment. Still, our opinion of Duvedan is mixed. Some months ago we raided several homes to flush a few suspected terrorists out into the open. A Duvedan team was supposed to close off a portion of the city with a checkpoint, but they failed to arrive on time, and the suspects were able to flee. They didn't even let anyone know that they had failed to reach their objective.

If given the chance, our unit could successfully complete the same missions Duvedan is asked to undertake. I'm sure of it. And here's our chance to prove it.

As usual, we are taken by truck to a point several kilometers from our target. With Yoav in the lead, we follow behind in two columns. With a bright moon increasing visibility, we spread out almost as far as if it were day. I'm a little more than ten meters behind the guy in front of me. Yoav navigates us to our target. Every so often, we pause and kneel low because of a passing car or to let Yoav radio our position to his superiors.

We reach the hill, which turns out to be very steep. We aren't going to be able to climb up from here as planned. While Yoav pauses to consider our next steps, we kneel facing outward. All of us look for any movement that would indicate that we're in danger or have been discovered. Moments later, Yoav has made his decision. He makes the low clicking noise with his tongue to inform us that it's time to start moving again. The clicking, which sounds a little like a chicken quietly clucking three times, is much quieter and carries a shorter distance than a whistle or a whisper. We walk to the north and toward the base of the hill. After a little more than five hundred meters, the hill flattens out enough for us to scramble up the slope.

It still isn't an easy climb, but we make it. By the time I near the top, I can see the other teams have nearly reached their objectives. Crouching low on firm ground, I see one team making its way along the ridge toward the east side of our target, while the other team, moving slowly and deliberately, edges toward the northern side. When they reach the building, the members of this team slowly stretch out against it. They form a long line to the left of the entrance. The only artificial light comes from the street, but the moonlight makes them quite visible. We slowly approach and pass the team that waits along the northern wall.

Since streetlights illuminate the west side of the building, we are going to be visible the moment we turn the corner, so we wait until we all can move on the target together. Menachem radios Yoav that we are in position. A moment later, Menachem says, "Third platoon, after me."

As we move quickly to the entrance on the west side of the building, I see first platoon move in the opposite direction toward the door near the corner of the north wall. Unsurprisingly, the door at the entrance is locked. It's a metal door. Menachem orders Dror to bring him the heavy metal rod that is used as a battering ram. Barak and I heave the metal rod at the door. On our second try, the door opens, and we pour inside.

Menachem doesn't need to give verbal commands. We've done this enough to know our jobs. Menachem takes the lead. When he finishes climbing the first flight of stairs and starts on the second, Yiron moves quickly but quietly up the first flight. When Yiron starts climbing the second flight, I start up the first with the battering ram in my hand. When Menachem, Yiron, Barak, and I reach the third floor, there are six men spread out on the staircase and three guarding the door below.

With all three teams now in the building, we will open fire only if we are shot at from close range and can clearly identify the shooter. Better to let someone get away than to injure or kill one of our own.

On the top floor we encounter another locked door. Barak and I swing the heavy rod and the door gives way immediately. Menachem enters the room moving toward his right; Yiron follows just after, moving left. Barak follows while I cover the entrance. I hear them shouting "Clear" as they move inside the room. Moments later they exit. No one is home. The place is empty. We work our way down to the second floor. We're making our way down to the first floor when Menachem says, "They got them. Second platoon has them."

We complete our search of this side of the building, just in case, but we know the tension and excitement have passed. Now we're just curious to find out what the second platoon has found. From the moment we reached the hill until now, the end of the operation, about thirty minutes has elapsed. The second platoon brings their two captives to the front of the building, one a tall and imposing figure, the other of medium height and build with no distinctive features. Even after looking at him closely, I think he'd be difficult to pick out of a lineup.

They are both blindfolded and handcuffed. While we wait for the Shin Bet to arrive, we learn from some guys from second platoon that the captives were trying to burn papers when the door burst open. They didn't put up a fight but focused on the papers until they were pushed aside. The guys said that they saw fax machines, stacks of money, and weapons. It makes us all curious. I can tell by the look on the faces of Yoav and Menachem that they don't quite know what to make of our discovery, either.

Taking possession of the building, we place guards on the rooftop and inside. It takes several days for the Shin Bet to search the building thoroughly. They find a list of names believed to designate people who were slated for murder. Some of the people are already dead, and they have a mark against their name. Everyone on the list is a Palestinian. A cache of weapons is found as well, including several Kalashnikov machine guns and literally hundreds of thousands of dollars in cash, in various denominations.

Before we vacate the building, we learn that this has been the PLO headquarters in Ramallah. According to Yoav, the men we captured have not spoken yet. He gives them grudging respect for not collapsing immediately under the pressure of interrogation, but he sounds confident when he says, "They'll talk. It's only a matter of time."

Our commanders are quick to mention that our accomplishment has been noted, and I have to admit that I'm quite proud to be a member of this unit. I didn't do much more than open a few doors and run up some stairs, but I think it's okay to share in the glory of the moment. In a few days, we'll be back to training and this will fade into a distant memory. There will be other raids. If there's one thing I've learned about the military, it's that the successful completion of one mission only leads to more.

Chapter 11

Final Training

In July we begin training at a base called Nebbe Musa. It's situated in the Judean Hills, about twenty minutes from Jerusalem. Some believe that this is where Moses died just before the Israelites made it to the Promised Land. Since the Muslims recognize Moses as a prophet, a small mosque was established to commemorate him. I expect to see the mosque and the base before dawn. We were driven to the training bases at Sanur, Cha'mam, and Yerocham. To reach Nebbe Musa—Moses' Hill—we're going to march from this small gas station and sandwich shop outside Jericho.

We won't be marching alone. The entire 202nd Battalion will be joining us. The battalion consists of four companies. One comprises administrative staff, including the battalion commander, intelligence officers, supply officers, logistical support teams, mechanics, and cooks. Another is a company of soldiers who, like me, enjoy training hard and spending time in the field. They are the battalion's primary assault group. A third is made up of the battalion's reconnaissance unit, mortar team, and anti-tank group. And then there is our company, which is still in training. In about six months, when we complete our training, some of us will be sent to officer training school. The rest of us will be sent back to the battalion. Those of us who complete the training will become sergeants.

Our training continues where we left off at Yerocham. We train with tanks and the air force. We navigate our way for kilometers to rendezvous with Chinook helicopters that carry us several more kilometers before dropping us off to walk several more kilometers to our objective.

The days and nights last longer than at Yerocham, but I am enjoying myself despite the lack of sleep and the thousands of flies that join us for every meal. Besides our training, we engage in long runs every morning. Before the military, I never ran. For this reason, I struggled during the first few months, but now only two others consistently run faster than me during our morning exercise. I wouldn't mind so much, but they are both smokers. And at the end of most nights, we run with stretchers.

The Israeli military culture places the highest value on acts taken to save the lives of others. Having been brought up with American images of war that seem mostly to honor valor on the battlefield, it's interesting that Israeli culture takes it for granted that we will fight bravely. Honor, commendations, and medals are largely reserved for those whose actions have saved lives.

As with our training at Cha'mam and Yerocham, we often leave the base for exercises at various sites around the country. This week we are training near Cha'mam. As we drive toward the place where we will set up camp, it feels like a lifetime has passed since we were last here. It's hard to believe it's only been about five months. Opposite our makeshift camp of two-man tents in rows, I see the beginning of a mountain range that seems to continue for kilometers. After we've run eight kilometers with the stretchers, Menachem points to the mountains before us and says, "We'll know this area very well before the week is over."

The next few days are torturous. It is extremely hot, and we make coordinated nonstop assaults on the nearby mountain range. For hours, we run up the foothills until we reach the summit. And as with any exercise, we follow a dry run with live ammunition and repeat at night everything we've done during the day. Each night, when the battalion is finished with us, Yoav has us running with the stretchers. If the goal is to test how far they can push us mentally and physically, our commanders are succeeding. I'm enjoying the challenge, but I keep that to myself. No one wants to hear it.

On the third day of training, we're standing in a column and just about to start a live-ammunition exercise when we hear a shot fired. It looks like it came from Nir, a member of my platoon. He may have forgotten to switch on his safety, or perhaps the lever rubbed against his assault vest. In any case, his finger shouldn't have been anywhere near the trigger. Luckily, he was standing in the left column and his gun was pointing to the left. If he had been on the other side, the person across from him could have been hit. We all halt. Menachem tells us to raise our weapons ninety degrees and check that our safeties are on.

Nir steps out of line and Menachem sends him back to the camp. We probably won't ever serve with him again. The accidental discharge of a weapon is an unforgivable mistake. He won't serve in a combat unit again. I'm sure he's embarrassed and miserable right now, but I know from our conversations that life as a combat soldier doesn't suit him. In the end, he might be happier.

On the fourth day, after completing our dry run, we discover that there is a water shortage. Normally there are several containers, each holding hundreds of liters of water, waiting for us when we complete an exercise. Today a member of the logistics team made a mistake. If I've learned one thing over the last six months, it's that you can live without food and sleep for an extended period of time. But without water, you're in a really tough spot.

Several of us make the issue known to Menachem, but there isn't much that can be done at this point. We're going to start the exercise in about ten minutes. It's a particularly hot day and I know I'm going to be parched by the time this is over.

Over the next two hours, we practice assault tactics, leapfrogging our way uphill and firing our weapons at targets as we move. I'm hot, thirsty, and exhausted. I would love to stop. I imagine how good it would be just to sit in the shade, but I keep moving. What would I do if we were in the middle of combat, tell Menachem *I'm sorry, but I'm too hot and tired to fight?*

My fatigue disappears as we move farther up the hill, but I'm happy to hear over Yiron's radio that our company has reached its objective. The exercise is over. I sit on the nearest boulder and coax the last drops of water from my canteen. It's hot and smells musty, but it tastes delicious.

As I walk down the hill with Yiron, I hear the crackle of the radio. Yiron stops to listen. He shakes his head and looks frustrated. I assume the worst. "What? Please don't tell me we have to do it over again."

He tells me, "Eleven people fainted during the exercise."

On the way down, we find Omri leaning against a rock and looking embarrassed. We sit with him while he receives fluids intravenously and help him down the hill. When we return to camp, we learn that Zohar, a member of our platoon who served as Yoav's radioman, passed out the moment he confirmed that the exercise was over. He was brought to Cha'mam and required six liters of fluids. We give him a great deal of respect because he hung in there long enough to complete his duty.

We continue training at Cha'mam for a few more days before returning to Nebbe Musa. A week later, we join the entire paratrooper brigade for a weeklong exercise.

I assume that our training with the brigade will be at least as tough as our training with the battalion. After our first day, I see that I'm only half right. The exercises last longer than those with the battalion and they are far more complex than anything I've experienced thus far, but every group actually has a relatively small task to perform.

If you look at the division from a general's perspective, you see an intricate strategy and a powerful force at your disposal, but a soldier experiences the exercise differently. Even though I walk several kilometers between each objective and I'm active from sunup to the following dawn, there are relatively long periods of rest between them. As with my first exercise with tanks, working with the entire division demonstrates that I am merely a small cog in a big machine.

Walking from one objective to another, I enjoy watching .50-caliber tracer bullets paint red lines across the night sky and hearing the buzzing of remote-controlled anti-tank missiles before they slam into their targets. The division is "capturing" kilometers of territory and destroying a mind-numbing number of targets along the way, but I feel more like a sightseer than a participant. That's okay, because I'm enjoying the view and can always use the rest.

After four days of training as a brigade, the various paratrooper companies now compete with one another in field exercises. We are timed, and the quality of our performance is being quantified. The company that gathers the most points, wins.

Since we are competing against units that have been serving for two years, as well as special units like the Sayerit, we don't expect to win, but we're going to try our best. We enjoy extraordinary luck. Everything works in our favor. Even when I shoot a mortar round of smoke to provide cover for Yoav's advancing assault team, the wind changes at exactly the right moment. The smoke stays one step ahead of them and keeps the team hidden right up until they reach their target. Pure serendipity. After eighteen hours of shooting, jumping, and running, we're actually in the lead.

The last exercise consists of a two-pronged attack on a built-up defensive position at the top of a hill. Yoav navigates the company most of the way. When we are a few kilometers from the target, Menachem takes our platoon along a route that will enable us to attack from the west, while Yoav and the rest of the company make their approach from the south.

Since timing is critical, Menachem moves fast. We expect to march a few kilometers through several wadis before reaching the indentation in the mountain, called a *guy*, that we will have to climb. I think we've walked too far and I'm not alone. Although we must maintain silence during nighttime, I can hear a few mutterings from the middle of the column. We press on for another twenty minutes before Menachem stops. He kneels down and we follow suit immediately. Kneeling closer together than we should, David says, "I think we're lost."

Before we have a chance to speculate further, Yiron runs to the back of the column. He doesn't look happy. Moments later, he returns to the front with our sergeant. A quick conference takes place. The sergeant returns to the back, and moments later Menachem turns our two columns around. About five hundred meters back, we enter another wadi and continue for another twenty minutes before we stop. We're all shaking our heads. Menachem isn't the world's best navigator, but this is not the time for a mistake. All of our efforts over the last twenty-four hours will be for nothing if we don't arrive on time.

There's another quick discussion. This time I see a dull red light emanating from the front. Menachem must be using his map. Moments later, he gathers the platoon in a circle and says, "I'm sorry. I screwed up. But I know where we are now. We can still make it, but it's not going to be easy."

Pointing at a hill in the distance, he says, "That's our hill. To reach it, we need to get over this hill here and make our ascent to our objective. I believe we can do it. Are you willing to try?"

His forthrightness changes our attitude immediately. None of us hesitates for an instant, sprinting to the hill in front of us. Our exhaustion evaporates as quickly as our exasperation and we attack the climb as if we had fresh legs. We're smiling and laughing all the way up, all the way back down, and all the way up the next hill that leads to our objective.

We're about thirty seconds late. Yoav doesn't wait for us. He starts his attack and when we arrive, we just keep running toward the target. In the end, the company completes the task and no one seems to notice the slight change in plans. We're told that this is the first time a company still in training has won.

Two more weeks of training at Nebbe Musa pass. Although we don't see many papers or listen to the radio much, we are aware that Hezbollah has ambushed several Golani units in Lebanon over the last couple of months. Tens of soldiers have been killed and dozens more have been wounded. The frequency and success rate of these attacks is new and troubling.

It's late in the afternoon and I'm lying down on my cot. Menachem pulls the flap open and says, "Herman, David, Yiron, and Omri, come here for a moment."

I assume he needs us to grab equipment from the base's weapons store or wants us to take care of some other minor task.

When we step out of the tent, Menachem looks a bit serious. I'm wondering if we're in trouble when he says, "You four have been selected for a special assignment. You'll receive a briefing in thirty minutes at the main quad. Congratulations."

Not knowing quite how to react, I say, "Thank you."

We get to the main quad twenty minutes later. Over the next ten minutes, six others arrive. It looks like three people have been chosen from each of the other platoons. At 4:30 PM, Yoav, the commander from the first platoon, Harel, and our sergeant Yotam arrive. Yoav says, "As you know, Golani has been hit hard over the last few weeks. We have been asked to buttress Golani and expand our presence in Lebanon. You have been selected from the entire company for this mission. Harel and Yotam, who have deep experience in Lebanon, will be leading you. I wish you all luck. I know you'll do our company proud."

When Yoav finishes, Harel says, "We're leaving tonight for Kibbutz Dafna. We will train in the area for three days to prepare for our mission. We'll be working with a team from the 101st Battalion. They have operated in the region recently and know the area well. We'll be setting up an ambush for a Hezbollah hit team."

Harel lets each of us know our responsibility during the mission. Almost everyone has useful expertise as a medic, a radioman, or a machine gunner. I'm being taken as a soldier. Mortars aren't used in ambushes. I'm sure I'll be carrying the water. I'm proud and glad to be selected for the mission, but I don't feel like I add much value to the team.

On the way to Kibbutz Dafna in northern Israel, we talk about the rise of Hezbollah. Until recently, PLO terror groups based in Lebanon were the largest threat, but that appears to be changing. I ask Harel if the military is sending additional teams from the other infantry brigades. He doesn't think so. "Out of the four infantry brigades, only the paratroopers and Golani conduct ambushes in southern Lebanon.

The other two brigades, Givati and Nachal, stay along the border much as your platoon did at Dalameyah."

We arrive at Kibbutz Dafna late at night, by civilian standards. There's nothing to do until the morning. Those who can sleep take advantage of the opportunity to rest indoors on a real bed. Most of us walk around, forage for food, and speculate about the coming week.

The next morning, we join Harel and Yotam in a small classroom. Over the last several months, we have learned how to capture kilometers of territory and work in urban environments. Today we're going to learn how to maneuver in enemy territory and set up an ambush.

We are brought to a small training area along the northern border and Harel and Yotam have us position ourselves in a "stomach ambush." Eight of us spread out in the shape of a crescent. Lying on our stomachs, with faces and guns pointed forward, we pretend that we're scanning the area in front of us. I'm on the end of the formation.

I need to position my body a little askew so that I'm looking more to the side than to the front. The guy on the opposite end of the formation does the same. About five meters behind us, two guys from second platoon and Yotam lie down to protect our rear. In this way, we create a protective circle. Anyone outside the circle is considered an enemy. And unlike the West Bank and Gaza, where the rules of engagement insist that you don't fire unless your life is in danger, in Lebanon we shoot as soon as someone is in our sights.

Over the next twenty-four hours, we train with Captain Liran and the ten men he selected from his paratrooper company. Until now, we've only been practicing our particular role in an ambush. Now it's time to learn how to coordinate with other units. Our team will be positioned in a valley while they remain on a nearby ridge above us. We will ambush the terrorists as they approach. They will serve as lookouts and provide support during an attack.

The coordination tactics we employ are not complicated, but we have to get it right. We're not concerned about the hike to the objective or how we'll deal with separating into two teams when we reach the ridge. We're not even worried about what will happen if we encounter terrorists along the way. The dangerous part occurs when we regroup after the mission is over. We need to make sure that we don't shoot each other by mistake.

While we were at Yerocham, two paratrooper units conducted an ambush in Lebanon much like the one we're now planning. When those two teams regrouped, a member of the lookout team thought the people approaching him with weapons were terrorists. He fired, killing the ambush team's officer and radioman. Both teams reacted instantly. Within ten seconds they all realized that they were shooting at other soldiers, but it was too late. Two officers and three soldiers were dead, several others wounded.

At Yerocham, our commanders used the incident to reinforce the value of the procedures we employ. They made sure we understood that the tragedy could have been avoided if the teams had followed procedures. Over the next several days, the incident remains a topic of discussion and debate. We argue over who was primarily at fault and consider ways to improve procedures, but almost every conversation ends with one of us praising both teams for their quick and effective reaction during the incident. The soldiers and commanders made critical errors, but we still credit the soldiers for picking their targets well and for shooting accurately.

Of course we regret the needless loss of life, but we remain emotionally detached from the deaths. For more than six months now, we have been trained to kill efficiently. For this reason, we respect the fact that the soldiers on both sides of this horrible incident functioned effectively: They remained focused, didn't panic, and quickly realized their mistake.

Besides, focusing on the actions of the living is more productive than dwelling on those who have died. Only a fool refuses to recognize the ways in which he is vulnerable to an enemy's fire, but a soldier on his way to ambush Hezbollah in Lebanon must lock away thoughts that make death personal. Those soldiers on that dark night could have been us. In several days, they will be us.

At the same time, reminding myself of this incident keeps me alert to carelessness on the part of my commanders and fellow soldiers. I will do my part to make sure we do not repeat the tragedy.

Throughout the day, we review the map, our route, and all the radio frequencies we need to know. This isn't a training exercise. All of us need to know how to navigate, contact Liran, direct artillery officers, and guide an air force rescue helicopter. Once Harel is satisfied, we make one final check of our weapons. We're as ready as we'll ever be.

I'm more anxious and excited than ever before as we are taken to the base from which we will launch our mission. I realize that Lebanon is different from the West Bank and Gaza and it isn't that it's a foreign country. The West Bank and Gaza don't feel like they are part of Israel either, but I enter those places in a bus or a car, not an armored personnel carrier. In the West Bank and Gaza, we are threatened by Molotov cocktails, stones, knives, or a sniper's bullets. Here, the enemy uses guided missiles, roadside bombs, and tactics learned from the Syrian and Iranian military.

Until the mission ends, we'll have a bullet chambered in our weapon at all times. Packed inside armored vehicles, we are driven to a small base that is about seven kilometers inside Lebanese territory. It is late afternoon when we arrive. We eat, review maps of the area, check our equipment once again, and rest until it's time to leave.

Several hours after dark, we leave the base. Walking in two columns, we make our way down a steep hill, through a large field, along a ridge, and across a flat tract of vacant land. Each time we complete a leg of our route, Liran calls in our position. Our eyes are always watching the perimeter. I'm on the right side of the column. My body points straight ahead, but my head is slightly angled to the right at all times. I've learned that you shouldn't actually look where you're going if you want to arrive safely.

We were taught early on that it is dangerous and unnecessary to look down or straight ahead while on a mission. If I'm looking down or in front of me, I won't be able to see the terrorist hiding behind the trees to my left or on a rooftop. I'll lose the precious second that I need to react. I don't know if it's my peripheral vision, but my feet seem to know what they need to do. I don't have to look down to know that I need to lift my foot a bit higher to avoid a large stone or extend my gait farther to avoid a small ditch. I don't stumble or fall and I feel more confident knowing that I can focus on my surroundings.

Our route is circuitous to ensure that we avoid two small villages. When we arrive at the point of separation, where Liran's team will start walking east to their lookout position and we will continue down the valley, we've covered nine kilometers. When they depart, Harel has us count off. Twelve in all.

Over the next forty minutes, we walk seven hundred meters down and into the valley. When we are one hundred meters from our planned ambush site, Harel calls Yotam forward. While we wait kneeling in two columns, they investigate the area to make sure it is clear of unwanted guests, and to select the precise spot of our ambush. When they return, Yotam walks to the back of the column and Harel says, "Half of you can take out your warm clothes now. The rest will guard. Then switch."

It's cool, but I'm going to be comfortable even if the temperature drops several more degrees. I drink water while the others take their coats out of their backpacks. When everyone is ready, we form into a single line and follow Harel to the site. As we've practiced many times, nine of us spread out in a crescent while Yotam and two others protect our rear. I'm on the extreme left. I remove the pack holding our water supply. Once I've settled into my spot, I place my right foot near Goldstein's left. Although we will communicate verbally when necessary, we will gain each other's attention with a light tap on a boot.

During the first hour, we just lie there and peer into the darkness, hoping and fearing that we'll notice movement. Afterward, Harel gives us permission to start our sleep cycle. Until one of us sees something to indicate that our targets are nearby, one-third of us will be permitted to sleep. Every hour one group signals another. I'm in the third group. We call it "Gimel" after the third letter in the Hebrew alphabet. Over the next two hours, I look into the night. There are small stones in the dirt near my head. To pass the time, I see how high I can pile them before they fall. Random thoughts enter and exit my head as if I were taking a subway to work, but forgot to bring a book. Luckily, I enjoy the solitude and the quiet.

I'm searching and listening for movement, but I'm not imagining what will happen if members of Hezbollah actually walk into our ambush. I'm thinking about searching for the aurora borealis with my sister Wendy and my parents over a year ago on a night just like this. I'm reminded that the avocados on the kibbutz will be ready to be picked in about a month. It occurs to me that I should have been relieved about an hour ago. I give Goldstein a light tap with my foot. "Has Harel signaled that it's Gimel's turn yet?"

He says, "No."

I suspect that Goldstein's sleeping, but it's not worth making a fuss. I'm awake and don't need to sleep much anyway. If he needs the rest, let him take it.

Another hour passes. I hear some shuffling before Goldstein taps me with his foot. Someone must have seen something. A moment later, Goldstein whispers, "One hundred meters straight ahead. Three figures."

My eyes are well adjusted to the night, but I'm not surprised that I can't see anything at that distance. Harel scans the area with his night-vision binoculars. Unfortunately, one hundred meters is quite a distance for an ambush. The goal is to let them approach within twenty or thirty meters before striking. Lebanese citizens know not to be outside at night within the Israeli security zone so we know that these aren't civilians. I'm ready for the order to fire and charge. Harel continues peering through his binoculars.

Several minutes later, Goldstein whispers, "False alarm."

I feel like I've been cheated. I wonder if Harel simply decided that it wasn't prudent to try to attack, given the distance.

Of course, for all I know, someone woke from a dream and thought he saw something. Maybe Liran's team saw movement using their sophisticated night-vision equipment, but the figures chose not to walk toward us. Here on the edge of our formation, I won't know what happened until we debrief later.

The next few hours pass without incident. As dawn approaches, it's clear that tonight was a bust. I know that the military sends out tens, if not hundreds of ambushes every week in Lebanon. It's a rare thing for intelligence to select the right spot, and a unit to be there at the right time, but I'm still disappointed.

Before dawn, we pack up our things and move about one hundred meters up the hill. The area has heavy brush. We use the brush and camouflage equipment we've brought to keep ourselves hidden. Since the military may want to use this area again for an ambush, it's vital that no one know we were here. We have already removed all evidence of our presence from the spot where we lay and will keep out of sight until late tonight.

An hour after night falls, we slowly rise from the bushes, form a single column, and quietly count off. We radio Liran to let him know that we are leaving the valley, and make our way to the rendezvous point. When we arrive, we divide into two columns, kneel, scan our perimeter, and wait. A few moments later, we hear a familiar scratching sound that means that Liran and his team are waiting for us several meters ahead. In reply, Harel twice lifts the Velcro that covers the magazine pouch on his assault vest; it makes two quick scratching sounds. We give Liran a moment to make sure that everyone on his team is aware of our approach and slowly move forward.

We warily form up behind Liran's team, and as we begin our journey back to base, our greatest fear is being ambushed ourselves. If someone had noticed our presence, they may have been able to deduce our route back to the base. We are now at our most vulnerable.

Before I know it, I can see the lights of the base in the distance. One last hill and we're back. We may not have reduced Hezbollah's numbers, but at least we relieved Golani of having to undertake another mission and our company demonstrated that we're able to perform in the field as well as any other paratrooper unit. For now, that will have to be enough.

Chapter 12

Richan

After completing our training at Nebbe Musa, we return to Beit Lid. There Yoav announces that we have been given a great privilege. Instead of rejoining the battalion, we are going to occupy the farthest base in the eastern sector.

He pauses while we process this. "The base has been abandoned for years. We're going to reoccupy it, leave the command structure of the battalion, and join the command structure of the special units."

We don't know exactly what this means, but we hope that we'll receive the same food and vacation schedule as the special units. Of course, it probably means that our responsibilities will be greater, too. Yoav tells us that we have been given this honor because of our many successes.

I'm excited and proud. I may have failed to win a position with one of the special units, but at least the unit with which I serve performs at the highest standard. Having the opportunity to carry out the same missions as the special units means a lot to me.

Even though the frequency of terrorist activity in the West Bank and Gaza is increasing, the terror organizations in Lebanon seem like a more pressing threat to Israeli security and regional stability. Every attack by Hezbollah on the communities along the northern border leads to a reaction by the Israeli military that could possibly spiral into a wider conflict with Syria.

I know we're not going to make much of a difference. Israeli forces have been in Lebanon since 1982, and little has changed. Israel initially invaded Lebanon after enduring years of almost daily bombing along the internationally recognized border. Within a matter of days, the PLO was defeated and Israel was on the outskirts of Beirut. Within a few months, fifteen thousand PLO terrorists were forced to flee the country, but Israel maintained a presence in Lebanon. Israel stayed because Syria refused to withdraw the tens of thousands of troops in the country and because attacks from other terror groups continued. By 1983, Israel had withdrawn from most of Lebanon, but created a buffer zone up to fifteen kilometers deep in some areas. Since that day, Israeli infantry, armor, navy, air force, and intelligence units patrol the area. Recently, due to the success of Hezbollah, Lebanon has become exceedingly dangerous.

Whether Israel should have invaded Lebanon in 1982 is rarely debated in Israel, but many people question the wisdom of our continuing presence. In my unit alone, we discuss this issue often. Even those of us who think Israel shouldn't remain in Lebanon agree that the growing threat of Hezbollah to the towns along the northern border gives our work in the field a purpose. We're not going in order to defend government policy; we're going to protect the citizens who only want to lead lives without fear of a Katyusha rocket landing on their roof.

As part of our preparations, I scrounge around paratrooper head-quarters at Beit Lid for additional batteries for our radios. I pass by one of the officers. He looks vaguely familiar. I don't know him, but he approaches me.

"Herman, right?"

"Yes. Can I help with something?"

"No. Yoav talked to you about the Hebrew course, right?"

I am taken aback and fear that I'll need to pass an exam I'm sure to fail. "No. He hasn't mentioned it. Not to me at least. Perhaps he said something to Menachem."

Scowling, the man says, "He hasn't said anything. Listen, an order has been issued. You are to attend a Hebrew course in two weeks."

Then, smiling as if he's doing me a favor, he adds, "You don't have to go to Lebanon. I'm going to talk with Yoav. Don't worry, they can't deny you. It's an order. You have to go."

He walks away and I stand there for a moment, stunned. I don't know what to think. Luckily, in Israel an order isn't exactly an order. It's more of a strong suggestion. If I'm determined, I know I can fight it. The Israeli military is not inflexible. But do I want to fight it? I'm proud that we've been given the chance to serve in the same place as the special units, but I'm conscious of the risks as well. I could avoid those risks without anyone thinking the worse of me. Later that day, both Menachem and Yoav approach me. Menachem says, "Adam, I understand that you heard today about the Hebrew course."

"Yes. It came as a surprise."

He says, "We were going to tell you. We know that you have every right to go, but we'd like you to consider remaining with your platoon. You're an important part of the platoon and you'll be missed."

"I don't know about that. I'm sure you'll all get along without me."

Yoav says, "How can you say that? You've come all this way and accomplished so much."

Menachem chimes in, "Don't you want to finish up with your platoon?"

I say, "Yes, I do. I want to go. Can I think about it and make a decision by dinner?"

"Certainly."

And as they turn to walk away, I say, "You know what, I don't need to wait. I know. I want to stay with my platoon and serve with them in Lebanon. I can't imagine leaving now."

When I return to the company, I discover that we are being divided into two groups. Second platoon will man the northernmost base in the western sector while the rest of us reestablish occupancy at the northernmost Israeli position in the more active eastern sector. The base is in the middle of a small Lebanese village called Richan. Those of us going to Richan meet up at the Good Fence. Established in 1976 near the Israeli border town of Metulla, the Good Fence was meant to be a gateway for Lebanese citizens into Israel, for better medical care and better jobs. Now the fence mainly serves as an access point for Israeli soldiers who are serving in the eastern sector of the Israeli Security Zone.

We are ferried to Richan in a convoy of armored trucks. Leading the convoy is an armored personnel carrier from a Golani unit that specializes in anti-tank warfare.

I can look out only by standing up and peering through a small slit. There are verdant valleys and high peaks, and I can see why people from around the world flocked to the country prior to their civil war. On the left, I see a large mountain. The PLO led operations against Israel from there prior to Israel's invasion in 1982. During Operation Peace for the Galilee, this was the site of a difficult battle. Many elite soldiers from Golani were lost in its capture. A member of my kibbutz was part of that operation. He doesn't talk about it, and I can understand why. Now the mountain is used as a base of operations by Israeli military units.

After a little more than forty minutes of slow going, we arrive at I'shia.

I'shia used to be the northernmost Israeli outpost in Lebanon. That honor will now go to our base, Richan. Before continuing on our way, we will receive a briefing by the outgoing officer in charge of I'shia. We crowd into the base's small headquarters and listen as he recounts the number and types of incidents they have encountered over the last two months. He suggests that the frequency of attacks will now rise because the terrorists will try to take advantage of the fact that a transition of personnel is taking place.

He wishes us luck. We return to the trucks, which take us part of the remaining five kilometers, until the road becomes too narrow and muddy to go farther. We'll have to dismount and carry our equipment the rest of the way. Walking there we pass two homes on the left and another on the right. Across from the base sits the skeleton of a home. Two floors have been built and I can even see the stairs, but it was left unfinished. I don't have to wonder why.

Yaki opens the red-and-white gate with an affable grin. He and a small crew of seven have been working tirelessly here for about a week to prepare the base for our arrival. They have made this abandoned outpost into a home for us. Yaki says, "Welcome to Richan."

I ask, "How is it?"

"It's been worse. It's livable now. The generators are up and running. The ovens work. You'll have heat."

There's about twenty-meters square of open space between the unfinished building and the two small structures that will serve as our headquarters and sleeping quarters. In the middle of the minuscule quad, I see the sign that has followed us all the way from Sanur. The red-and-white metal has been shaped and painted to look like a viper. I guess this is home. Pointing to a rusty contraption at the edge of the quad, Yaki says, "There aren't any toilets, but that's the bathroom.

There is a hole, plenty of toilet paper, a faucet, and a shower, but we don't have hot water. The rooms are warm, though."

Richan is certainly smaller than I'shia, but what does it matter? We're going to spend most of our time out in the field anyway. Walking in the entrance, I see in front of me a room the size of a closet where several radios are set up. This must be our command center. To the left of this room, I stick my head inside our dining area. There are five tables and, to my surprise, a small TV attached to the far wall. This is the first time we've had access to a television. I'm sure it will provide a welcome respite. Still standing in the entranceway, I turn right, toward our sleeping quarters. On the left, our commanders will be sharing space with much of our equipment.

Walking down a short corridor, I catch a glimpse of a narrow tunnel penetrating the wall. It is dark so I can't tell how far it goes. I doubt it goes far. As we pass it, Omri says, "That's in case of a mortar attack."

We think about that as we file into the two small rooms we're going to share. Fifteen bunk beds are squeezed into rooms that are each about six-meters square. For the most part, first platoon takes over one room and we take over the other. I grab a bottom bunk against a wall, shove my duffel bag under my bed, sling my weapon's strap around my neck, and return to the dining area for our first briefing.

Using the large, highly detailed map hung up on the wall, Yoav demarks our area of responsibility. Before he leaves, he says that there will be a briefing in two hours for tonight's missions. He suggests that we use the time to organize our equipment, familiarize ourselves with the base, study the maps, and learn the radio frequencies we'll be using.

That night, Menachem takes a team out on an ambush. We walk five kilometers. It's just the twelve of us. There won't be another team looking out for us. The night passes much like my first time in Lebanon. Once during the night, someone thinks he sees movement, but we aren't that lucky. We lie there until two hours before dawn then pack up. We march back to base, hoping no one knows that we were here.

We trudge through the gate just before dawn. Menachem tells us not to bother taking off our assault vests as by first light we'll be spread out around the base. Throughout the history of warfare, dawn has been a favored time for attack. Morning provides a chance to catch an enemy off guard, as soldiers stir from a night's sleep. The light is also valuable; as many modern militaries don't emphasize night fighting, their soldiers are more comfortable fighting during the day. Our training has focused on nighttime operations. In fact, our daytime exercises seem like they are merely a preparation for the night actions. But recent history shows that Hezbollah and the Palestinian terror organizations tend to prefer the day.

Menachem says, "Wait out here a moment. I'll find out where we need to be positioned."

When he returns, we are divided into two groups. Half of us spread out along the eastern edge of our base. I'm with the group facing north toward an open field. Two hundred meters farther, there is a forest. There's no reason to be particularly quiet, but we don't raise our voices. We stand protected only by the layers of barbed wire that surround the perimeter of our base, daring an enemy to approach. No one comes. After an hour, we leave the perimeter to Oz, Asaf, and Ariel.

Along with the daily ritual, a small team is gathered to clear the road that links Richan and I'shia of roadside bombs. Chagai, Yoav's new second in command, has replaced an officer who completed his military service just before we left for Lebanon. He walks into our room and calls for six volunteers to clear the road plus a radioman and a machine gunner. We're leaving in ten minutes.

Given the types of operations we carry out, military strategists have decided that the mortar doesn't play a useful role in Lebanon. So, the mortar rests easy at base while I begin a new career as a radioman. I've come a long way since someone insisted that "the American" should be kept off the radio, but I'm still a little uncomfortable knowing that I'm the main link between my unit and the rest of the Israeli Defense Forces (IDF).

I grab a radio, check its batteries, make sure I have an extra. I put Kevlar body armor over my shirt, slip on my assault vest, grab my gun, and walk outside. It's sunny and already warm. While I make sure our own command center and I'shia can hear me over the radio, Barak, David, and the others file out. Moments later Chagai exits and says, "Okay. Oren and Barak, you're with me. David and Yigal, you two are trackers. Shauli, close up our rear. Understood?"

Chagai isn't one for discussion. Without waiting another moment, he turns and walks toward the gate. Once we're past the gate, Barak walks on Chagai's right, Oren on his left. I'm right behind Chagai. The rest are divided up into two columns. We walk slowly, watching the ground closely for evidence of wires or devices buried in the mud alongside the road.

As we reach the paved road, I can see the small South Lebanese Army (SLA) base. The SLA, a militia comprised of both Christians and Shi'ite Muslims, has been allied with Israel for years. During our original briefing, we learned that the units in this area have been hit hard by Hezbollah over the last year, which has impacted their ability to recruit quality soldiers. I've met the people serving with the militia. Mostly men in their forties, they don't look highly motivated or disciplined. Their equipment is even worse than ours. They don't look much like soldiers, but then again I'm sure we don't look very imposing, either. The code word for them over the radio is *mastic,* which means "gum." It doesn't seem very complimentary, but I'll give them the benefit of the doubt. I'm just glad to know that we have some allies in the region.

As Chagai starts down the hill, David and Yigal are flanking the road. They are about thirty meters in front of us. Their job is the most dangerous: They're looking for telltale signs of improvised explosive devices planted to wipe out any patrol vehicles using the road.

I radio the base at I'shia and our command that we have left our base. We'll call in our position at three different points along the way. Aside from the danger, it's a pleasant morning walk. We chatter among ourselves some, but we do not relax our guard. We're a small group walking on a known path at a fairly regular time. We're an attractive target and we know it.

As a protective measure, no Lebanese vehicle is allowed to come within fifty meters of an Israeli vehicle or patrol. The inhabitants have been warned to keep their distance. Our rules of engagement during the day are similar to those we employ during emergencies in the West Bank and Gaza. If a vehicle encroaches, we instruct those aboard to stop by using hand signals or by aiming our weapons at them. If they keep advancing, we shoot at their tires. If they keep coming after that, we shoot to kill.

We've walked a little more than a kilometer. As we pass a bend in the road we see a Mercedes sedan driving at high speed toward us. We keep walking, assuming they haven't seen us yet. They're about three hundred meters away. Given that the road is now straight, they have to see us, but they don't reduce speed. They are now 150 meters away. My hand tightens around the grip of my rifle. Chagai waves his hand slowly and then holds it out to indicate that they must stop. They keep coming. They are only a hundred meters away. Barak and Oren stand still. Like me, they are probably waiting for orders. Chagai raises his weapon as if he's going to shoot, but he doesn't say anything. Finally, I ask him what he wants us to do.

Gruffly, he says, "Go, all of you on the side."

We take positions on the side of the road but Chagai stands there. The car is still coming. I don't care what he says; I'm not going to let him stand there alone. I run to his left, kneel, and aim at the car. Chagai doesn't speak, but when I hear the first bullet leave his weapon I start to fire one bullet at a time. The car keeps coming. I can't believe we haven't hit a tire yet. The two of us keep firing until the car screeches to a halt. Six men jump out of the car shouting, "South Lebanese Army! South Lebanese Army!"

"Idiots. Those idiots."

The entire incident, from start to finish, has taken place in a matter of seconds. Barak and the others take their positions on the road. Barak looks a bit sheepish. Chagai turns around and with a sarcastic, grim look on his face says, "Thanks for your help. I thought you were all supposed to be such great soldiers. What happened?"

We all know what we should have done. Chagai shouldn't have had to tell us what to do. We certainly weren't supposed to line up on the side of the road. He probably told us to do that out of frustration, in the way that a father might try to protect his children from coming danger. The moment that car advanced, Barak and I should have positioned ourselves on either side of Chagai. Barak, with his heavy machine gun, and me, as Chagai's radioman, should have backed up Chagai immediately. The others should have spread out on either side of the road. We all hesitated, and that is a cardinal sin for a soldier.

None of us says a word. Like everyone else, I'm embarrassed that I didn't react perfectly. I never should have left Chagai's side.

We speak briefly with the very apologetic members of the militia, and Chagai has stern words for them. Thankfully, the rest of the walk to I'shia is uneventful. As usual, we are given a ride back to Richan in two armored personnel carriers. None of us has much to say. When we return to Richan, we debrief with Chagai and Yoav. It isn't an easy discussion, but we all know it's essential to our becoming better soldiers and critical to our survival. This time it was the militia; next time we won't be so lucky.

Over the next month, we conduct ambushes, tramp through the hills in broad daylight to demonstrate our presence, keep roads open, and guard our base. Our days are long, but if we're not assigned to a specific task we're allowed to relax. Compared with our training regimen, we have a fair amount of downtime.

Although we're in range, our base hasn't yet been bombarded by mortars since we arrived. We think it's because we're nestled close to the Lebanese civilians living in Richan. Hezbollah mortars are deadly, but they aren't accurate. They're just as likely to hit our neighbors as they are to hit us and injuring civilians isn't going to benefit their political ambitions.

Along with infantry units, the Israeli army operates several tanks in Lebanon. With their sophisticated optical sensing equipment they can locate terrorists at great distances, day or night, and with a gun that can deliver munitions kilometers away. They are used as artillery pieces, lending fire support for infantry units in trouble.

But to be able to lay down accurate fire, the tanks need to be positioned in known geographic positions. Therefore the Israeli army has pre-positioned several platforms from which these tanks can operate. Of course, the terrorists know where these platforms are located and so they are perfect places for a Hezbollah ambush.

Our company's job is to protect the tanks. Before the Merkava tanks arrive, we enter the area first in APC's and use special equipment to search for bombs planted near the platform. When we're sure it's clear, we radio the tank crew that they can roll in. During the night, we form a perimeter around the tank and keep watch.

At two in the morning, it's my turn to rest, but I'm not tired. Instead, I climb onto the tank and chat with the guys. They give me the grand tour. It's an impressive beast, but I'd never want to serve in one. I don't care that it is one of the fastest, deadliest, and best-protected tanks in the world. It's still a tin can and a huge target. I might be more exposed as a paratrooper, but at least I'll see my enemy coming. Hopefully.

While I'm sitting on the turret with the commander and the munitions loader, the driver's head pops out. He catches the commander's attention. "Gadi, I think we've got something."

Gadi puts down his sandwich, enters the tank, and asks me if I'd like to take a look.

I don't need another invitation. They make room and I slide down. Sitting in the driver's seat and looking through the padded scope, I can see three distinct figures walking together. They are far off and in an area known for playing host to terrorists. Gadi calls in a description and the precise coordinates and asks for permission to fire upon the figures. I assume that someone is checking to make sure that we don't have a unit conducting an ambush or some other operation in the area. Ten minutes later, Gadi gets his permission. I leave the tank and let the crew make their preparations to fire.

After Gadi's men have let loose, I return to the tank and ask how it went. Gadi says that between the computers and the munitions they couldn't miss. "They didn't have a chance," he's proud to say.

When we first arrived in Lebanon, the weather was temperate. It was perfect for long hikes, and lying out all night was fairly comfortable. We're now well into our second month and it is cold. It's even cold for me. I can't imagine what it's like for Rada, who is Ethiopian. He's never seen snow.

We put on sweaters and thick jumpsuits once we arrive at our ambush site. Still, our boots are merely thin strips of leather and my feet feel like solid blocks of ice. Standing up requires effort, and I walk more like Frankenstein than a soldier ready for battle. If we have to engage the enemy, I doubt that any of us will be able to move effectively but I also doubt Hezbollah is sending people out on nights like this. Of course, Iran and Syria may be outfitting them with great winter gear. From intelligence briefings, I know they have better night-vision equipment than most Israeli units.

While I muse on the cold and convince myself that Hezbollah wouldn't be foolish enough to come out on a night like this, Shimi, who is looking at the valley below using the long-range night-vision device, taps me on the foot. "Do you see something?"

Two figures are walking near an abandoned building on the other side of the valley. They are too large and are moving too deliberately to be wild boar. I pass the information along and Menachem takes a look. He agrees with my assessment. Unfortunately, they are about three hundred meters away, too far to engage them, but Menachem has an idea. He has Yiron bring over the radio. He requests that a nearby South Lebanese Army half-track move toward us and fire its machine gun in the direction of the building. Menachem's hope is that the fire will disrupt the terrorists and possibly drive them toward our position.

The figures haven't moved far when the half-track approaches. We can hear it from over a kilometer away. It makes more noise than a tank. Spread out on the ledge, we look down the valley below expectantly. Through the night-vision scope, I see the half-track approach and the gunner swing his heavy machine gun toward the structure. The muzzle flashes, intensified thousands of times, obliterate any other details through the scope. I look up to see the tracers streak across the night sky. Several strike the building. Shimi grabs the scope back from me and looks for the figures, trying to track their movements; then he says, "Wait."

Before I can ask what he means, I see the tracers arc toward us. A single .50-caliber bullet would literally tear your head off, and hundreds are being fired in our direction. Menachem, in a quiet but decisive voice, orders us, "Down. Everyone down. Find cover."

I bend down to take the night-vision scope, but Menachem grabs me by the shoulder and pushes me back. "Forget it. Get to cover."

I should be very concerned, but strangely I'm not. I make my way back and search for a nice-sized boulder to get behind, but I'm not in any real hurry. I even pause for a second to turn around. If you can forget for a second what the bright lights are, it is quite beautiful to watch.

Moments later, the shooting ends. I assume that Menachem got through to the militia on the radio and ordered them to stop. Five minutes later, we have the militia search the area. They don't find anything.

One week later, it begins to snow. We're all ecstatic. It is truly beautiful. Some, like Rada, dance in the snow. We make a snowman and have snowball fights. Whether it is the beauty of the white snow or the change it brings in our routine, we are filled with joy. And then it snows some more. Then again and again. A tank parked in the quad can barely be seen. It is covered with deep snow.

What at first made us so ecstatic, now presents us with new difficulties. When on ambush, there is little conversation. Your own thoughts are your only company. Quietly we share the bits of chocolate and other rations we have brought, but nothing much is said beyond a brief thank you. It is only while doing guard duty, having long conversations, or completing math puzzles that the misery of the cold can be held at bay. For me, guard duty becomes my first opportunity to learn more about the men with whom I have served for more than a year.

I discover who wants to learn physics, who can't wait to travel to Peru, and who wants to become an officer once he's completed his compulsory service. The members of my platoon also find out that they don't know me nearly as well as they thought. They assumed that I have been dedicated and self-disciplined throughout my life. When I tell them a little bit about my days in college, they are surprised. They find it hard to imagine my carousing all night around Washington, DC.

The weather worsens. We are told that a militia base even farther north is facing morale issues because of the harsh conditions. The military has decided that members of our company will relieve them for two weeks. Ten members of first platoon and Gadi's tank team are the first to go. A week later, it's our turn. As usual, Menachem has more volunteers than he needs.

The militia's base is even smaller than Richan, but because of its proximity to several villages known to be sympathetic to Hezbollah, the base is constantly under threat. When we relieve the first platoon they look very weary. They tell us that they were barely able to sleep because of the need to be on guard duty all the time. There is also almost no food left on the base. I certainly wish someone had thought to mention that to us before we came. We would have brought more food with us.

Gadi and his men are here with their tank. They volunteer to guard with us, even though they are under no obligation. The night is cold. The small shack where we are supposed to be sleeping has a small kerosene heater that needs to be maintained every hour. We keep it lit, but since the door doesn't fully close and it lacks insulation, the room doesn't retain heat. I now know why the first platoon looked so tired. We're going to shiver in here, not sleep. Still—it's only a week.

At this high elevation the snowfall is very heavy. The next day adds another foot of snow on top of all the snow we've already had. The small quad is filled with snow, and if we were to be attacked now, it would be difficult to move from one defense position to another. We also learn that the road is impassable; we will not be resupplied for several days.

In the past few days we have gone through most of the food that we brought with us. The base kitchen contains only a huge bag of carrots and another filled with beets. We can heat water and make tea.

Although our situation could provide an opportunity for arguments and dissension, we take it in stride. You can either laugh or cry, and we choose to laugh. On our fourth night, at 1 AM, the eight of us on guard duty start singing. I don't know the words, so I hum along. We're freezing, we're tired, and we're hungry, but we're in this together. We make the best of it.

It continues snowing. We are told that they can't even send a helicopter. Menachem radios that we'll be all right. On the ninth day, it stops snowing and the sky clears. Menachem asks us to try to clear the base of snow. He reminds us that as paratroopers we are obligated to leave the base in better condition than we found it. We find small shovels and start with the pathways. I work in one area for an hour and clear a path from one station to another. Menachem and Yiron walk up to my position to check on my progress. I watch Menachem's jaw tighten. He stays for just a moment, but before he turns to leave, he says, "Good work, Herman."

As Menachem makes his way down the steps, Yiron holds back a moment, smiles conspiratorially, and says, "It's just that he's been working for over an hour and has only cleared a meter."

I say, "Well, if he says anything, remind him I grew up in New Hampshire. I was brought up shoveling snow."

Yiron slaps my shoulder and rejoins Menachem.

The next afternoon, Yoav and a team of ten others arrive, all with backpacks filled with food. The trucks still can't make the trip and no other solution could be found, so they marched. A few who have suffered frostbite here are relieved. We remain for another two days before the roads are finally cleared.

In March, the harsh winter is replaced with rain and mud. Our time here at Richan—our time together as a company—is nearing its end. In about a month, each of us will move on to the next phase in our military service. Before any decisions are made about our futures, Yoav takes time to speak to each of us. He thanks us all for our service and asks us what we want to do next.

My understanding of what it means to be a soldier is so closely tied with my experience in this company that I simply can't envision wanting to be anywhere else. The part of me that strives to excel still finds fault that I failed to win a spot in one of the specialized units and wonders what opportunities to contribute I missed, but I am very grateful and proud to have served with this company.

Completing our duty in Lebanon in March is the last step in a long march toward becoming a trained paratrooper. We're now moving on to the second phase in our compulsory service. Some will go to school to become officers, while others will complete their service as sergeants in the 202nd Battalion. We've graduated and are moving on. I have a green piece of plastic underneath my metal wings that proves it.

After a weeklong break, I make my way to my new base. Called Machveh Alon, it's situated on a hill just outside a small but fast-growing town in northern Israel called Karmiel. Here I'll take the two-month Hebrew course I missed five months ago. I walk up the road to the main gate. A few cars pause to see if I want a ride, but I prefer to walk. The sun is shining and I'm in no rush.

At the gate, I am greeted by a soldier who has probably not served in a combat unit. He scrutinizes my paperwork and allows me to enter. I ask for directions, and he provides a complicated set of instructions. Walking along, I can't help but notice the manicured lawns and the buildings. It's not nearly as big as Tel Nof, but it looks more like a campus than a military base.

Arriving as directed, at the second building opposite the infirmary, I see that I'm not the first. Two dozen others have unsurprisingly divided themselves into two groups; the seven with red berets on their shoulders stand apart from the rest.

Among the seven, I feel right at home. They are from France, Brazil, Costa Rica, Ukraine, Russia, Denmark, and Argentina; there is one other from the United States. We each speak different languages, but we all speak Hebrew, more or less. Like me, most of them left their family when they moved to Israel.

Milton, who is from Brazil, tells us why we are here. Normally the military has provided new immigrants with two months of Hebrew instruction prior to sending them to an induction center. However, the military was overwhelmed by a massive wave of Russian immigrants in 1990. To ease the pressure of this indoctrination phase, it was decided to let people like us, who had scored well on the intelligence and psychological exams, through, with the proviso that we would be dealt with later. Now that the military has absorbed and adapted to the wave of immigration, it can provide us with instruction. Of course, given the fact that we have all completed our training and most are already nearing the completion of their military service, it's a little absurd to pull us away from our units now. But none of us are complaining.

Over these two months, we've taken several short trips as part of an effort to learn about Israeli culture and history. The last trip we take is to Jerusalem, and one of the places we visit is Ammunition Hill. The instructors think it would be appropriate for one of the paratroopers to give a lesson about this place. They ask for volunteers and despite my fear of embarrassing myself, I raise my hand.

As the thirty-five members of the course and our instructors sit in the shade, I stand up and provide the historical context of the Six Day War. In Hebrew, I talk about the Israeli effort to gain control of the entire city of Jerusalem, and describe the battle that took place in this very spot twenty-five years ago. I am not communicating perfectly by any measure. I make many mistakes along the way, but I can't help but feel like I have overcome a significant difficulty.

I feel a deep sense of accomplishment. This moment will stay with me for the rest of my life.

When I return, the battalion is training on the Golan Heights. I am assigned to the battalion's main assault group, whose cavalier attitude is a bit disconcerting to me, but I am impressed with their performance in the field. I'd feel better if more members of my old platoon were beside me, but it's clear that these men know what they are doing.

The next few months pass quickly, and I am nearing the end of my compulsory service. The battalion's new commander asks to meet with me. He wants to discuss my plans. I don't have any. I moved to Israel to become a citizen, not a soldier. Being a soldier was just something I had to do. Only afterward did I discover how much I enjoyed marching through the night, conducting raids, and training for conflicts I hoped would never come to pass. Now I feel that being a soldier and being an Israeli are synonymous. Staying in the military would be very rewarding, while returning to civilian life will force me to think through difficult questions. Do I stay on the kibbutz or move to a city? If I move, where do I go? How will I make a living? What do I want to do with the rest of my life?

When I do meet with the battalion commander, he wants to know if I'd like to go to officer training school and become an intelligence officer. The intelligence officers I've met have been map readers for the most part so I thank him for his recommendation, but I tell him that if I'm going to continue being a soldier, I need to be in the field.

A month before my discharge, I call Yoav to let him know that I'm thinking about staying in the military. I tell him that I talked with a member of Israel's most elite commando unit through a friend, Matkal, about the possibility of my testing for his unit. I want to know his opinion. Does he think I could ever meet their high standards? He tells me that he believes in me. In fact, he encourages me to consider joining the Israeli SEAL team. He offers to help.

A part of me is certainly eager to test for one of these elite units. It's like a second chance. I'll be able to serve my country and challenge myself in new ways, but ultimately I decide to complete my compulsory service on time and start living my life as a citizen. I love the Israeli people and the culture, and have felt more at home in Israel than anywhere else I've been. It's time for me to focus on the reason I came here in the first place.

On the day of my discharge, I return to the induction center near Tel Aviv. I bring my rucksack filled with clothes and basic equipment. A bored clerk reviews my papers and spills the contents of my bag onto the counter. I know that I'm missing a sweater and that he's going to charge me for it. Luckily, his phone rings and he walks into a room in the back. I see the piles of sweaters, uniforms, and other equipment in a bin against the wall. Like a good soldier, I grab one of the sweaters and add it to my kit. The clerk returns, examines my pile, stamps my paperwork, and says, "Congratulations. You're a civilian now."

In 1993, Israeli and Palestinian leaders sign the Oslo Accords, and Israel withdraws from the West Bank and Gaza. During nine years of negotiations, Palestinian terror increases. During the first five years of negotiations, more Israelis are killed than in the previous fifteen years. In July 2000, Palestinian and Israeli leaders meet at a Camp David peace summit, which ends without agreement. A second Intifadah begins in September 2000.

Chapter 13

Citizen Soldier

Thanks to the ever-generous help of my parents and the financial aid provided by the government, my transition from soldier to civilian has been relatively smooth. I now live in an apartment near Ammunition Hill with two roommates, both of whom I know from the Hebrew course.

I support myself by guarding the public schools.

Like many who have served in combat units, I find that working as a security guard is a convenient way to earn money. The hours are flexible and if you're a student it's even possible to study while at work.

It's 1993, and I completed my compulsory military service a year ago. Generally, the military waits until a year after discharge before calling you up for reserve duty, but friends who completed their military service at the same time as me have served in the reserves for a month already.

I haven't even heard from my unit and feel guilty for not serving while my friends are fulfilling their obligation. I call the local military administration office and provide my serial number. The soldier says, "I see you. You're attached to a reserve paratrooper unit at Yerocham."

"You mean the training base?"

He says, "I don't know. I see it in the system, but I don't have any other information."

"What's that mean?"

After several more phone calls, I discover that the reserve unit is indeed attached to the training base in Yerocham. Since they aren't part of a reserve division, they operate under the radar. With some effort, I contact the unit's commanding officer and learn that they will be training up north in two months. He takes down my information and tells me to expect my orders in a few weeks.

When I report for duty, I find that the men in this unit are not highly motivated. They don't take the training seriously and are delighted that the unusual pairing of a reserve unit with a training facility results in their not having to serve very often. In fact, I'm told that this is the first training they've had in two years.

The reserves are vital to Israel's security. The standing army of conscripts and career soldiers is meant only to hold the borders for forty-eight hours after an attack. By then, the bulk of Israel's military, the reserves, will defend the nation. For this reason, I want to train hard and serve with men who are able to perform their duty. Maybe I'm setting my standards too high, but I don't think this unit will be of much use if we ever go to war.

Another year passes. It's 1994. After taking English literature courses last semester on a lark, I officially become a graduate student working toward an M.A. To earn money, I take a job as a security guard for a Jewish community in East Jerusalem. The Arab residents call the neighborhood Silwan. The Jewish residents call it the City of David because Silwan is built atop King David's ancient capital. The Jewish settlers are also quick to point out that the red roofs scattered throughout Silwan are the remains of a thriving Jewish community that was driven out by the Arab riots in the late 1930s.

I'm not here for political reasons. The security company pays me twice as much to work here as when I was guarding the school. The other guards who work here have all served with a special forces or special operations unit. I don't have the same pedigree, but I'm confident that my experiences have adequately prepared me for the position.

The situation in Silwan is potentially explosive. The last thing anyone wants is a security guard who is quick to pull the trigger. I think the security company appreciated the fact that I resolved a situation where a school principal was attacked by several thugs without even considering using my weapon. Armed with handguns and Uzis, we are authorized to protect lives by any means necessary, but we should have the confidence and ability to defuse situations without them.

The guards at Silwan drill regularly with urban warfare experts who also train Israeli SWAT teams. During our first training session, I'm concerned that I'm going to embarrass myself. Many have served in Duvedan and its counterpart in Gaza, Shimshon. Others have gained extensive urban warfare training from their units. I assume that they will all outperform me to such an extent that some will question my ability to perform my duties.

During the first hour, we work on drawing, aiming, and pulling the trigger quickly. According to our instructors, we must return fire in less than 1.6 seconds. Much of the time, we practice without ammunition. Our guns are holstered until one of the instructors shouts that we're under attack. Like everyone else, I draw my weapon, pull back the slide as if I were loading a bullet in the chamber, take aim at an imagined target in front of me, and squeeze the trigger three times.

We practice the draw at least thirty times before we move on to pretending that the weapon is jammed or that we need to switch to a fresh magazine.

When we transition to live ammunition, I'm pleased to see that I'm shooting better than most of the others. I've always had a knack for urban combat.

Over the next year, we scuffle with the Arab population several times. Stones are thrown at us on a regular basis, but it's relatively calm. We walk the Jewish families to and from their homes, we guard their houses, and we patrol the neighborhood.

In the rest of the country, the peace negotiations continue. As Israel withdraws its military from the major Palestinian population centers, the new Palestinian Authority asserts its control in these areas with the employment of thousands of newly commissioned police officers. Yet as peace negotiations move forward, the number and severity of terror attacks only increase.

I hope that this is only a phase. As we close in on peace, radical Palestinian elements that refuse to recognize Israel's right to exist want to derail the peace process. They hope to goad Israel into a major offensive that will make it difficult for Palestinian moderates to compromise. Israeli hawks believe that the negotiations with Arafat are a farce and won't lead anywhere. They believe that Arafat isn't interested in genuine peace and suggest that he is directly involved in terrorism. I want to give him and the peace process the benefit of the doubt.

My reserve unit remains a source of frustration. The lack of motivation grates on me. I want to serve my country and personally enjoy tough physical training. The members of my unit just want to go through the motions, when we're training and when we're in the West Bank. I want to improve my skills and I take my service seriously. I start asking friends about their reserve units. If I find one that sounds like it'll be a good fit, I will try to transfer to it.

Roni, one of the paratroopers I met during the Hebrew course, joined an elite special operations unit called the Alpinistim. The unit is made up of some of the best commandos in the country. They reject most applicants out of hand and require weeklong testing before accepting candidates. Roni gives me the number of the unit's commander, Shimon.

I leave ten messages for Shimon. Eventually, I'm able to speak with him. The Alpinistim are best known for being able to maneuver in the snow. In a country like Israel, soldiers who ski and sleep in snow caves are a rarity. I mention that I've been skiing since I was three. He says, "I don't care. Skiing we can teach. I need fighters."

I say, "I'm a fighter. Speak with my former commanders. I'm a good soldier."

He says, "Well, I only want the best. Also, I can't pull you out of an existing unit. You have to get your current commander to release you. If you can do that, I'll let you test."

I thank him and call up the commander of my reserve unit. I tell him that I have a chance to join the Alpinistim and ask if he'd be willing to release me from the unit if I'm accepted. He readily agrees.

Two months later, I'm serving with my reserve unit in the West Bank in what is known as Area B. Territory under full control of the Palestinian Authority is called Area A. Area B is where the Palestinian Authority administers to the civil needs of the population and the Israeli military maintains an active presence. We're guarding buses that take children to and from school. Buses are a favorite target for terrorists; our presence serves as a deterrent.

When the unit is ordered to staff a nearby checkpoint for twenty-four hours, I'm quick to volunteer. After a week of traveling up and down the same stretch of road, I'm eager for a change. We quickly check people's ID cards and inspect the vehicles that pass.

Reviewing the ID of the seventh driver to pass through the checkpoint since our arrival, I notice that his number is on the list of wanted individuals. I double-check, ask the man to step out of his car, and call over one of the guys. While the suspect sits on the curb, I let headquarters know that we have stopped a wanted individual at our checkpoint.

In the past, that would be the end of the conversation. Now, in the spirit of cooperation, a discussion between Israeli and Palestinian military counterparts takes place. While the hours pass, we share our food and water with him. I call up headquarters to remind them that we're waiting to hear what they want us to do. I'm told to let him go. In the past, I would have assumed that the Shin Bet wanted him released for a specific reason. Now I'm wondering if the person on the other end of the phone simply doesn't want to bother with the paperwork. Feeling frustrated, I tell the man that it's his lucky day and let him drive off. I hope that he doesn't go home and build a bomb.

At midnight, a car approaches our checkpoint slowly. I put my hand up; the driver stops and pulls his ID card out of his front pocket. I ask him to step out of the car while we inspect it and verify his ID. Since it's a little odd for someone to be driving around at this hour, I carefully scrutinize his car. While I'm looking underneath his spare tire, he says, "I'm Fatah, not Hamas. I'm okay."

One day, perhaps, claiming allegiance to the PLO's leading faction will lead me to think I can trust a person. Unfortunately, right now I don't see a real difference between the PLO and Hamas. Unlike Hamas, the PLO has changed its rhetoric, but it is hard to point to any concrete steps that have been taken to create an atmosphere of reconciliation.

People feel more comfortable eating falafel in Jenin now, but the number of terror attacks only grows.

The media, politicians, and analysts all agree that the retreat of military forces from the main Palestinian population centers hinders our ability to strike at Palestinian terrorists. I believe that Prime Minister Rabin is correct and that our restraint will eventually pave the way to peace, but each attack makes it harder to believe that it's worth the price.

After the first heavy snow of the year, I test for the Alpinistim. I join fifteen other hopefuls, all of whom hail from various special forces and special operations units. We are given a weeklong course that includes snowshoeing, basic ice climbing skills with crampons, orienteering, the building of snow caves, backcountry skiing, and reconnaissance techniques. Officers evaluate fitness levels, determine how quickly we learn, and decide whether we fit the unit's culture.

On the last day, I cross paths with Shimon for the first time since I arrived. "Herman, come here."

I say, "Hi, thanks for—"

He interrupts, "I hear you don't suck."

I don't quite know how to respond. "Thank you," I say.

Without another word, he continues on his way. Later I learn that I've been accepted.

Unexpectedly, the commander from the paratrooper unit refuses to release me. I remind him of his promise; he tells me that he needs everyone in the unit right now and asks me to be patient. Since I don't want to give up my chance to join the Alpinistim, I decide to serve with both units until I can convince my commander to let me go.

During the next two years, I pull double reserve duty. Twice a year, I'm reporting to the reserve unit attached to the Yerocham as ordered and I'm also training with the Alpinistim as a volunteer. I continue working at Silwan, and keep at my studies. In addition, I build a community of friends and feel increasingly at home in Jerusalem. I finally wear down the commander of my reserve unit, who consents to release me. Finally, after two years, I am officially a member of the Alpinistim.

Over the next four years, serving with the Alpinistim gives me great pleasure. Like me, the reservists in this unit enjoy soldiering. The level of dedication, the professionalism, and the demanding physical effort remind me of serving under Yoav's command. I don't feel like I need to apologize for being highly motivated. From my days as a raw recruit until I joined the Alpinistim, most of the people with whom I served were only fulfilling an obligation and as a result, they had every right to gripe about serving.

The bombings in Israel become more frequent and deadly. I see the carnage and check with friends to make sure that everyone is safe, but I am detached, hardened by my experiences.

Afterward, I put the images and even the stench aside and tell myself that the violence will pass once we start living side by side as two sovereign nations. But the negotiations only lead to more negotiations and more broken promises. And when Rabin is killed, we mourn him by rededicating ourselves to the dream that peace is possible. Most of the nation ignores the Palestinian Authority's incitement and the rise of a Fatah-sponsored competitor of Hamas suicide bombers, the al-Aqsa Martyrs' Brigades. Instead, we focus on the booming economy and tell ourselves that we are on the verge of peace with the entire Arab world. Despite the bombings, there is a kind of euphoria. Many people begin to suggest that reservists are suckers who are wasting taxpayer money.

There's something about hiking all night, managing without much sleep or food, and being indifferent to the climate that makes me feel more connected to myself and my surroundings. As a citizen, so many things compete for my time that I am barely able to give my studies, employers, friends, family, or self the kind of attention we deserve. In the military, I'm able to step back from many of life's demands and focus on the task at hand, the person sitting next to me, or the colors of the setting sun. And I'm beginning to see that being a member of the military is the most rewarding part of living here, apart from the friends I've made.

My employer owes me several months' salary by this time. The Histradrut, the government agency that is supposed to protect workers' rights, agrees, but it seems powerless to help. I watch my limited savings quickly dwindle, and since my employer won't fire me, I can't even collect unemployment.

Over the next few months, I take on additional freelance work, but it's not enough to pay the bills, and given the economy I can't find a job that will pay me a living wage. By November 1999, I've completed my course work and I need to write my thesis. My aunt and uncle offer me their summer house in Ogunquit, Maine. At this point, it seems like the only viable option.

Given that Clinton, Barak, and Arafat are on their way toward creating a framework for peace at Camp David, I don't feel I'm deserting my country in its time of need. So I pack my bags and return to the United States.

Chapter 14

Operation Defensive Shield

My stay in the States was meant to be a brief break, but I've been here now for two years. While working on my thesis, I get an opportunity to develop a small marketing campaign for Microsoft. The success of that campaign leads to steady work as a copywriter.

I enjoy my work immensely. While in Israel, I tried to work in advertising, and failed. My fluency in Hebrew increased tremendously over the years, but not to the point where I could write a striking headline or develop compelling content. Yet I advance quickly in the United States and join a Boston-based firm. In Israel I'd be unemployed or, at best, underemployed.

For the first time, I understand what it must be like for the Russian architects, engineers, and other professionals who end up working at Israeli supermarkets. I tell myself that I'll stay just long enough to earn some money and establish a track record that will position me for success when I go back.

In September 2000, news of another Intifadah chills me to the bone. In the past, Palestinian defiance and violence achieved tangible gains. Palestinian leaders were warmly received in capitals around the world, and an increasing number of Israelis recognized the wisdom of a Palestinian state. But this new round of violence is causing people to wonder if the Palestinian leadership is interested in achieving peace at all.

The Israelis of course don't expect the Palestinians to be grateful that Israel now accepts their claim to the West Bank and Gaza, but an increasing number of people are questioning the logic of the virtual autonomy given to the Palestinians as part of the Oslo Accords.

In September 1993, the Israeli government agreed to withdraw its forces from the West Bank and Gaza. In addition, Israel allowed the PLO leadership to form a proto-government, called the Palestinian Authority, which would govern the Palestinians while a long-term solution to the conflict was negotiated. In the nine years since the Oslo Peace Process began, terrorist attacks against Israeli citizens spiked. In the five years immediately following the signing of the accords, more Israelis were killed than in the fifteen years preceding the agreement. Throughout this period, people like me called on the Israeli government to show restraint. I believed that the increased number of terror attacks was part of the transition process. I hoped that the Palestinian leadership would turn inward toward nation-building and move away from embracing extremism. But nine years is a long time.

I'm beginning to wonder if Israel's restraint only encourages more violence. It's a horrible thought, and the kind of thing my best friend, Uri, might say. I've invested too many hours seeing the world from the left of center to start agreeing with the right.

After an attack during 2002's Passover, Sharon orders a massive call-up of reserves. Operation Defensive Shield is under way. I e-mail Roni and ask if the Alpinistim have been activated. He hasn't received a call and will let me know the moment he learns anything. I speak with Uri and ask if his reconnaissance unit has been activated. It hasn't.

I can't get any work done. I'm completely focused on the unfolding events in Israel. I want to go and serve, but there is little I can do if my unit isn't activated.

As Israel gears up to destroy the terrorist infrastructures that the Palestinian Authority has allowed to flourish, commentators in Israel and abroad suggest that thousands of Israeli soldiers may be killed. They discuss how the Palestinians have built up well-constructed defensive positions in the major cities, and that the Israelis may be facing well over fifty thousand heavily armed Palestinian policemen.

In only a week, Israeli tactics succeed magnificently and the military is in the process of taking back the territory ceded to the Palestinian Authority with minimal casualties. Two days later, Uri tells me that his unit is being activated. When Roni verifies that the Alpinistim aren't being called up, I tell Uri that I want to join his unit. He calls his commander and gains his support.

That night I purchase a plane ticket and tell the vice president to whom I report that I'm leaving for Israel in three days. He and the firm are completely supportive of my decision. I call my parents and tell them I'm going to visit Israel. They ask if I'm going to serve in the army. I don't exactly lie when I tell them that my unit hasn't been called up and that I don't have any orders to serve.

When I board my Swissair flight, I'm feeling anything but neutral. Nilly Barelli, whose family more or less adopted me ten years ago, picks me up at the airport. She has a hair appointment at a trendy salon in Tel Aviv. It is late afternoon on a beautiful day. Normally, the cafés are filled with people drinking coffee and talking on their cell phones, but today it's like a ghost town. It reminds me of the Gulf War. Nilly tells me that it's like this all over the country. People hardly go out and only patronize places where security guards are present.

Guards have always been posted at supermarkets, bus stations, malls, movie theaters, and any other place where large numbers of people congregate, but now small shops like this hair salon must either hire a guard or close down. Nilly tells me that many of my favorite places in Jerusalem have shut their doors.

When I tell Nilly that I plan on joining Uri's unit, she doesn't seem entirely pleased. She's an intelligent and practical person. But I can't help myself. My love for Israel runs deep. It is my home in the world and I can't stand by and do nothing.

While Uri and his unit prepare for their mission, I spend the next day dealing with administrative issues. To resolve them, I return to Israel's main induction center. It's been years, but the place doesn't look any different. Once I've taken care of the paperwork, I return to the Barelli home, thank them for everything, and make my way up north to Uri's unit.

Uri and his reconnaissance team are away scouting an area. I use the time to gather my equipment. I have to argue a bit in order to make sure I receive an M-4 assault rifle and find a place for target practice.

I practice for an hour, mostly without ammunition. I focus on how I'll respond to being under fire. I run a series of exercises until I'm satisfied with the speed with which I lift my weapon, flick the switch from safety to semiautomatic, plant the stock in the notch between my pec and shoulder, lower my eye to the sights, aim, and squeeze the trigger as I exhale. As usual, I practice exchanging magazine clips and transitioning to various firing positions.

Soon after I return to the unit's tent, Uri and his team arrive. They greet me warmly. I'm guessing that Uri has exaggerated my abilities. Later, I meet with the company commander. He is a bit too busy making sure I know he's the company commander to garner much trust from me, but his second in command, Sharon, is a professional—he's easygoing, bright, and eager. The members of the reconnaissance team think he's a little too eager, but they all respect and trust his judgment.

Over the next two days, we train for the upcoming mission. The members of this reserve unit aren't as fit, motivated, or highly trained as the Alpinistim, but they are committed soldiers.

During a briefing, we are told that our mission is classified and that we cannot discuss our objective with anyone. That's okay by me, because as far as my family is concerned, I'm camping with Uri on the Golan. I don't think my dad believed me, but he lets me keep up the illusion. I'll tell them what I can when I return to the United States. Right now, I don't want to worry them any more than necessary.

After three weeks, we achieve our objectives. The West Bank and Gaza are now firmly under Israeli control and the government demobilizes the reserve units. Uri and I return to Jerusalem. I'm going to return to the States but before I leave, I coerce Uri and his wife, Tali, to join me at a restaurant-bar called the Shanty. Patronized by some of the city's best and brightest, it has great food, and its bar is stocked with a wide variety of Belgian beers.

The Shanty's armed guard searches us when we enter. I am surprised to see that the place is packed. We ask the waitress if the restaurant has been busy despite the situation. She tells us that there has been a decided increase in customers since Operation Defensive Shield began.

I'm glad to see that more people are venturing forth and feel safe. They don't have any illusions about their vulnerability, but they know that the Palestinian ability to strike has been greatly diminished since the military reestablished control over the West Bank. With the military in close proximity to the terrorists, Israeli counterterror forces are better able to gather intelligence and create a buffer between the terrorists and Israeli civilians.

Watching people come up to thank a table of five reservists for their service reminds me how times have changed. Once again, reservists are heroes and the country is grateful. Talking with Uri and his wife about their son Yohonatan, I can't help but wonder how long this feeling will last.

Chapter 15

Returning to Help Maintain the Quiet

After Operation Defensive Shield, I return to Massachusetts and go back to work the very next day.

I don't know if it's because I've just returned from seeing how happy Uri and Tali are together or if it's because I simply haven't been in a relationship for a while, but I take my search for love more seriously. I don't need to stay in the Boston area. I've been here for more than two years and haven't met anyone. Knowing my job affords me the opportunity to work from anywhere in the States, I log on to an online dating service.

I don't narrow my search to Boston. Instead, I look at the profiles of the newest members. On the first page, I see a profile for a woman whose user name is Blond Booklover. I can't tell what she looks like from her photo, but from what she's written in her profile I can tell that she and I have a lot in common. She's in Knoxville, Tennessee, but I write her anyway.

The next day, I receive a thoughtful response from Jennifer. Over the next few weeks, e-mails lead to long phone calls. I fly out to Knoxville. From the moment I see her at the airport, I'm hooked. Over the next three months, we visit each other regularly. We're both deeply in love. My position is being eliminated. I gladly accept a generous compensation package, pack my belongings in my car, and move to Tennessee to be close to her.

An e-mail from Uri lets me know that his reserve unit will be the primary reconnaissance and assault team in the Jenin sector. The unit will be called up in February and will remain active for a month. He reminds me that I am not obligated to return and serve; he's just letting me know.

I give him a call to say I plan on joining him. He insists that I don't have to come. Certainly there is no legal obligation, but I feel a moral obligation to watch his back and help protect my people. If I don't go, I will feel like a deserter, but my life has changed considerably since last year.

When Operation Defensive Shield began, I couldn't wait to be in uniform, but my duty as an Israeli now conflicts with my obligations to Jennifer. I shouldn't be giving her reasons to worry. She knows I have been serving in the reserves, but up until now it has been an abstract idea. In a little more than a month, she'll wave good-bye to me at the airport and wonder if I'll ever come back.

This is our first real crisis. I know that my leaving is causing her great pain and could possibly end our relationship, but my need to serve my people is greater than my desire to make her happy.

After she and I have said our final farewell at the airport, I realize that I could die in the West Bank. This is the first time I've allowed this thought to creep into my consciousness. I have few assets and realize that it may not even be legal, but I draft a will on the plane to New York. I make Jennifer the beneficiary of my (laughable) estate and ask my family to treat her as if she were my wife. I ask them all to understand why I find it necessary to continue to go, and to forgive me for all the anxiety they've endured over the years.

When I land in Tel Aviv, the first thing I do is purchase a cell phone. Last year, I was able to use Uri's phone every few days to put in a quick call to my family. This year, I plan on calling Jennifer every day. This will, I hope, make my being here easier for her. I don't care how much it costs.

Beyond the customs area, I see Uri waiting for me in the crowd. After a quick embrace, we walk toward his car and pepper each other with questions. We're just two friends who haven't seen each other for a year. We speak about the military only once during the hour it takes us to reach his home in Jerusalem. He tells me the unit will assemble in El Yakeem. The last time I was at El Yakeem, I barely slept, it rained every day, and I spent the entire time knee-deep in mud. Needless to say, I have very fond memories of the place.

Even before we enter Uri's apartment, I smell my favorite Moroccan dishes. Tali greets me with a welcoming smile and a warm hug, but over dinner, she makes it clear that she thinks Uri and I are fools for not avoiding our reserve duty. She reminds us that many people find compelling reasons to defer their service. Work, family responsibilities, even a vacation abroad, are all legal dodges. Then there are those who simply ignore the army's summonses. She recognizes the value of the reserves to the military and accepts that citizens are necessary to the defense of our nation, but she reproaches us for always being willing to show up.

At 6 AM, Uri and I walk out the door, wearing our well-worn military uniforms and army boots. When we arrive at the bus station, we pass through security quickly. The guards smile at us and wish us good luck.

When we arrive at El Yakeem, it's still early in the morning. It's been many years since I've endured the military's typically slow and torturous process of distributing equipment and filling out paperwork, but this is particularly bad. With the Alpinistim, induction was a breeze because a relatively large support staff was assigned to meet the needs of a small unit. It's also hard to get used to the fact that no one is eager to start.

Uri's reconnaissance unit has squatted in one of the six long tents being used by the battalion. He and I settle on two plastic cots and are playing cards with the others for about two hours when we learn that the supply staff is finally ready to distribute our gear. I put down my cards, but Daboosh says, "What's your rush? Are you afraid they're going to run out of canteens? Let's finish whist."

I resist the urge to run toward the oversized metal container that the supply staff has transformed into a distribution center. I want to be one of the guys. I am used to organizing my equipment immediately so I can start training, but this unit's culture is different. I must respect their ways if I am going to be a part of the team.

We play another few hands of whist before we leave the tent together and walk toward the supply staff. We are each given a canvas kit-bag filled with equipment. It's a basic package, but I have everything I need.

As we head back to the tent, Uri, who is the team's sergeant, stops to talk with the battalion's commander and the platoon's officer. When he returns, he hands me a small piece of white paper with a number on it. When I go to the armory, I'll exchange this scrap for a short M-16. This time, I won't have to argue or beg for it. I thank him for his effort. Over the next six hours, we play cards, drink tea, and walk around the

base. Every so often our leisure is interrupted by a request from an officer to sign for and lug equipment back to the battalion. In the late
afternoon, we walk to the gun range. My weapon shoots just fine, but
I'm not satisfied with my accuracy. I need to work on that if I'm going
to be of any use.

By the time we sit down for dinner, I've been productive for only
about two hours of the entire day. After dinner, we learn that we will
be training at El Yakeem for three days. As is the norm, we will not be
keeping a nine-to-five schedule. It's now about 6:30 PM. In thirty minutes, our first class will begin. We focus on orienteering. It's back to ba-
sics. Maps and compasses. No GPS for us. Obviously, none of us wants
to get lost in the middle of Jenin. We all pay close attention and brush up
on our skills. Two hours later, we follow the immutable law dictating that
every exercise that takes place during the day must be repeated at night.
We return to the range to shoot some more. Later that night, I call Jen
and my parents. This time, I tell them the truth. I let them know that
we'll be training for the next few days. I make it clear that this means
I'll be in no danger, but it doesn't seem to make them feel less anxious.

Even though we don't need it in Jenin, since we are the reconnaissance unit, we learn about advances in camouflage. Uri and I are familiar with all this, but some of the others marvel at the devices that look
just like a boulder and the suit that enables you to blend in with trees.
The only camouflage we'll be using are thin, wide tarps, green, black,
and brown, that we'll spread over our Hummers or attach to trees. They
aren't sophisticated, but if used properly they will enable us to conduct
surveillance from a distance without being seen.

After lunch, the fun begins with *la'shab* (urban warfare) training. As
with all other infantry tactics, surrounding and entering a home isn't all
that complicated. But unlike the demands associated with taking over a
ridge, this type of activity requires a great deal of coordination among

several small teams, flexible minds that can adapt to unexpected events, a keen awareness of your surroundings, and finesse. Urban warfare does not require athleticism. It demands creativity and teamwork.

I haven't practiced *la'shab* in several years. From the looks of it, neither have the members of Uri's unit. We start off looking like a bunch of raw recruits, but several dry runs change that. No one speaks of it, but I bet that all of us are reflecting on the truism that hard training makes combat easier. Being an effective soldier doesn't completely shield you during a fight, but I certainly don't want to die because I was too lazy to train, and the members of this unit seem to feel the same. We don't train nearly as long or as hard as I'd like, but we definitely make progress.

By the time we return to repeat the training at night, I feel more confident in our abilities. My one concern is the team's officer, Aviv. He served in an elite antiguerrilla unit and probably has the highest IQ in the company, yet he lacks common sense. I fear he might make decisions that will endanger us all, but I will try to give him the benefit of the doubt.

The company commander, Sharon, tells us that we're going to be very busy because we've been given the honor of serving as the primary assault unit in the Jenin sector. I have my doubts, but he seems very excited—and when a commander like him is smiling nonstop, you know you're not going to rest much.

On our third day at El Yakeem, Uri, as the unit's sergeant, travels with several officers to meet with the reserve unit we will be replacing. When he returns, he reassures us that we won't be sleeping in tents in the cold and wet; the army has transformed some storage containers into living quarters. He also confirms that our battalion will indeed be the primary assault force in the area. We will work closely with the Shin Bet, military intelligence, and special operations units. According to Uri, we will staff checkpoints, perform surveillance, and make arrests. He adds that while the terrorists' activity level is relatively high, so many people showed up for reserve duty that we should have adequate rest and opportunities for quick visits home.

As our last day of training winds down, we gather up our gear and head for the bus that will take us to our new home away from home.

Chapter 16

First Days at Mevo Dotan

Mevo Dotan takes up about twenty acres on the outskirts of Jenin. On the main roads, it is a few minutes' drive from Jenin or Qakilyah. We are also along a major highway linking Jenin and Nablus.

When we pull in, the company we are replacing hurriedly packs its gear. The soldiers look tired and that certainly isn't a good sign. Uri and I inspect the Hummers, making sure they are fully equipped, the radios function, and towing gear is stored in the back. When we're done, Uri signs a piece of paper that makes the three Hummers his responsibility.

It's hard to imagine us as anything other than a group of students, salesmen, administrators, architects, and marketing professionals. We are all in uniform, we all carry guns, but while walking down the paved road, we don't carry ourselves any differently than we did last week when we all came home after a hard day's work.

I know that the moment we go through the base's gate, it won't matter what we do as civilians 335 days out of the year. The moment we leave this base all of us will be seen, by both Jews and Arabs, only as Israeli soldiers.

Tonight a special forces unit, made up of nineteen- and twenty-year-olds performing their compulsory service, will be arresting a suspected terrorist in his home. While they make their way through the narrow streets, I'll be sitting in a Land Rover listening to the radio chatter with Uri and four others as part of the backup team. If something goes wrong, we will speed to their location where we'll join the fight until the terrorist and his cohorts are either killed or captured. That said, it's unlikely that we'll leave this vehicle. Knowing special forces, the situation will have to be dire. They'll suffer wounded or killed before anyone calls for the cavalry.

But it's been several years since my last mission in the territories. When I climb into the back of the Hummer, I am tense and alert. And I am not the only one. As we leave the base, we all pull back the T-shaped metal slide at the back of our rifles and flick the safety on. We now all have a round in the chamber. Still not trusting the men in this unit, I'm less worried about a firefight with terrorists than of one of the guys accidentally squeezing off a round.

As expected, we arrive at our station on the outskirts of town, turn off our running lights, listen to the radio, and wait. And wait. Thirty minutes goes by before the radio whispers that the special forces unit has reached objective C. They are now just a couple of blocks from the terrorist's home. We won't hear anything more until the task is complete or help is requested.

We exchange glances in silence. I keep looking at the radio. I'm waiting to see if the little orange bulb that indicates someone is talking over our frequency will light up. All is silent for the next thirty or forty minutes. Suddenly there is a short whirl of static and an orange light as the radio comes to life. The twenty-year-old commander of the unit declares that they have completed their mission and are on their way out of the village.

By the time he completes his message, we see the unit's two Land Rovers approach. When they link up with us, they let us know that they are about to fire a few rounds in the air under the pretext of checking their weapons. It's a small, childish act of bravado. As we leave together in a convoy, I see a massive yellow banner hanging from a telephone pole. On it is the image of a young boy with some Arabic writing underneath. I ask Uri what it means and he says, "It's the boy's name. It celebrates his being a *shahid*"—Arabic for martyr.

Fifteen minutes later, we're back at the base. The special forces unit leaves us and continues on to their area. They will deliver their captive to the Shin Bet for questioning. After parking our vehicles and unloading our gear, we walk the thirty meters to our container. We're all relaxed.

Over the next few days, we'll patrol the local roads and paths, and in the process push our Hummers to their limits on off-road expeditions. In the villages, youths taunt us and some pelt us with stones. It can be startling, but we're not under any real threat. We simply ignore them and drive on.

A couple of days later, we are told that we're going to conduct night surveillance on the town of Qabatya.

I beg and borrow until we have all the radios and night-vision equipment we need for tonight's mission. The skies are darkening. We're in for a storm. Once our equipment is gathered, several of us pore over the topographic maps. Even though we're going to be driven most of the way and will be picked up when we're done, we want to make sure that we're ready for any eventuality. We make sure to know the military's code names for the streets and junctions. When we report movement, we need to use naming conventions that are universally understood.

After dinner, we practice our marksmanship. Aviv walks over to check on my shooting. All ten of my bullets are grouped tightly in the center of the target. He gives me a surprised look of grudging respect. Smiling back, I say, "I just got lucky," although I'm sure someone else must have shot at my target by mistake. My night shooting is never that good, but I'm not going to let Aviv know that.

My evening oscillates between playing cards and making last-minute preparations. Every once in a while, Aviv opens the door and asks us to scrounge for extra radio batteries, or any one of the other small tasks that we need to complete before we leave. For the most part, either Uri or I leave the game to take care of the matter. By 10 PM, our equipment is ready and most of us have a solid knowledge of the area we're about to visit.

At 10:30 PM, we walk out the door. Besides my weapon and ammunition, I'm carrying a TAS-6 long-range night-observation device on my back. It's old, heavy, and awkward to carry. It's the kind I used about ten years ago, when I was a new recruit. We stand in the traditional U-shaped formation. Aviv doesn't waste time checking us, he just asks if everyone has ammunition, radios, extra batteries, and night vision. We nod. He makes an attempt to smile before turning toward the waiting truck.

One by one, we climb aboard. Since there are only twelve of us, we have plenty of room. When we arrive, we disembark slowly. Each man takes a position around the truck. Assured that we are secure, we all gather in a nearby field. Aviv whispers, "Two lines," and we form up behind him.

Uri takes up the last position in the rear and I'm at the back with him. The moment we move forward, he hits me on the back and hisses, "Zero." I know he told the guy on my left, "One." I immediately take a few steps forward and tap the man ahead of me and whisper, "One." This numbering continues up the line until the man in the front of each line taps Aviv on the back. If all is well, Aviv will come up with the number eleven each time. Every time we pause or make a turn, Uri initiates the counting again. It's not very high-tech, but it's the quickest way to make sure that no one is missing.

As we climb a hill, I peer into the darkness. I both hope and fear we'll walk into someone. I want to see danger in order to react to it quickly and effectively, but I'd much rather make it all the way up this hill having seen nothing but gnarled tree trunks. Thirty meters before we arrive at our destination, Aviv stops and kneels. We all do the same. Word is passed down the line for Uri to move forward: He and Aviv will check out the area while we wait here in the dark. A few moments later, they return and we split off into four teams. As far as I know, we're not looking for anyone in particular nor are we part of a coordinated mission, but this wouldn't be the first time that I didn't know the true purpose of my nocturnal activity.

Three teams spread out along the crest of a hill overlooking Qabatya. The fourth team guards our back, making sure we aren't greeted by unannounced visitors.

In less than thirty minutes, the rain starts pouring out of the sky. We all put on our bargain-basement rain slickers, which soak through in ten minutes.

Over the next couple of hours, we take note of a few moving cars and people. Aviv passes some of this information along over the radio, but it doesn't sound like anyone is very interested.

When it's time to pull up stakes, we gather our gear and make our way down the hill in two columns. We take a right when I expect to take a left. I hang back a moment and confer with Uri. He agrees that Aviv has probably taken a wrong turn. Mistakes happen and in this case it costs us only about fifteen minutes, but this serves to confirm my doubts about Aviv.

When we arrive at the road, the truck is already waiting for us. We all climb in and head back to the base. We debrief quickly before we head for our container. We're soaked and tired, but I think I'm not the only one who had a great time. On one level, activities like this are annoying because they don't serve any immediate purpose—such as making an arrest—but they do serve as reminders that we're now soldiers. And they're good practice for the time when we'll face something more fearsome than a cold, wet night.

Typical for this time of year, the weather seems to change from cold and rainy to warm and sunny in an instant. Today, there isn't a cloud in the sky and it feels like it's sixty-five degrees. After breakfast, Aviv asks for two volunteers to escort the Shin Bet. I raise my hand. I don't even know what will be required of me, but I'm eager to volunteer. This is an example of being *mor'al*.* If I were smarter, I would have asked a few questions.

Uri isn't in the room, so Daboosh volunteers. For the most part, Uri and I have gone out together every time, but I think it's a good thing for me to go off without him. We don't need a break from each other, but I don't want the guys to think that he and I are attached at the hip.

An hour later, we have our gear together and meet Guy, who'll be driving us. He tells us that the Shin Bet have their own driver. That's certainly not a surprise. Moments later, they drive up. Like me, their commander is in his midthirties. He is accompanied by two others who look like they completed their military service a couple of years ago. They are all wearing up-to-date light body armor, and have GPS signaling equipment. We don't. If something were to happen to them, the military could find them instantly; if something were to happen to

---

* From the Hebrew root *ra'al,* the word *mor'al* literally means someone who is "poisoned," but it's more politely used to suggest that a person is extraordinarily motivated.

Daboosh or me, it could take them hours. Of course, neither of us is carrying intelligence data, nor do we know anything of consequence. Our capture or loss would be inconvenient and the military would expend every effort to recover us, but these Shin Bet guys are another matter. Given the fact that Israel can afford only a small number of cool and useful gadgets, I don't resent the fact that they are given better gear. And yet I'm still a bit envious.

The members of the Shin Bet team shake our hands and tell us they are glad to have us along, but I get the feeling that they look at us as unnecessary baggage forced on them by regulations. I can't say I blame them.

We follow their Land Rover in our Hummer. They are guided by maps and GPS signals we can't see. We check out various dirt paths that connect to one of the main roads in the area. It is apparent that they are looking for a navigable route. What with the recent rains, many unpaved roads have turned into mud traps.

Since the Shin Bet never bothered to ask, they don't know that Guy was born and brought up in a nearby Jewish settlement. He knows this area as well as the Arab villagers. Before we even enter one of the paths, Guy says, "This place might be drivable for ten minutes, but after that it will be like a swamp."

He's right. At first, it seems like we've found a good road, but we soon encounter deep mud that extends all the way to the heavy woods flanking the road. There's no way the Land Rover is going to get through it. We drive off the path in several different directions, but don't find a way around it.

Stumped, the Shin Bet call a halt. When I step out into the sunshine, I move immediately to high ground. I'm probably being overly cautious, but I can't help myself. I am what the paratroopers made me. Meanwhile, Daboosh chats with our driver and the Shin Bet team open their maps. One says, "Any of you care for food or water? We've got plenty."

Daboosh and our driver are already on their way to the back of the Land Rover. I know it's unlikely that we'll receive enemy gunfire, but I don't want a preventable incident to occur just because bottled water tastes better than the musty stuff in my canteen. I join them but I keep my eyes peeled.

The Shin Bet ask our driver if he has any ideas. Unsurprisingly, he has plenty. He tells them he knows the perfect route. Soon afterward, we're back on the road. This time, our vehicle is in the lead. Every so often, the Shin Bet use the radio to tell us to stop. I assume they want to set their waypoints on their GPS.

An hour later, we arrive at the top of a hill overlooking Qabatya. The sun is shining. I grab some water and take a position on high ground. The area is wooded and we stay just inside the treeline. The members of the Shin Bet team talk among themselves and make a few calls. One of them asks Daboosh which unit he is from.

"Just your average reserve infantry unit. I'm with the reconnaissance unit." Daboosh points to me. "He's an Alpinist."

The Shin Bet officer looks at me surprised. "Really? Where did you serve during your compulsory service?"

"I was with the paratroopers."

He smiles. Knowing I serve with the Alpinistim, he probably assumes I served with one of the elite paratrooper reconnaissance units. I don't correct him. I like the idea of him thinking that he and I are at the same level. He says, "When did you start serving?"

"November 1990."

He thinks about it a bit, but has trouble coming up with the name of anyone I might know. I'm about ten years older than him so I'm not surprised. That's for the best. I don't want to have to tell him that I actually served in the 202nd Battalion. It's stupid and I know it, especially at this stage in my life. I should be proud of my service, but I'm not.

He goes over to his team and after a few moments returns to tell us they want to enter Qabatya. We get back into the vehicles and follow them to the outskirts of the village. I stay alert, focusing on windows and roofs that could be used by a sniper. I can't discern any movement. It's the middle of the day and this part of the village is quiet—no doubt due entirely to our presence.

A member of the Shin Bet team takes out a camera with a long lens and starts taking pictures. I probably should be concerned, since we are without any nearby support. It wouldn't be the first time that a group of soldiers was attacked, but I can't imagine ever being that unlucky.

All the same, I don't let my guard down for a second. Even after we return to our vehicles and drive off, my body is taut like a spring. There might be plenty of steel plating between me and a bullet, but an RPG would tear us apart. We were there for over thirty minutes, more than enough time for terrorists to set up an ambush farther up the road. This is the most dangerous part of the trip. I'm tense, but I'm not particularly fearful. Looking at Daboosh, I can see that he is completely relaxed. I wonder if he's aware of the possible dangers.

Fifteen minutes later, we're back on the dirt paths and returning to the base.

When Daboosh and I get to our container, we discover that tonight's activity has already been planned. We're going to demolish the home of a suicide bomber who blew up a bus in the north a little over a week ago. Suicide bombers were once comforted by the knowledge that their families would be enriched by local organizations and foreign countries such as Iraq, Iran, and Saudi Arabia. So the IDF established a policy whereby the homes of suicide bombers would be demolished. It's having an impact. According to most sources, there has been a steady increase in the number of family members turning in sons, brothers, and daughters who are preparing to become bombers.

I realize that the policy creates hardships, but if it deters a single terrorist, I can live with it.

The entire platoon will be used to secure the area while the demolition team places charges inside the house. During the day, we are broken into several teams, learn the route we will travel, and look at satellite maps of the neighborhood. Uri, Daboosh, and I will be in a Hummer; if the situation requires, we'll be called on the radio. We can get to the area in less than a minute.

By 10:30 PM, we have fully prepped. Sharon, the company's commander, will be just one of many officers on the ground. The demolition unit will have its own commander, and officers from division headquarters will be present as well as members of the Shin Bet.

After the demolition unit arrives, all nine vehicles move as a convoy to a small village outside Jenin. As the reconnaissance unit, our two Hummers take the lead until we reach the outskirts of the village where the rest of the team continues to the terrorist's home. As part of our small force, military lawyers and other administrative types validate our actions and make sure we conform to standards prescribed by Israeli law. Subject to their approval, the demolition team makes preparations and members of the company establish a secure perimeter around the home. In the meantime, I'm feeling stuck and left out, patrolling the streets as a rear guard.

Over the next half hour, I hear the progress over the radio. The perimeter is secure, the family has been given time to remove their belongings, and the neighbors have been asked to leave their homes temporarily in case something goes awry.

Our vehicle's designation, Gimel 2, is called over the radio. Sharon asks where we are. Uri answers that we're fifty meters west of Tag'lit (the designation for the terrorist's house).

Sharon says, "I need a *gafor** at Tag'lit right now."

Before Uri has a chance to ask, I say, "I'll go."

It's a dark night, but the streetlights are bright. On the side of the road are about fifty Palestinians. Facing them are several soldiers, but for now everyone seems calm.

Sharon approaches and tells me to follow him.

I step right behind him, excited and curious. This is the first time I've experienced a demolition up close. Until now, it has only been an abstract idea, a matter of policy to consider and discuss. Now I'm witnessing it.

We walk toward a home nestled between two other buildings. It's about forty meters from the main road. I can hear the bustle of activity before I see it. Even though the perimeter is relatively secure, Sharon isn't relaxed. Following his example, I kneel every time we stop and search the dark for a possible enemy. I see the demolition team going about their business and several soldiers guarding the perimeter. Administrative officers are speaking with the family whose home we're about to destroy. I can't help but feel sympathy for them, but I remind myself that this is the result of their son's mad wish to murder. And this mad desire to murder indiscriminately was encouraged by his leaders. I am convinced that Israel must be resolute on its path to peace.

As Sharon and I approach the house, I watch members of the demolition team busily place and check their charges. Sharon asks me to wait one moment. He walks into the large house while I watch the activity on its first and second floors. Then, without even telling me why I was needed in the first place, Sharon tells me that I can go back to my vehicle.

When I climb in, Uri says, "What was that all about?"

"Heck if I know."

---

* Literally meaning "cigarette," over the radio *gafor* refers to a soldier.

When we resume patrolling the main intersection, we are told over the radio to expect an explosion. A moment later, we hear the blast. Soon we're leading the convoy back to Mevo Dotan.

The next several days are filled with an assortment of activities— staffing surprise checkpoints on auxiliary roads, patrols, searches for weapons, and surveillance. For the most part, it's routine. We don't expect to find anything or anyone of interest to the military. Our real purpose is to make the military appear ever-present and deepen our knowledge of the area, but the company's mortar team actually hits a Bingo. The Shin Bet is brought in to pick up the wanted individual.

While we drive around, I think of Jen and enjoy the scenery. It was a wet winter, so the olive fields are lush with purple, red, and yellow wildflowers. Tal says it's a shame we're going to leave this land one day; Daboosh says he can't wait until there is real peace so that he can come back to hike here as a civilian. We talk about it as we drive around. One thing is clear: We can't wait for it to be over.

Chapter 17

Capturing the Leader of Islamic Jihad: First Attempt

It's the middle of the afternoon and Sharon enters our container looking for volunteers. The Shin Bet need an escort tonight. We'll probably be with them until the morning.

When Sharon walks out the door, Uri turns to me and says, "Do you have any plans tonight?"

An hour later, Uri has seven other volunteers and is ready to provide us all with details regarding tonight's operation.

The Shin Bet have information that should bring them to the leader of the Islamic Jihad in Qabatya. After Operation Defensive Shield, many terrorists from Jenin fled there. The Shin Bet will use advanced technology to track him, while the arrest itself will be carried out by Duvedan.

It's going to be a long, cold night.

Before we leave, we divide ourselves up into two groups of four men: Uri, Oren, and I will be in one vehicle with a driver from the base. Daboosh and the others will be in another vehicle.

Beyond this, we don't undertake any preparations. We won't even know tonight's destination until we meet up with the Shin Bet at a well-known checkpoint. We're supposed to arrive at 7 PM and find a Shin Bet officer called Moti.

When we arrive, we see that we're not the only ones. There are at least ten other military vehicles here, including command cars. Finding Moti might not be all that easy. We park on the side of the road near the checkpoint. A few minutes later, a command car parks nearby. The type of body armor worn and the demeanor of the men suggest that they are with the Shin Bet.

Uri and I walk over to them. Uri, with a slightly embarrassed, bashful smile spread across his face, says, "Are you Shin Bet?"

The man looks at us appraisingly. He isn't smiling. "Who are you?"

Uri says, "We're reservists from Mevo Dotan. We're supposed to meet Moti here."

The man in the passenger's seat leans over his friend, takes a good look at us, and says, "That's not us. You may want to try over there."

He points to a lighted area about five hundred meters away. It's worth a try. We drive up to the gate and tell the guards who we are; they let us in without questions.

We drive straight into a large parking lot. At the far end of the asphalt is a well-lit tent and several portable toilets. Along the side, there are some containers. It's clear that this base is used as a storage facility and transition point for units entering and leaving this part of the West Bank. We park our Hummers near a large group of young soldiers who are relaxing next to their own vehicles.

Given their demeanor and weapons, it's pretty clear that these soldiers are from an elite unit.

I tell Uri, "I can't believe we were ever that young."

"Neither can I."

"They look like kids. Did we look like that when we were young?"

"Maybe you did. I haven't changed a bit."

"Do you miss those days?"

"Not really, but they were good times."

I tell him that I miss the clarity of purpose, the sense that what I was doing had a purpose beyond selling more widgets. But being a reservist has its advantages. How many hours' sleep have they had this week? How many minutes' downtime have they had this month?

Raising his plastic cup of tea, Uri says, "Cheers to that."

The Shin Bet team finally arrives in two specially modified vehicles, and we all gather for a quick briefing. The commander's vehicle that will lead our small convoy quickly becomes a subject of interest with us reservists.

Our guesses as to the purpose of the odd-looking devices on their vehicles range from a cooking stove to a brain-wave vibration receiver. We're having a good time as we all climb aboard and start up our vehicles.

About two hundred meters from our destination, the convoy is halted. Lights out. Uri and I step out together and walk to our objective. This is the most dangerous part of the mission. Walking with our guns at the ready, we sweep the area. When we are convinced no one is waiting in ambush, we radio that the area is safe. Without using their lights, the vehicles edge forward.

I begin to realize that this is where I escorted the other Shin Bet team several days ago. Using my night-vision binoculars, I scan the area for enemy movement while Uri organizes four two-man teams. Three will be placed at points along our perimeter; the fourth will stick close to the Shin Bet.

A little after 4 AM, I hear dogs barking in the village. As with most villages in the West Bank, many people have dogs. These are not pets, but guard dogs. The number of dogs that have picked up the Duvedan team's scent increases as the minutes go by. I turn to Uri and grumble, "That's not good."

"Maybe they're close enough to keep him from escaping."

Moments later, the Duvedan team announces over the radio that they have reached their jumping-off point. While they wait, Shin Bet confirm the whereabouts of the terrorist. More dogs join the throng. The Duvedan team must be on the move.

Over the next twenty minutes, I scour Qabatya with my night-vision binoculars. I know the Duvedan team is too far away and too deep in the bowels of the village for me to see them, but I keep looking all the same. I listen for gunfire or the sound of a concussion grenade; the village remains quiet, except for the dogs. Finally, the Duvedan team comes in over the radio. They are all safe and have reached their extraction point. Unfortunately, the target has escaped.

The Shin Bet take it in stride. They acknowledge Duvedan's report and start packing up their equipment. We say good-bye to the Shin Bet as the sun just becomes visible along the horizon. It's going to be a beautiful day. Hopefully our target will spend it shivering in someone's basement.

Chapter 18

The Checkpoint

It's the afternoon and I've had just four hours of sleep to keep me going. Sharon enters our container looking for another volunteer. He says they've just received information that a high-value target is on the move.

I say, "I'm happy to come."

He says, "Okay. Grab your gear and meet by my Land Rover."

"Do you need two?" Uri asks.

"No, just the one. Don't worry, there's work for everyone. We're setting up checkpoints on all the main roads. Your team will receive instructions momentarily."

And with that, he leaves. Before I walk out the door, Uri says, "Have fun."

He knows I will.

Thirty minutes later, I'm bumping along a dirt road with Sharon in his Land Rover heading to a small village near Qabatya. The target has been sighted there driving a dark Toyota sedan with two others. Sharon radios two checkpoints that the target is moving toward them and orders another mobile force toward the area. We cut through dirt paths between small agricultural tracts in an attempt to intercept the target ourselves. Sharon's driver is tenacious and experienced, but ten minutes later our initial excitement is dampened by the fruitless spinning of wheels deep in mud. We're stuck.

While the driver works to extricate us, I position myself on high ground nearby. After a few minutes, I see a local on a tractor driving toward us. I tell Sharon that we have company, and he takes advantage of this opportunity. Waving my arms, I direct the Arab farmer to drive toward us. I have him stop about twenty meters away from our vehicle. While I watch the driver's every movement, Sharon asks the dark and wizened farmer for help. With a good-natured smile, he helps drag us out of the mud. We give him our thanks and continue on our way.

The target hasn't passed any of the checkpoints. It's possible that he turned back.

Only after we've been at it for almost two hours do I ask Sharon, "Who is this guy?"

"He's the one the Shin Bet missed last night. He knows they're close, and he's trying to flee. They are going after him again tonight and want to keep him boxed in."

"Does that mean we're going out with them again tonight?"

"If that's all right with you."

"Of course."

While we're traveling around, we hear over the radio that one of our checkpoints stopped and arrested someone on the Shin Bet's Bingo list. Sometimes that happens. While we're trying to capture or limit the movements of one person, someone else is caught. I don't know who he is, but if he made it onto the Bingo list, he must be relatively valuable.

Sharon grins wide with pride when he makes arrangements for the captured individual's transportation to our base. After a couple of hours, it's apparent that our target is not on the open road. He may have gone back into hiding, but he could just be waiting for us to pack up our checkpoints. If we were to go now, he might bolt. We need to stay long enough to convince our quarry that he isn't safe on the road today.

Passing the crossroads that connects Sanur, Jenin, and Nablus, we weave past an armored personnel carrier in the middle of the intersection. Sharon stops briefly and talks with the captain in charge of the area. The captain, Eldad, says that he could use additional men on a section of road that originates in Sanur.

This section has been closed off to all automobile and truck traffic to trap the target. As a result, inhabitants of Sanur who left in the morning for work or school, or to visit friends and family, are unable to return. Many have turned around in hopes of finding an alternative route, but many more are waiting for the military to pack up.

When we stop at the checkpoint, we are greeted by Ari, a mortar team sergeant originally from Argentina who has been living in Israel for nearly fifteen years. He is in charge. Sharon asks him if there has been any trouble.

"No. No trouble, but there are a lot of people here. Most are waiting to get home."

Sharon twists his head back at me. "Adam, want to help out?"

Before I even have a chance to answer, Ari says, "Glad to have you join us, Alpinist."

With that, I get out and Sharon takes off. As I collect myself, I notice a line of cars, vans, and trucks along the side of the road extending as far as the eye can see.

Offering a bag of sunflower seeds, Ari tells me, "It's very calm here. No incidents to speak of. I've been lying down by the trees. We have one radio. With you, we're now four."

All I see is one other soldier standing about twenty meters ahead of us. "Where are you all positioned? Where is everyone else?"

"We're trading off every once in a while. Yoni is up now and we're sitting back. If anything happens, we're right here."

It's not my place to criticize; I'm just a guest of the unit. But Yoni is exposed and alone. If the civilians turn into a mob and get ugly, he could be seriously injured or killed before Ari and the others get to him. Moreover, the Palestinians take a long look at the soldiers with whom they interact. When our soldiers fail to act professionally, the civilians often grab the chance to circumvent their authority. I take a few sunflower seeds and say, "Do you mind if I join Yoni? I'll keep him company."

Ari shrugs and points to a small grove on the side of the road. "Sure. Whatever you want. I'll be over in the shade if you need me."

Yoni's rifle is swung behind his back, his hands are inside his pockets, and his stance is relaxed. I'm not surprised to discover later that he is a medic. Medics tend to be relatively easygoing. When I meet up with him, he is quick to let down his guard and ignores the long line of cars and anxious people as he greets me.

He tells me that the traffic has been stopped for about two hours. I can see for myself that there are hundreds of cars parked alongside the road. Despite all the people, it's relatively quiet. As expected, we are under orders to stop all cars except ambulances and UN personnel. Yoni also tells me that we should expect increased friction since more and more people will be returning home from school and work.

We exchange opinions regarding best practices of soldiering for several minutes, but soon our conversation evolves into personal chatter and I discover that Yoni is married, has two kids, and works as an engineer.

It doesn't take long for several Palestinians to notice me—a new soldier standing next to Yoni—and clearly they hope I will have the authority or naïveté to let them through. Four men in their midtwenties approach.

I tighten my grip on my weapon and raise the muzzle slightly. It's not pointed directly at them, but if necessary I will be able to disperse them with a couple of rounds by slightly shifting my arm and pulling the trigger. My pointer finger is resting against the trigger guard. It would take me less than a second to fire the first shot. The four of them are now only ten meters away.

I'm comfortable with my task and ready to act, but I still don't like the idea of inconveniencing so many people. Almost every one of them simply wants to go home. I know that. I also know that checkpoints serve a vital function. Right now this checkpoint is keeping a senior terrorist from fleeing.

The Israeli military has been trying to influence Palestinian communities by making a clear linkage between the level of terrorist activity and the level of Israeli military presence. For instance, there is a barely discernible Israeli military presence in Jericho, because the people of that city have consistently shown a keen disinterest in terrorism. Time and again, Israel has withdrawn from areas where there is no threat to the lives of Israeli citizens. But Nablus, Jenin, Qabatya, Sanur, and the surrounding villages here are not like Jericho. They harbor and support terrorism. As a result, Israel has no choice but to treat these communities differently. When they decide to stop killing Israeli citizens, we'll stop inconveniencing their people.

Watching the young men approach, I focus on appearing relaxed, confident, and alert. I will listen attentively to their questions and concerns, but they must understand that they have only two choices. They can either wait patiently or return to where they've come from. When they are ten meters away, I raise my hand. They stop immediately.

As is common with people in their age group, they are able to communicate freely in Hebrew. One in a leather jacket, jeans, and a mustache asks, "Are you the officer?"

Pointing at the distant crossroads and the armored personnel carrier, I say, "No. He's over there. How can I help you?"

"I need to get through. I'm on my way back from school and need to get home. We've been waiting here for over an hour."

"I know. But we can't let anyone go yet. And it could be several hours before we can let the traffic through."

"But what are we supposed to do?"

I tell him I wish there was something more I could do. They're going to have to go back or be patient.

They don't look like they are feeling particularly patient, but they realize that they won't be able to accomplish anything beyond expressing their frustration. They leave. Over the next thirty minutes, several others approach Yoni and me. They all express their frustration and ask that we allow them to pass. Each time, I have to say no. There is nothing I can do.

It isn't easy.

I look at the young children with their mothers and am sure that letting them continue would not pose a threat—yet I know, too, that I'm not competent to make that decision.

When I notice a white car's slow approach, I know that a delicate situation is about to unfold. Fifty meters before it reaches me, I raise my hand. The car stops. I ask Yoni to move to the right and cover me. I'm not confident in his abilities, but he will serve as a deterrent. I approach the car slowly.

A few meters from the car, I see two big, bold, black letters painted on the side—UN. The majority of people who administer UN programs in the West Bank and Gaza are local citizens, and there have been a number of instances when UN vehicles ferried known terrorists. As a result, Israeli soldiers check IDs and search all cars for explosives or other illicit equipment. UN officials take offense at this and, aware of my need to strike a balance between security and diplomacy, I start by saying, "Good afternoon. How can I help you gentlemen?"

The driver, a thin forty-ish man in a well-worn dark suit, says, "We need to get through. We're on our way to Nablus."

I'm hoping to appear both friendly and professional at the same time. "As you can see, the road is closed. We can let you go, but I'll need to see your papers. After that, we'll need to search your car. Could you gentlemen step out of the car and provide me with your identification?"

The driver is all smiles. "Yes. Absolutely. One moment."

As they exit the car, I motion Yoni to join me and ask him if he has the Bingo list. He doesn't.

"No. I'll get it, though."

As the Palestinians exit the vehicle, I ask the driver to collect all the IDs and hand them over to me. A Palestinian traveling without identification is usually held for questioning by the civil administration, so it is very rare to find someone without documents. After Yoni returns with the watch list, I stand a few meters from the men and briefly question each one. I verify that the picture on the ID is the same as the face in front of me. I verify his name, where he lives, and so forth. I feel more like a bouncer than a soldier, and I don't have extensive experience at this. I'm sure I'm easily fooled, but I do my best to look for any signs of anxiety that would suggest extra scrutiny. My questioning lasts no more than five minutes. When I'm done, I hand the IDs to Yoni and ask him to check the numbers against the Bingo list.

In the meantime, I ask the driver, who functions as the group leader, to open the car's trunk. I stand back about ten meters. I highly doubt the car is booby-trapped, but better safe than dead. After a good look at the trunk, I check out the car's interior. I don't see anything of interest. I ask Yoni if everything is in order.

"Yup."

I hand all the IDs back to the driver. "You're all set. Drive slowly until you reach the other checkpoint. The soldiers there will stop you briefly—they may even ask you a couple of questions—but they'll let you go. They probably won't need to check your ID or car."

The driver thanks me and gives me a friendly wave, but I'm sure he's unhappy that he's been stopped and questioned. I don't blame him for that, but Israeli citizens must also be checked before entering shopping malls, taking public transportation, watching a movie, or meeting friends at a restaurant. Most Israelis don't mind the inconvenience because they see the disruptions as necessary for their own safety. But the Palestinian perspective is different.

After the UN car passes several more people approach with renewed hope. Most of them are students and laborers who just want to continue on their way, but a family of three—a woman in her seventies, her son in his fifties and his wife—arrive with a valid request. They approach in a large white van. He stops before us, but before I can even open my mouth, he is already out of his car. He speaks Hebrew. "Sir, please, my mother, she is very sick. We take her to hospital in Nablus. Please."

I could be wrong, but this man's anxiety seems real to me. I believe him. I take his identification, but before I even glance at it, I take a look inside the van. Besides the two women, the van is empty. It is probably used to transport laborers. Maybe he's a contractor. It doesn't matter. What matters is that his elderly mother is ill and needs to get to a hospital. Unfortunately, I can't let their vehicle through. I ask him to give me the women's identification and I pass all three IDs to Yoni. Yoni has already stopped covering me and walks over. "What's wrong with your mother?"

"I don't know. She feels very bad. My doctor told me to take her to hospital."

"How long has she felt ill?"

He says, "Since last night."

"I may not be able to let you go, but I'll try to figure something out. Do you have water?"

"Yes."

"Okay. I'll check with my officer. In the meantime, you can wait in your car. If your mother needs water or something, just let me know."

I realize that the offer of water and the knowledge that I'm going to try to help is probably small consolation to a man trying to get his mother to the hospital. As expected, I am told that I cannot let anyone pass unless it is clear that their life is in immediate danger. Unfortunately there is no way for me to know, but given the fact that she's on her feet and only appears uncomfortable, I have to hope that our keeping her here doesn't cause irreversible harm.

An hour passes. By his calm face, I know the man has experienced this situation many times before.

People are beginning to abandon their cars and start walking toward their destination. This is fairly typical. They are hoping that we won't care enough to walk the necessary distance to intercept them. Sometimes this works, though not with me. And not while we're trying to quarantine a leading terrorist. I know my decision to stop them will not be popular with Yoni, Ari, or the Palestinians, but today isn't about making new friends.

I point out to Yoni that several people are cutting through a field about two hundred meters from us. As I expected, he isn't interested in stopping them. I don't know if it's laziness or a sincere belief that we should be letting them go. He is probably thinking I'm being overzealous—and he might be right. He relaxes a bit when I tell him to keep an eye on me. I walk as fast as I can through the muddy field. Within seconds, the Palestinians see me; some turn back, but others continue. I pick up my pace, being careful not to fall. I don't mind being overzealous, but I don't want to look like a klutz.

In Arabic and Hebrew, I shout at them to stop. Some of them listen and turn back; others trudge on. I walk forward, now pleading for them to stop. When I am a little over fifty meters away and it's clear that those that remain are ignoring me, I shoulder my rifle. Looking through the sights, I aim at the front of the line and again I shout to them in Arabic, then in Hebrew. This time, they listen.

I can hear them cursing me as they turn back, but I am relieved. If they hadn't stopped, I would have been forced to face them down. I would not have the will or the authority to shoot at them—and certainly they know this as well as I do—but none of us wants to let our confrontation escalate.

When I return to Yoni, I feel as if I've accomplished something, but that feeling evaporates when the son of the sick woman approaches me and asks again to be allowed through. This time he's agitated. I meet his eyes and say, "I'm sorry. There is nothing I can do. But the minute I can, you'll be the first to go."

After several minutes of discussion, he returns to his van and lights up another cigarette. Yoni and I talk some more, but I'm not really listening. I'm thinking of the man and his sick mother. I'm wondering if I should talk with the officer at the main intersection. While I'm thinking this over, another van approaches.

There are three young Palestinians, all men, in their midtwenties to early thirties. Yoni approaches them and takes their identification. While he checks their papers, I stand by the side and watch closely. They tell Yoni that they are on their way to a nearby village. Since we have established checkpoints around it, we are permitting movement between this position and the village. We've let several cars like this pass in the last few hours.

After Yoni is satisfied that the vehicle is clean, he waves them on. I radio the officer manning the checkpoint at the main intersection and let him know that this vehicle will be heading toward him. While I'm speaking, I watch the van drive slowly past us on the deserted stretch of road. The officer confirms receipt of my message and lets me know that he can see the van approaching.

Five seconds pass and Yoni says, "Where are they going?"

Only then do I hear the van speed up. I turn my head and see the van veer onto a small unpaved road. They are attempting to circumvent the checkpoint and make their way to Jenin. I immediately start sprinting across the field.

The unpaved road slows them down, and by running diagonally across the field, I am sure that I will be able to intercept them. My eyes are locked on their progress as I race across the muddy field. I am not going to let them go. Not on my watch. I consider firing my weapon in the air. Given the fact that they are deliberately circumventing our roadblock, I have the authority I need to do so. And the moment I open fire, other soldiers will move toward this position. But this would only create an opportunity for miscalculation on the part of a soldier or a Palestinian. The day ends better for everyone if I don't shoot, so I keep running.

When I make it to the road, my gun is pointed down, and my hand up, indicating that they must stop, and I hope that I look determined. They keep coming. I raise my rifle. I am already imagining how this might play out when the van stops five meters in front of me.

I walk toward the vehicle, my weapon raised and pointed at the driver's head. I'm seething mad. They lied to me and created a potentially explosive situation. I hate them for that.

"What the hell are you doing?" The driver, whose window is already rolled down, puts one hand out and waves, like he is waving a white flag. "I'm sorry. I just want—"

"I don't care what you want. You knew the road was closed. You lied and tried to break through. Give me your IDs now."

While they rustle up their papers, I watch them closely. I am ready to shoot them. All I need is a reason to. When the driver has gathered all their documents, I step back and point to the man in the passenger's seat. "Hand the documents to your friend over there. Everyone but you steps out. We're all going to walk back to the road while you slowly drive back. Understood?"

I hear a "Yes sir."

Once the men are out of the van, I motion for them to walk ahead of the vehicle. I walk a little off to the side as we slowly return to the road. We're greeted by Ari, who says to me, "Alpinist, you're crazy."

He gives me a hard slap on the shoulder and I return to my post. Soon afterward, a Red Crescent ambulance approaches. As with the United Nations vehicles, we let the ambulances pass through our checkpoints but not without first checking papers and the vehicle for weapons. The driver tells me that the ambulance is on the way to Jenin.

While Yoni checks their identification, the man and his mother approach. The man asks if there is a doctor aboard. The driver tells him that his passenger is a hospital administrator. Their conversation continues in Arabic and I am soon lost, but it's clear that the man is upset. His voice is raised while the hospital administrator continues speaking to him calmly. The woman's face is impassive. I would be hard put to say that she is even sick. She appears strained and fatigued, but hers is no different from the hundreds of other faces I've seen here today.

I have forgotten the man's name. I learned it for a moment when we initially checked his identification papers, but I forgot it almost as soon as they were handed back. Now I only think of him as the man with the sick mother. I ask him what the administrator told him. "He says he can't help."

"What did you ask him?"

The driver and the administrator are listening to our conversation, but I ignore them for now. I focus on the man, who says, "I ask them to take me Nablus. But they say no. They go to Jenin."

I turn to the driver. "His mother is sick. You need to take them to the hospital in Nablus. The checkpoint up ahead will let you through. When you drop them off, you can continue on your way to Jenin."

The hospital administrator smiles, stretches out his palms in a warm, welcoming gesture, and says, "Yes, I understand, but we are in a rush. I need to get to Jenin immediately. I can't go to Nablus."

Hoping to coax him, I say, "But she's sick and needs to be in a hospital now. Nablus is close. It won't take you long. You want to help her, don't you?"

His smile widening, he says, "Of course I do. But I can't. I am late already. Why don't you just let them through?"

He has an excellent point. I certainly wish I could let them pass, but I have orders. Yet I can allow ambulances through. If I put her on this ambulance, she'll reach a hospital.

He and I go back and forth several times. The more he argues, the more I wonder why. This is an ambulance and these are hospital personnel. Aren't they supposed to care about the welfare of the sick? I assume that they are simply a bunch of bureaucrats who care only about their own convenience.

I decide to abuse my authority. "Listen carefully. You're going to take those people to Nablus or you're not going anywhere."

The hospital administrator says, "You can't do that. You have to let me through."

I ignore him and say to the man with the sick mother, "Get your mother. These people will take you to the hospital."

The man thanks me and returns to his van. When he leaves, I look at the ambulance driver sternly. "You're going to take them to Nablus. I'm going to tell the commander at the other checkpoint not to let you through if you don't turn left and head for Nablus. Do you understand me?"

He realizes that the discussion has ended. "Yes. We'll take them."

I say, *"Deer'balek.*"*

The man and his family are greeted fairly warmly by the hospital administrator. After they all pile in, the man turns to shake my hand and says, "Thank you. Thank you."

Another hour passes. Earlier in the day, individuals or small groups of three or four people were approaching us. Now thirty or more people are coming. They are in their midtwenties to early thirties—mostly men, but a few women also. In fact, a woman is out front and seems to be leading their advance.

This is the nightmare situation I've always hoped to avoid. If the group turns violent or if Yoni and I respond incorrectly, the confrontation could end in civilian deaths. I don't want any part of that. Keeping my eyes on the group that is now 150 meters away, I say to Yoni, "It looks like we have company."

"I see them."

He looks the way I feel. I hope I'm doing a better job of hiding my fears. I say, "This won't be a problem. Stand a little to the side. Be ready, but don't worry. I'm sure we'll talk this through."

I'm lying, but I hope to instill some confidence in us both.

When the group is less than twenty meters in front of us, I put my hand out as I have dozens of times this afternoon and try to appear

* Arabic for "Be warned."

friendly, but serious. I say in Hebrew and then repeat in Arabic, "Stop. You must stop now."

Given their speedy walk and the tense looks on their faces, I'm not surprised to see that they keep walking. I tighten my grip on my weapon. I have less than ten seconds before they reach me. "Stop. Stop now."

Not even five meters in front of me, the crowd stops. The woman, who's in her midtwenties, shouts at me rapidly in English, "Why do you keep us here? Do you have any idea how long we've been waiting? You have no right."

It takes me a second to respond. She is almost shaking with rage. The men surrounding her look grim and their faces are taut, but I recognize that they are shouting and not shoving. In English, I say, "I understand. Believe me, I do. I don't blame you for being angry. If I could let you go, I would. But I can't."

She is taken aback. It is clear that she did not expect to meet a soldier who speaks English fluently. She may have chosen English because she didn't want to speak in her "occupier's" language. She may have hoped that the language would give her an advantage over an Israeli soldier. Whatever her reasons, she quickly overcomes her surprise and continues shouting at me. For more than ten minutes she shouts while I try to calmly explain that I can't let anyone pass. The two dozen men standing beside her are content to let her do the fighting for them.

"You keeping us here, forbidding us from going home, it's inhumane," she cries. "Who are you to come here and tell us what to do? You're just like the Nazis."

I know enough not to start debating the political muck she's probably been spoon-fed since she was a child, but she's getting to me. I yell back at her for the first time. "Do you think I want to be here? Don't you think I have something better to do than stand here? Do you really think I want to keep you all waiting? I've been standing here for hours.

I'm tired and hungry and nothing would make me happier than to leave, but I can't. I have orders to stay and I can't leave here until I'm told otherwise. And until I'm told to leave, I can't let you and your friends through. If you want to stand here and yell at me for the rest of the day, that's fine by me. Just don't think it's going to make a difference. We're both stuck here."

She is, for the first time since she confronted me twenty minutes ago, silent. The men are looking at her. I'm looking at her. Turning around and heading back down the street, she yells back to me, "It's not right."

I say, "I know. I'm sorry, but that's the way it is right now."

Thirty minutes later, I hear the order we've all been awaiting. The APC's engine revs as the team controlling the main intersection prepares to leave. I turn my head and see Ari and a few of his friends climbing out from the shade. After their long day, they're eager to return to the base. Indeed, everyone is anxious to leave, and there doesn't seem to be an organized method of retreat. It's more like a mad dash, as if we all hear a dinner bell ringing in the distance. When a Land Rover stops and asks if Yoni and I need a lift back to the base, we don't hesitate to accept. We drive past a line of vehicles stretching nearly a kilometer.

Yoni is talking, but I'm still thinking about the checkpoint. I assume that military intelligence or the Shin Bet have learned that the man we're after has decided to remain hidden in Qabatya or they know where he's going. I would hate for all this to have been for nothing.

Later I learn that our random checks did lead to the arrest of another terrorist on the Bingo list. He just happened to be in the wrong place at the right time. We got lucky. Hopefully the Shin Bet will gain useful information from him. In any event, that's one more bad guy off the streets. Not bad for a day's work.

Chapter 19

Capturing the Leader of Islamic Jihad: Second Attempt

R eturning to the base after the checkpoint, I'm not surprised to
discover that my day is actually far from over. Uri tells me that the
Shin Bet is still tracking the leader of the Islamic Jihad. The Duvedan
team is going to make another try for him tonight; we've been asked to
provide escort again.

After dinner, Uri and I make our way to the small army convenience store on the base. We purchase cookies, Coke, and chocolate,
adding them to the pita, sandwich meat, hummus, and tea that we lib-
erated from the kitchen supply closet. Since we're going to replicate last
night's operation, we don't need to spend much time planning. I replace the batteries in our radios and night-vision gear, but I have plenty
of time to call Jen, speak with the family, and play cards. Like Uri, I
should be working, but playing cards is a good opportunity to
strengthen my bond with the men in the unit. That's more important
than achieving my daily word count.

When it's time to leave, I hear the rain splattering against the wooden slats that have become an improvised awning outside our door. The dirt path to the latrine has already turned to mud. It rains throughout our drive to the rendezvous point.

Tonight will be just like yesterday in all ways but one. We're working with the same people. We're given the same instructions. We're after the same terrorist. And we're even conducting our surveillance from the same spot. Only the weather has changed. That will make reaching our destination more difficult, but it will give the Duvedan added cover during the arrest.

The minute we leave the main road and start driving on the path, I feel our Hummer slip in the mud. Luckily, tonight's drivers are highly trained and able to slog through.

I'm not so sure about the Shin Bet's Land Rover though. In general, these vehicles aren't as mobile as the Hummers, and theirs is also weighed down by a lot of equipment. Taking the lead, we adjust our route along the way for the Land Rover's sake. This adds time to our journey and if it takes us too long, the Duvedan assault team will be literally left waiting out in the cold.

The longer they wait on the edge of the village, the more likely that their presence will become known—and we could lose our chance to capture the terrorist once again. If we don't capture the suspect tonight, moreover, I'm afraid we will not have another chance tomorrow. Given the suicide bombers and other terror organizers he could identify, failure is not an option. I find myself wishing I were on the Duvedan team. I'm certainly not as spry as they are, and I realize that I'm not needed, but the desire to personally capture one of these bastards is particularly strong. This is a new sensation.

Up until now, I've never felt emotional about my work. I've felt proud of my service, but my attitude changed with the start of the second Intifadah. The Palestinians received extensive autonomy in 1993 as

part of the Oslo Accords and could have started building their home-
land in 2000 after Camp David. Instead, the violence continues. Now
every time an Israeli is killed or wounded, my anger and frustration
increase. I regret having to sit in this Hummer while others have the
privilege of bringing a criminal to justice. I don't like watching sports,
but I like playing. Tonight, I learn that I feel the same about soldiering.

Cutting through a thick wood, we are about two kilometers from
our destination. The mud is deep. Even our Hummer has trouble, but
we haven't traveled more than three hundred meters before learning
that the Shin Bet are stuck. Uri orders the driver to pull over to an area
that is relatively firm. Uri and I exit the vehicle. He helps the drivers
link the vehicles with a steel cable while I walk up ahead to make sure
no one is waiting in ambush.

As I walk, I hear the Hummer engine roar as it drags the Land
Rover out of the mire. It's a good thing that no one lives close by; we
certainly aren't being particularly quiet tonight.

Unfortunately, this scene repeats itself three times and we haven't
traveled more than five hundred meters when it happens a fourth time.
Once again, Uri and I exit the vehicle. While he helps the drivers, I
walk ahead. I'm particularly concerned about an ambush tonight because we are returning to the same place we were yesterday. While I
walk, I try to identify a path to our destination. It's very dark out and
the mud seems to be everywhere, but I come across a narrow strip that
has been partially protected by several trees planted relatively close together. It will be a tight fit for the Hummers, and the additional equipment on the Land Rover will brush against the low branches, but I
think it's our best bet.

When I return to our small convoy, almost everyone is out of their
vehicles. Uri and Daboosh are congregated with the Shin Bet. The others stand together on the periphery while the commanders discuss our
options. It's been very frustrating these last couple of hours and I know

from our earlier conversations that the Shin Bet commander is ready to give up.

Walking up to Uri, I ask him what's going on.

One of the Shin Bet officers says, "I think we're going to have to call it off."

"Why?"

"Even if we make it through, it's going to take too long. We need to be set up in the next thirty, forty minutes."

Speaking with more confidence than I really feel, I tell him that I scouted a way close by, and I can walk ahead on foot and show the lead driver where to go.

Uri trusts that I know what I'm talking about and supports me. "Sounds good. Let's give it a try."

The Shin Bet commander agrees, but doesn't look enthusiastic. He's trained to discover the truth, and he can probably tell by reading my face that I don't know what I'm talking about.

Uri walks with me to the front of our Hummer, and I show him the way. The Hummer pushes past the branches and the Land Rover follows without incident. We walk until we reach the rocky ground just before our destination. Once the drivers feel comfortable, they race ahead so that the Shin Bet can unload their equipment and keep to their schedule.

When we catch up, the Shin Bet team is hard at work setting up their equipment while our guys are fanning out along the perimeter. Uri and I greet the members of our team. Uri reiterates the rules of engagement and reminds everyone how we're going to handle rest periods. I let them know that I'm going to make a wide patrol of the area in the next few minutes and ask them not to shoot me. Everyone eventually agrees to let me live.

Over the next couple of hours, the rain returns. It's not a heavy rain, but we're all going to be soaked before the end of the night. Uri distributes tea and cookies to everyone. While he's making the rounds, I stand several meters from the ledge overlooking the village, stare down at the distant streetlights, and take a moment to recognize how much I enjoy my work. It's raining, it's cold, it's very late, and I've had little sleep, but standing here alone on a hill with a gas generator's hum in the background, I feel at peace. If Israel is my home, soldiering is my hearth. It's like a dark green cloth that shields me from the cold, the wet, the hunger, and the fatigue. While I'm on duty, none of that seems able to penetrate and reach me.

I return to our Hummer ostensibly to forage for food, but I'm really looking for information. One of the Shin Bet officers sees me and says, "How are you guys doing?"

"We're just fine. The question is, how are you doing? How is it coming along?"

"We're nearly there. We're zeroing in right now." He conveys this news with the deadpan calm of a professional.

The sky is beginning to lighten. It will be dawn in less than an hour. The Duvedan team have been out there too long as it is and I'm wondering if this has been yet another wasted night when I hear the Shin Bet officer over the radio. He has identified the terrorist's exact location. The Duvedan officer acknowledges. Minutes later Duvedan has the terrorist's home surrounded and secured. After several minutes of flurried communications, the radio falls silent. We wait. Finally, Duvedan signals that they have the terrorist in custody and are on their way out of the village. Uri and I stand smiling like idiots. No one shouts for joy, but we are all feeling giddy.

Just after dawn, our gear is packed and we are ready to leave. The roads haven't improved, so we battle the mud as much as we did when we arrived. This time, though, there is no sense of urgency and no one really cares how long it takes. We're all smiles and laughter now. The only thing waiting for us is a warm shower and a bed. By the time we arrive back at the base, it's lunchtime.

As Uri and I walk together toward our container, the adrenaline has begun to wear off. I'm tired and looking forward to several hours of sleep. When we pass the container used by the officers, Sharon, who is lying on a bed, sees us through the open doorway and calls out, "I've got something special for you both. Are you interested?"

Uri rolls his eyes at me. I know he's thinking about his bed when he says, "No, not really. What do you need?"

Sharon tells Uri that several terrorists are going to take part in a funeral procession today and a sniper team will take them out. He'd like Uri to take command.

Uri doesn't pause, but he does look a bit sheepish when he says, "I'm sorry, Sharon, but I'm tired. It's been a long night. Do you mind finding someone else?"

Without thinking, I blurt out, "I'd be glad to do it."

Uri raises his eyebrows. I have to admit that I'm a little surprised at myself as well, but I'm anxious to take part in the mission. I want to be the one looking through a pair of binoculars and telling a sniper that he has permission to open fire.

When I first put on a uniform thirteen years ago, I joined a culture that deeply held that while force was a necessary tool, killing was the last resort and considered a sign of failure.

But times have changed.

Today, targeted killings of known terrorists have become part of an Israeli strategy to eliminate "ticking bombs" and decapitate the enemy's leadership. Although the policy is hotly debated in Israel and around the world, it is widely reported to have worked. The resultant measures taken by terrorist leaders to stay alive deny them the time, resources, and contacts needed to plan attacks. Leaders can be replaced, but that, too, takes time and disrupts the organization's ability to act.

Sharon looks at me for a moment and says, "Can you be ready in an hour?"

Uri and I walk back to our container and as we sit on our bunks, he says quietly, "I'm concerned that this is a half-baked idea. There's no solid plan. No briefing. You can't just organize something like this at a moment's notice. At least, you shouldn't. I'm not sure it's a good idea."

Until now, I assumed Uri only wanted to sleep. Now I realize that he has reservations regarding the assignment. As usual, I haven't even thought about the feasibility of the plan, but I'm thinking about it now.

"I have the feeling that this is just someone's bright idea and no one has thought it through," says Uri.

"You're probably right, but I said I'd go. And if it's going to be poorly organized, I'll only feel worse if I make someone else go in my place."

Uri thinks for a moment.

"I understand. I'm going to talk to Sharon. Learn what I can."

After twenty minutes, Uri returns. Sharon is still committed to the operation and the details remain fuzzy, but Uri has decided to join me. He's going only because I am. He says, "If anything happened to you, Tali would kill me."

I say, "That's funny. She said the same thing to me about you."

We both lie back in our bunks and try to rest. An hour later, Sharon comes in, taps Uri on the feet, and says, "You have two snipers. They'll meet you by the Hummers in ten minutes."

We both rise, shake our heads at each other, and smile. Sometimes you are sent on an operation before you even establish a coherent plan, but it's unusual.

Uri and I greet the two snipers. It doesn't take long to establish that they have very limited experience with the .50-caliber Barrett rifle. I probably have as much experience shooting one as they do. Uri and I share a sideways smirk, although I'm sure we're both thinking that a bad situation just got worse. Shooting a person in a crowd takes expertise. These two guys are not up to the task. My desire to help a terrorist find a quick path to hell quickly turns into a hope that this mission will be scrapped. If these guys are asked to pull the trigger, I'm almost certain that they will miss and kill a civilian.

Together, the four of us drive to the Jewish settlement near Sanur. The settlement is protected by a platoon from another reserve battalion. When we arrive, we will be under someone else's command, but Uri and I have both agreed not to follow any order that doesn't make sense.

Right now, I'm especially grateful that Uri has joined me, because I already regret my impulsive decision.

When we meet the officer who originally devised the plan, the phrase *deep thinker* doesn't come to mind. Uri and I both assumed that we were going to snipe from a hill near the street. As it turns out, we are being asked to fire from the perimeter fence that surrounds this tiny community.

Along the fence, we meet six more soldiers. Four of them have Barrett rifles. Two of them are officers who will serve as spotters. We're told that in about an hour the terrorists are expected to be walking along one of two roads that are clearly visible from our position. Uri and I scan the area and help our snipers prepare. An hour passes and there is no discernible movement in the village. After another hour passes, Uri and I gratefully take a seat on the gravel. Happily, the intelligence was faulty. No funeral procession, no crowd, no nothing.

Unfortunately, the officer in charge isn't convinced. While he spends his time looking through his binoculars, Uri and I, completely giddy from lack of sleep, are having the time of our lives joking around and laughing—being most unprofessional.

Another couple of hours pass and Uri and I are ready to pack up. We tell the officer that we need to head back. By now, even he must see that it's a bust. He looks disappointed. I'm not. When we're back at our base, I put my hand on Uri's shoulder and say, "Sorry, buddy. That was my bad. I don't know what I was thinking volunteering for this."

Uri says, "I do. And I understand, but you still owe me a few beers."

"It'll be my pleasure."

Chapter 20

Preparations

At ten o'clock this morning, I learned that I'd be arresting a suicide bomber in less than twenty-four hours. I've done this countless times in the past, but that was nearly ten years ago. And, I'll be doing it without Uri. In "real life" Uri is with the Israeli Foreign Service, and he's being sent to Africa.

It's now 9 PM. Since morning, the team has been planning the raid, simulating every conceivable eventuality, testing weapons, studying aerial photos of the village, hovering over topographic maps, entering coordinates into the GPS, and scrounging around for any additional equipment we'll need. The reserve unit I've been assigned to has been a little lax, but to be honest, I've enjoyed the relaxed and casual atmosphere. With this unit, everyone is usually satisfied with the bare minimum. But not tonight. Everyone takes the assignment and preparations seriously.

We are leaving the base around 2 AM. I'll sleep until 1, stretching out on one of the five bunks squeezed into our metal shipping container. I shield my eyes from the ever burning fluorescent light with a fleece mask I bought before I left Tennessee. The room is unusually quiet considering the early hour, a time when army activity picks up, but I can't seem to rest.

I experience intermittent insomnia. Tonight is unlike the countless other nights that I've faced during my thirteen years of military service because tonight, feeling the wire mesh of the bed frame through this thin mattress, I can't shake the fear that I may not live to see tomorrow.

For the first time in all my years of service, I actually conjure mental images of my own death. Kalashnikov-toting terrorists ambush me in an orchard. I'm burned to death by a glue-filled Molotov cocktail. Shot in the head the moment I enter the terrorist's home. Blown up by a booby trap.

Like almost every combat veteran, I've encountered moments of fear and tension before a mission or training exercise, but this is different. In the past, my apprehension has been far more general in nature, and I have always quickly shaken it off by clinging to the irrational belief that my luck would shield me from harm.

Instead of recognizing the statistical probability that eventually my turn would come, I looked at my good fortune as an affirmation that I led a charmed life. It was the same irrational conviction that convinced me it was safe to hitchhike as a teenager in New Hampshire, that it was a good idea to avoid the designated trails while climbing alone in Switzerland or walk around the most dangerous parts of Washington, DC, while at college.

I knew I'd never step on a landmine, be shot, knifed, blown to bits by a rocket-propelled grenade, or die in any of the myriad ways awaiting a soldier. That happened to other people.

Now, tonight, I have several reasons to worry. In the past, I've trained and served with some of Israel's best combat units—and this isn't one of them. Many members of this reconnaissance unit have impressed me with their skills, intelligence, and professionalism, yet it is clear that they have limited experience with urban warfare. Just as disturbing is my realization that it's been ten years since I've been on such a mission.

During our training sessions two weeks ago, I definitely felt rusty. It also doesn't help that I have very little confidence in the commanding officer, Aviv. Although he probably has the highest IQ in the entire company, he has consistently shown poor judgment. Over the last few weeks, my impression of him as both stubborn and rigid has only strengthened. If we encounter something unexpected in the field, he may be unable to adapt our plan effectively. He also doesn't listen to suggestions made by the members of his unit. This is unusual in the Israeli military, and it is always the sign of a bad commander.

Still, it's dark, windy, cold, and raining: a perfect night for a raid. As part of my efforts to fit in, I too complain about being wet, but I know that bad weather increases our chances of success tonight because it limits movement in the village, decreases the likelihood that Palestinian watchdogs will catch our scent, and diminishes visibility enough that we're unlikely to be noticed while we hike into the village four hours from now.

And yet I'm worried.

I try not to, but I keep thinking of Jennifer, the love of my life, and fear I'll never see her again.

Three months ago, when I learned that this reconnaissance unit was being called up to serve in the West Bank, it took me more than two weeks to tell Uri that I would join him. Less than a year ago, during the massive reserve call-up for Operation Defensive Shield, I didn't hesitate for an instant when I had an opportunity to serve my adoptive country.

At that time, I had a good job I could have lost and the dangers I expected to face were far more severe than those waiting for me now.

Only nine months has passed, but so much has changed. My love for Israel and sense of responsibility are still there. If anything, those feelings have only grown stronger since my participation in Operation Defensive Shield.

Now that I've found the person whom I plan to spend the rest of my life with, I'm terrified that I won't live long enough to marry her, play with our kids, and pamper our grandchildren.

I now understand, for the first time, the sacrifice of all the fathers and husbands with whom I have served over the years. I have heard reservists talk about missing their children and their wives. I have listened as they discussed how difficult being in the army makes life for their loved ones. I was paying attention, but I never really knew what they were talking about until now.

I have three sisters, a mother, and a father who love me dearly and with whom I'm very close. I have always known that my death would be hard on them and felt guilty because I knew that I put them through hell every time I donned my uniform. I knew that if anything happened to me, they would be devastated. Over the years, I justified the emotional burden I dumped on my family by telling myself that it was right to subordinate our individual needs for the greater good of our people. What was the importance of my life when compared to all the lives that would be saved because I performed my duty as a soldier? What did it matter that my parents would live in intermittent fear for my life, if it meant that thousands of other parents could send their children to school without fear because people like myself serve in the military? I told myself that my personal sacrifices and the anxiety my family endured were a fair price to pay if it meant that even a single person was kept safe because I chose to be a soldier.

But knowing that I am going to put the woman I love through a month's worth of anxious days and fearful nights is different from putting my family through that same hell. I don't know exactly why. Perhaps it's natural for a child to cause a parent pain and drive siblings crazy, while a lover is supposed to bring joy and lighten burdens, not bring sorrow and add worry. As a son and brother, it always seemed acceptable for me to strike out on my own path, even if it involved danger. As a lover, I should be tending to Jennifer's needs and building a home, not trekking across the world to slay dragons.

My determination to be an effective soldier tonight will have more to do with my desire to return to the woman I love than my need to stop another terrorist.

Since I've been here, she's been upbeat and supportive, and I've been blasé about our operations. I hope I can pull that off again tonight. Because the reception inside this metal container is poor and because it's the only way to have any privacy, I put on my winter jacket and head outside. I pick a spot behind our container where the reception is good. Every few meters, someone else is talking on the phone with a loved one. It makes me feel better knowing that almost everyone else is feeling the same fears as me. I speed-dial Jennifer's work number. It's late at night here, but early afternoon in Tennessee. When I hear her voice, my tension dissipates and I feel relieved. It's as if I have been transported to her side.

I tell her we've had a good day. I tell her how much I miss her, how much I love her, and how I can't wait to be back in her arms again. We talk for about thirty minutes and my sense of purpose strengthens. I tell her everything that is in my heart, but I don't talk about my fears, or the coming mission. Instead, I let her know that I might not be able to call her tomorrow until late. I tell her we're going to be busy, and I may not have access to a phone for a while.

Afterward, I call my parents and sisters. I make sure to say how much I love them and miss them. I warn them, too, that I might not be able to call for a while. They know what that means. When I hang up, I'm emotionally exhausted. I've been on the phone for almost two hours. I close my phone, put it in my pocket, and wipe my boots before reentering our hovel away from home.

All day long, we've talked and joked about tonight's mission, but almost everyone is now locked away in his own private world. I nod hello to those who are still awake. They nod back. One of them asks me if I've learned anything new about tonight's mission. I tell him that I was just on the phone with my family and girlfriend in the States. He closes his eyes and returns to sleep without saying another word. I walk the six steps it takes to reach my bunk, sit down, take off my jacket, pull off my boots, and lie down. I feel myself drift off to welcome sleep.

Daboosh gently nudges me awake. He's a good guy. He's a salesman in the construction industry. He is bright, friendly, levelheaded, and good-humored. More importantly, he's six foot one and weighs 190 pounds. That will be important in about three hours when he enters the terrorist's home with the unit's commander and me. I look at my watch and see that it's 12:56 AM.

Earlier today, Daboosh confided that this is his first raid. If it had been anyone else, that information would make me nervous, but I've spent enough time with Daboosh to know that he'll be all right. Although experience enables a soldier to react quickly and effectively to threats, being able to think clearly and make good choices despite pumping adrenaline, confusion, and fear is something you can't learn. Generally, the real concern is that an inexperienced soldier will be quick on the trigger because he mistakes a civilian running toward him with a broom for a terrorist with a rifle. Usually, the more experienced soldier is coolheaded enough to take his time and respond only to real threats. Daboosh might not have a lot of urban warfare experience, but I trust his judgment.

Right now, he's waking me because Aviv will be here in four minutes to review tonight's mission plan, make sure that we all have the necessary equipment, and provide us with any last-minute intelligence updates. I smile up at Daboosh, slowly slide my feet to the floor, and say, *"Bo'ker tov"* (Good morning).

Four minutes later, my boots are laced up and I'm sipping water out of my canteen when Aviv opens the door. In an Israeli unit, no one considers jumping to attention or saluting. Rank doesn't mean much to Israelis. We respect the man, not the uniform. That said, we do immediately arrange ourselves along the bunks to ensure that we can all see and hear Aviv.

Over the last few weeks, Aviv has almost managed to smile twice. This isn't one of those times. He's all business right now.

As it turns out, he doesn't have much news to add. One of the guys asks whether intelligence has provided any new information about the people who will be in the house we intend to raid. What he really wants to know—what we all want to know—is whether these people will be armed and if they'll put up a fight. Aviv just repeats what we already know; that we don't know for sure who is in the house or whether or not there may be weapons inside the house. In short, it seems that intelligence doesn't really know much beyond the identity of the suicide bomber.

Thirteen years ago, when I was still functionally illiterate in Hebrew and didn't know much about the Israeli intelligence community's methods, I was usually vaguely suspicious when they designated an individual a terrorist. Like most graduates from American universities, I thought of these people as "suspected" terrorists and "alleged" murderers. Now I better understand how the Shin Bet and the military gather their evidence, and I know that they would put the lives of Israeli soldiers at risk only if they had definitive proof that an individual was indeed a threat. In this case, I'm particularly sure that the Shin Bet has concrete information because of last week's capture of the Islamic Jihad leader in Qabatya. The Shin Bet's long conversation with him no doubt led to this mission, as well as three others also taking place tonight.

After Aviv leaves more questions unanswered, the meeting ends and we all take another look at the topographic map and aerial footage. It's important for everyone to know the route we are taking since if we are attacked along the way, any one of us may have to assume command and direct support teams to our location. We review our plan again and test each other on the rules of engagement.

We also discuss the mission plans of the three other teams operating in Qabatya tonight and study aerial footage of their areas. There are two vital reasons for this. First, it will minimize the possibility that one of us will accidentally shoot a soldier from a different team. Second, it will enable us to quickly understand where we'll need to go if any of the other teams require help. We don't stop until we're sure that we recognize every house, every building, every street, and every alley.

Being able to visualize the territory is vital, but we will be coordinating our actions with the other teams by using a shared radio frequency. We'll also use a second frequency unique to our team. Our unit of fifteen men will be divided into five three-man teams. Only one member of each team will have a radio, but everyone studies the frequencies in case the radioman is killed.

By the time we feel ready, we have less than an hour left before it's time to leave. We spend our time chattering away like children before the first day of school. Ever since we first learned about this mission, the members of our unit have been open and honest about their fears. I have been impressed by their candor, their lack of bravado, and their determination to see the mission through. I haven't been very honest with them. All along I've played the part of the experienced combat veteran. I have done my utmost to appear unconcerned. Knowing that courage, like fear, is contagious, I act confident, self-assured, and relaxed. That's what they expect from people who serve in special operations units. So the last thing I want to do is tell them how difficult it is for me to understand why I was never accepted to that unit in the first place.

They know I've served with the Alpinistim for several years, and these guys assume I'm an expert. It makes them feel good to know that a member of a special operations unit has joined them.

One of the younger guys, Tamir, looks at me with a smile before addressing the group. "Adam, I hear your girlfriend told you not to return without a terrorist's ear as a souvenir."

Keeping up the tough-guy persona, I smile right back. "No, she demands that I bring back two. She wants a matching set for earrings."

This prompts some banter, and several jokes are made at my expense. It's all in good fun. Someone suggests we play a few hands of cards before we leave. While I shuffle, I think about Tamir's suggestion that Jennifer expects me to come back with heroic tales. It makes me smile because I know she, like all of our loved ones, only wants us to return home in one piece.

The hour passes quickly. Before I know it, it's time to throw on my heavy bulletproof vest. Its ceramic plates will protect me from most weapons we are likely to encounter, shy of an RPG. Over this vest, I sling my assault vest. In its pockets, I carry eight magazines that hold thirty bullets apiece, two fragmentary grenades, two concussion grenades, a flashlight, and various medical supplies. A massive hammer tied snugly to my back will take care of any locked doors in our way.

Fifteen minutes before we depart, we're all standing outside in the main quad. It's raining. Members of the three other units are milling about as well, but we're the only unit that's ready to go. We alternate between relaxed conversations and taut predictions of what we'll be facing in the next few hours. For myself, all my fear and concerns faded into the distance the moment I stood to suit up. I am now conscious only of my determination to survive, my belief in my own skills, my trust in the members of this team, my conviction that a successful mission will save lives, and my faith that the same luck that has kept me safe over the years will continue to shield me while I do what I can to serve my people.

A few minutes later, Aviv joins the team. He looks very serious, but manages a smile.

This reconnaissance team is one of three units that combine to make an IDF infantry reserve company. Each of these units has a specialty. The reconnaissance team is meant to be especially good at navigation and intelligence gathering. There is also a mortar team that specializes in firing mortars over great distances, and an anti-tank team that uses remote-controlled weapon systems. Tonight the mortar and anti-tank teams won't be bringing their toys; they'll be walking with the rest of us.

In stark contrast to most of us, whose ages range from twenty-three to thirty-seven, two of the company's administrative staff, who have been with this unit since before the Yom Kippur War and are now in their late forties to early fifties, are running around laughing, shouting, and handing out camouflage paint like candy. Given the rain and the fact that we're going to be working in well-lit streets, the camouflage is unnecessary. The men either don't know this or are trying to have fun, because almost everyone gladly accepts the paint. Even members of the reconnaissance team, who certainly know better, darken their faces with several different shades of green and black. Trying to be one of the guys, I join in.

While everyone is busy finger painting, the members of the fourth unit that will take part in this raid are sitting down quietly and drinking tea. Unlike us, who are all in the reserves, these are nineteen-year-olds who have been in the service for only a little over a year. They serve with Duvedan. Their commander is twenty years old. A week ago, when I worked with another team from this unit, I thought they all looked too young. Tonight, they are too far away for me to hear their adolescent voices and it is too dark for me to see their baby faces. Right now, they just look like good soldiers.

Each of the four units has been assigned a specific target. Our own reconnaissance team and the mortar unit will capture two suicide bombers who live only a few houses apart. The anti-tank unit will try to capture a terrorist leader who lives nearby, and the special operations unit will arrest yet another suicide bomber several streets away.

When the time comes, Sharon says a few words. He reminds us why this mission is important, that we've been chosen for this operation because we have proven ourselves over the last several weeks. He urges us to stay focused, and tells us that he's proud of us. I've heard speeches like this ever since I was a raw recruit. Most people reach a stage where they are no longer affected by such rhetoric, but I often hear phrases that are still meaningful to me.

When Sharon is done, our reconnaissance team takes the lead as we form two columns. More than sixty soldiers stand behind us. When I look back at them, I see why it is easy for journalists, foreigners, and Palestinians to forget that we are mostly husbands and fathers who are civilians 335 days out of the year; generally decent, caring men who spend most days worrying about work and most nights enjoying the company of friends and family.

Most of the men here grumble about having to serve, but they all believe that it is a duty and an honor to serve their country. The men walking with me tonight might not have the enthusiasm, the diligence, the skills, or the luck to count themselves among Israel's elite, but I am proud to serve with them.

Chapter 21

The Last Raid

S tanding before the base's front gate, we are given final authoriza-
tion for the mission. Almost in unison, seventy bullets are pushed
into the chambers of our automatic weapons. Everyone using a radio
has a headset. Observing the rules for nighttime operations, nobody
talks and everyone maintains a maximum distance from the person in
front of him. The goal is to stay just close enough that you don't lose
sight of him. Any closer and we'd give a sniper two easy targets instead
of one. Given how dark it is tonight, we'll walk about three meters
apart.

Six kilometers separate us from our targets.

We pass the edge of our base. Even though it is dimly lit, as always,
and despite the tall eucalyptus trees that keep it mostly hidden, I can
see the Israeli flag flapping in the wind. The blue star and the blue bars
are illuminated by a soft yellow light. I can't stop looking at the flag.
Perhaps it's because of all my fears; maybe it's because I'm among Jew-

ish soldiers being sent to remove a threat to the lives of other Jews; but right now, I feel a deep emotional connection to the millions of men and women who have willingly risked their lives over the millennia for the freedom and safety of my people. In this moment, time collapses and I feel present within every moment of Jewish history.

This could be when Abraham first came to Canaan in 1850 BCE. It could be when the Israelites made their exodus from Egypt five hundred years later; or when David made Jerusalem his capital.

It doesn't matter. It's as if all these moments in Jewish history exist right now and I, like all the nameless and faceless people who have come before and all those who will take my place, don't matter as an individual. As far as history is concerned, it only matters that seventy men showed up to hike toward Qabatya tonight. Thousands of years ago, perhaps on this very field, another Jewish soldier came to secure his country's northern border.

I doubt that the men walking with me would be interested in my thoughts. Like most Israelis, they live in the present. Right now, I assume that they are completely focused on the mud and are just trying not to fall down.

After twenty minutes in the field, we are given the signal to kneel. I am smiling. I'm enjoying myself. I know enough to keep this to myself, but I turn my head to Daboosh and grin. He smiles right back at me and gives me the thumbs-up sign. Maybe I'm not so alone in my thoughts after all.

In pairs, we cross Route 60, the last major road we'll see tonight. After walking a couple of hundred meters, we discover that the entire area has been flooded by the rains. It takes the commanders several minutes to select an alternative route. While the officers talk quietly among themselves, the rest of us are completely silent. We're in enemy territory now.

The officers decide to take us south of a flooded barrier, even though this will force us to march very close to several houses we originally planned to avoid. When we are about three hundred meters away from these houses, we stop again because Aviv thinks he has seen movement. He doesn't have to speak; he simply kneels and points his gun in the direction of a building. In an instant, the rest of us are down on our knees as well. Those of us with night-vision scopes scour the area. We sit still for several minutes. There is some quiet chatter on the radios as people along the column report in; they don't see anything. With our earpieces and microphones, the noise barely ripples the night. Concluding that it was just a tarp moving in the wind, Aviv stands up and continues to walk. We all follow.

Every once in a while, thoughts creep into my head that don't serve my needs as a soldier, but they are no longer morbid. Right now, I'm thinking that it would take a civilian only thirty minutes to reach our objective, but since we take our time crossing streets and are forced to stop intermittently, it will take us about two hours. The clouds have dispersed, and major constellations are clearly visible. I see Orion, the constellation I loved as a child, and Cassiopeia, which has helped me to navigate as a soldier. Although the improved visibility increases the possibility that we'll be seen, I'm not worried about it.

Every few minutes, I scan the countryside with a binocular-sized night-vision device we call the Owl. My rifle is slanted to the right, pointing out toward our flank. It would take me less than two seconds to find a target and fire a round, but since a civilian could be walking these orchards, even at this hour, our rules of engagement stipulate that we can't fire unless our lives are in danger.

Tonight, I can trust my own vision only up to fifty meters; the Owl extends that to more than five hundred. Having learned from experience, I keep my eyes lifted and constantly scan the perimeter rather than succumbing to the temptation of looking directly at the ground to avoid rocks, branches, or any other obstacles.

The more we walk, the better I feel about tonight's operation. It's probably the adrenaline. Suddenly we start to pick up our pace. Up until now, we've been marching, but this is a brisk run. Perhaps we're behind schedule. Since this area is deserted, the extra noise generated by our running is unlikely to be heard. We run for about a kilometer. I'm glad that I decided to train for several months in Tennessee by running with stacks of books in my backpack. Soon enough we reach a small dirt road less than a kilometer from our objective. We are given time to drink water, take off our light windbreakers, and make final adjustments to our equipment.

About to enter the village, I feel relaxed and focused. I chat quietly with Daboosh while sharing water from his canteen. He seems in good spirits as well. We say good-bye to a few members of the reconnaissance unit, who will hike to a position where they can provide visual support. Using specialized equipment, they will be able to tell us where a target has fled, or if a crowd is mobilizing against us. Our own eyes will be on the windows, the alleyways, the walls, the doors, and the roofs.

We're now on the final leg. Within fifteen minutes, we see the first house. Set on a hill about two hundred meters from the road, it is two stories tall with more than two dozen windows, and three balconies from which someone could shoot. A few lights are on. It's still dark, but visibility increases long before the sun rises. We should be finished and on our way by then.

We stop. I cannot see around the curve of this dirt path, but I've studied all the aerial footage and know exactly what's there. Two large single-story houses lie on the right, less than seven meters apart. A two-story house on the left is surrounded by a large plot of open ground.

We've arrived at our final break-off point. The special operations team that has been bringing up the rear needs extra time to reach their objective.

While they hike past us at a brisk clip, I turn my head to look at them. I don't begrudge them their youth or their light armament, but I wish I had one of those new bulletproof vests they all wear instead of the bulky, heavy, cumbersome antique I was given.

Once the youngsters are out of sight, we wait five minutes. When it's time to move, we find ourselves on a road illuminated by streetlights. As a result, the distance between each individual is increased. Although soldiers naturally feel safer walking close together, the opposite is actually true. It's tolerable for an individual to be an easy target for a sniper, but not for several of us to stand close enough to let him shoot more than one. I'm about fifteen meters behind the person in front of me.

We are now in a heavily populated area. Before we arrived, I could smell it. Arab villages have a distinctive smell. Given their poverty and inadequate infrastructure, residents must burn much of their rubbish. Strangely, I like the smell. There is something warm and welcoming about it.

We are still in two columns as our eyes scan the rooftops, windows, doorways, trees, lawns, and stone walls that line the street. Our weapons are raised and pointing toward every potential threat. By being alert and assertive, we may spot an enemy before he attacks and react effectively. Moreover, by looking like competent soldiers, we may cause an individual to decide against attacking us in the first place.

After passing about one hundred homes, we arrive at our intersection. We take a left; our target's house is the second one on the right. Aviv signals us to move. Crossing the street one by one, our team spreads out on both sides of the pavement. I'm with Aviv, Daboosh, and a Russian immigrant who was loaned to us from the mortar team.

At three-meter intervals, we kneel against the waist-high stone wall that runs along this side of the street. Six other guys are opposite us and have no cover.

Right now, our job is to keep our eyes peeled and provide cover for the other two units whose objectives lie farther down the road. Aviv and Daboosh are looking ahead and up at the house across the street. The Russian and I watch the houses and intersection behind us. The mortar unit passes us quietly. They make their way three houses down from our objective because intelligence believes that another suicide bomber is sleeping there tonight. The anti-tank guys and two old-timers, who are tagging along enthusiastically, stream past us. One of the older men, who has taken a particular interest in me because he appreciates, and probably identifies with, my decision to fly from the United States to join this unit, stops by to pat me on the back. He gives me a big toothy grin. I smile right back at him. I can see that this makes him happy and he scoots off toward his objective, the second house on the left side of this street. One of the primary organizers of terror activities in this area is supposed to be sleeping there tonight. He will definitely be armed and he may not be alone.

Although we always have to be prepared for trouble, arresting the leaders is particularly risky. It certainly requires an incredible amount of hate and determination to become a suicide bomber, but these types are generally less likely to take out a gun and shoot you. When it comes right down to it, anything is possible.

The Russian starts delivering hand signals straight out of some hokey war movie: He points two fingers at his eyes, holds up three fingers, makes a circle with his index finger, and then points toward one of the roofs. I don't care what he's trying to say but I'm beginning to understand why he's been moved from one unit to another over the years.

I think about giving him the signal I use to express frustration, but I refrain. He repeats himself. I nod and smile at him. This shuts him up. I know he just wants to be heard and feel like he's contributing. I'm glad he won't be entering the house with me.

Since our target is the closest, we wait for the other units to report that they have reached their own objectives. It's time.

Oren and Tal, each commanding a three-man team, cross the street for a last-minute conference with Aviv. Such short discussions among all the commanders are standard procedure before any action—a last chance to deal with any potential problems.

Oren's team moves first. The three of them crouch low, cross the street, and hug the rock wall for about seventy-five meters then climb over the wall one by one. Using an Owl, Aviv watches our target's house while Daboosh backs him up with his rifle. The Russian and I are covering everyone's backs. Oren and his men are over the wall and lying down behind a small shed within five minutes.

Now it's Tal's turn. His team, also crouching low, crosses the street, and slinks along the house to the back. They keep their distance and move deliberately, watching out for the random bricks, branches, rocks, and shovels lying about. We are very lucky in a particularly important way: These people don't have a dog, and neither do their closest neighbors.

Tal confirms over the radio that he and his men are in place. The perimeter is secure. If someone were to leave the house, he'd be spotted and easily captured. Now we must wait for the three other units to report that they are ready. We scan the house and the surrounding area for about ten minutes. Without listening to the radio's chatter, it feels longer.

I carried a radio during much of my compulsory service and later, with the Alpinistim. There was something calming about hearing commands given and received over the radio. In part, it reminds you that you are not alone. You also know what's happening. When you're crouching low in the middle of the night surrounded by enemies and engulfed in silence, it is terrible to be left waiting and not know why.

I'm now seriously considering shooting the Russian, who continues to gesticulate. The more he tries to use sign language to tell me to look at the windows on the second floor of the house across the street, the more he looks like someone acting the part of a soldier and less like a guy I can depend on. I'm fantasizing about seeing a gun pointing at him from one of the rooftops and wondering if I could be blamed for reacting *just slowly enough* for him to get shot in the leg, when Aviv motions for me to join him and Daboosh.

Now the fun begins. The art of arresting wanted individuals has evolved a bit since I began serving thirteen years ago. Breaking into dark dwellings with little or no intelligence about the threats awaiting inside is now deemed too risky. Today the favored method is called the Pressure Cooker.

The idea is to put the terrorist under an increasing amount of pressure until he gives himself up peaceably, reducing the risk to Israeli soldiers and Palestinian civilians. In the first stage, we surround the house completely. Now that there is no way for the terrorist to escape, time is supposedly in our favor. Of course, the longer we're here, the more likely it is that we'll meet organized resistance, but by then the military will have placed a large number of troops in the area and closed off the neighboring streets if necessary.

Aviv begins the process by throwing pebbles at the metal door and calling out, *"If'tach el bab!"* (Open your door!) He throws a few more pebbles and has to repeat himself several times before a light turns on and we begin to hear movement inside.

If the residents ignore the request, we will intimidate them into complying with our demands by setting off explosions near the house, and, should that fail, firing into the air or at the house's stone walls.

Luckily, none of that is necessary tonight. Within a couple of minutes, the door creaks open slightly. The hands of a middle-aged man wave at us furiously. We can hear him say in Hebrew, "One minute. One minute," before closing the door again.

I look at Daboosh and try to give him a reassuring smile, but I'm wondering if the man wants this minute to gather and distribute weapons. We don't have to wait long for an answer. He steps outside, still pushing his shirt inside his jeans. Aviv, who speaks Arabic, tells him, "We need everyone to come out of the house. Now."

The man, who must be the head of the household, nods in agreement. He reenters the house, and more lights are turned on. Within moments, we can hear people moving about inside. The man comes out again and explains that the women need to get dressed. Although he is polite, Aviv makes it clear that the man needs to hurry them up.

Another five minutes pass. Enough noise is being produced to possibly wake the neighbors, who may or may not be armed and hostile. During these tense moments, I scan the surrounding area for threats. I'm concerned enough to actually pay attention to the Russian now.

Suddenly we hear the loud bang of a stun grenade down the road. One of the other units may have met with resistance. A few seconds later, shots are fired from the same area.

I don't have time to wonder what's happening down the street, because the door of the house right in front of me opens wide. The father walks out followed by three boys, four girls, a woman who may be his wife, and an older woman who is probably the kids' grandmother. They all stand together by the entrance. Aviv stands out in the open at the edge of what would be a driveway if the family owned a car.

Aviv, talking to the father, says, "Stand in the light and lift your shirt."

The father moves a little to the right. He's underneath the bulb that lights up the entrance to his house. He lifts his shirt up to his chest. Aviv says, "Turn around and lift your shirt higher."

The father does as he's been instructed. I can see his pale pudgy belly, his sunken chest, and his pockmarked back. It's clear that he doesn't have a suicide belt on him. Aviv says, "Step to the left and send your boys forward one at a time."

One by one, the boys step forward and expose their stomachs and backs. Like their father, it's obvious that they have done this before or have seen this done before. When we decide that they aren't concealing anything, we tell them to stand next to their father. Now that it's the women's turn, the father starts arguing with us from a distance. He's upset because he knows that we are going to expect the women to expose themselves as well. I don't blame him, but female terrorists are not unknown. They will have to be checked, but Aviv makes it clear that they won't have to raise their shirts as high as the boys.

Understandably, the father is still upset, but he relents. His willingness to accept the situation probably has a lot to do with the weapons aimed at him and his family. Although it's not our objective, we certainly aren't winning any new friends here tonight. One by one, the women lift their shirts slightly. They lift them higher than their modesty would normally allow, but I can't say that we've seen enough to know with any confidence that they aren't concealing an explosive belt or any other weapon.

The family seems to be cooperating, but we know this can change within a matter of seconds. We need to treat them with understanding and respect, but we also need to keep the situation under control. If we can do that, no one will be hurt. I am thinking about how difficult and frightening this must be for them to be awakened in the middle of the night by heavily armed soldiers.

Since we're here to take away their sixteen-year-old boy, their night is only going to get worse.

As each family member is cleared, we ask him or her to step farther from the house. As a group, they are now at the midpoint between their house and the street. Aviv has called in Tal's team from behind the house. They will monitor the family while Aviv, Daboosh, and I enter.

Just as we have practiced, I stand right behind Aviv, and Daboosh behind me. We're lined up against the house's wall on the right-hand side of the door. Aviv enters first. My right hand is on Aviv's shoulder and I give him a slight shove to the right as I move toward the left side of the room. Both of us aim our weapons at the center of the room and then slowly swing our rifles and gaze toward the sides. Alert for any movement or any explosive devices that may have been left for us, we make our way toward opposite corners. Once we reach them, we are both confident that the room is safe. We shout "Clear" and Daboosh, who has been waiting at the entrance of the house, repeats "Clear."

It's time to move on to the next room. The door is near me. This time, I'm the first person through it, and Daboosh lines up after me. Since we're on the left-hand side of the door, Daboosh gives me a slight shove to the left as he moves right. We make our sweep and shout "Clear" when we're done. Aviv, in the main room, responds "Clear."

We make our way through the seven rooms of this one-story home. It doesn't take us even ten minutes to determine that it's secure. We are now reasonably sure that no one is waiting to ambush us from inside. I am greatly relieved that we have reached this point without incident, but we're still in the middle of a large and militant village that could mobilize thousands with the simple flick of a switch at the mosque's muezzin. I'm a lot more relaxed now than I was before we went into the house, but this isn't the time to let down my guard. That's how people get killed.

Aviv reports our progress. We learn that the nearby unit that threw the stun grenade has discovered why no one responded to all their noise: Their target isn't home. Israeli intelligence is very good, but no one is perfect. It's possible that he's staying at one of the other houses in the neighborhood. We might have to search a few more homes before the night is over.

Meanwhile, we need to keep this family secure and search the home more thoroughly. To facilitate matters, we three leave the house and call the father over to us. We tell him to join us as we search the house. We're going to have him open up drawers, pull back drapes, and open closets. If there's a booby trap he'll find it, not us. While we're outside, one of the sons, about thirteen, starts shouting at Tal and the other soldiers. They don't react. In and of itself, the boy's yelling doesn't constitute a real threat, but if we let him continue it could encourage others. His angry rants won't lead anywhere good, for him or us. Without thinking or asking Aviv's opinion, I move to defuse the situation.

Friends and family don't know me as a violent person. I don't instigate fights; I break them up. I'm relatively slow to anger and my first response is always verbal. This situation doesn't demand physical aggression, but it does require that I use my size and voice to assert my authority. I know only a dozen phrases in Arabic—the phrases every Israeli soldier must know. While still at the entrance, I say, *"Shtok"* (Shut up) loud enough to startle the boy, but low enough so as not to wake the neighborhood. I walk toward him briskly and look straight into his eyes. I'm standing only inches away from him. With a mix of Hebrew and Arabic, I warn him to keep his mouth shut. I don't specifically threaten him with bodily harm, but I play the part of the tough, scary-looking soldier well enough to cause him to lower his eyes and remain quiet until we leave.

Without another word, I walk back to the entrance and get ready to search the house. I notice several of the guys nodding and smiling as I pass. Until now, they have seen me only as a generally good-natured American. This is probably the first time any of them has seen me act aggressive in any way. I acknowledge them as I pass, but I still try to look gruff. A smile right now would destroy the persona I'm attempting to create for the benefit of the family.

I return to the house's entrance and join Aviv, Daboosh, and the head of the household. Daboosh, speaking to me in English, says, "The younger one is a suicide bomber in training. We'll probably have to come back for him in a couple of years." I agree, but I hope like heck that Daboosh is wrong. Unfortunately, he probably isn't.

He walks us through the house and we engage in a superficial search. I actually want to look around more thoroughly, but Aviv isn't interested. I start to argue with him, but I realize that there is no point. It's my turn to *shtok*. Soon we all emerge from the house. A command car arrives and a couple of Shin Bet agents jump out of the vehicle. They speak briefly with the father then talk with the sixteen-year-old boy for several minutes. They tell us that they have verified his identity. They want us to hold on to him while they make the rounds of the other units.

It's still fairly dark outside, but the sun will start rising in a little over an hour. Now that the boy has been identified as the suicide bomber, we place him under arrest. It's a simple matter. Within the hollow handle of my rifle, I have a thick white plastic cable tie that I use to bind his hands together behind his back. He won't be able to loosen his hands, but I don't want to cut off his circulation. I ask him if they are too tight. He tells me that they are fine. What else is he going to say? I take out a soft piece of flannel from one of my many pockets and use it to blindfold him.

Our unit has been asked to join the search for the missing terrorist. It's doubtful that we'll find him, but it is worth the effort.

We tell our prisoner's parents, brothers, and sisters to go back inside. Like any family, they plead with us not to take him away. And to someone not privy to the context of this event, this would truly be most horrifying to any parent. But as the parents of a suicide bomber, they certainly would have celebrated his murderous act and been rewarded handsomely for their son's martyrdom. They know he will be interrogated by the Shin Bet and then sent to prison. Whether they like it or not, we've just saved lives—his own, and his victims'.

After the family's door closes for the last time tonight, Aviv asks me to stay with the prisoner. Although there's a part of me that resents being left behind, I realize that it is probably for the best. While the rest of the unit heads off to keep searching, I guide my prisoner to a spot down the street. Given the fact that he can't see, it takes several minutes to walk thirty meters. When we arrive, I help him sit down on the sidewalk. He is quiet, but he tells me he's okay.

This spot provides good cover and will be easy to defend, but I doubt that this will be necessary. I'm still wary, but the area has been quiet for the last couple of hours. If we were going to be confronted, it would have happened by now. The hard part is over. We're just wrapping everything up.

Thirty minutes later, Aviv and the rest of the unit return. Daboosh tells me that the search was indeed fruitless. Now that all the other teams have completed their missions, we're just waiting to be picked up by the armored trucks that will return us to our base. We set up a perimeter and are still wary of attack, but our level of intensity has diminished. The sun is rising. It is a new day and it feels like all the danger is now behind us. Our work tonight led to the capture of three suicide bombers and two terrorist leaders.

Some of the guys are standing together, chatting and drinking water. In the daylight our face paint makes us look more like Halloween revelers than soldiers.

Three trucks and several command cars arrive. The prisoners are placed in the command cars while we soldiers clamber into the trucks.

I am purposely one of the last to climb aboard because I don't want to be squeezed in the middle. I much prefer the more roomy and airy section in the truck's rear. When I climb in, everyone is smiling and patting each other on the back. No one is swaggering, but everyone is pleased, proud, and greatly relieved.

I'm standing next to Itzik, one of the two fifty-something men who voluntarily returned for reserve duty even though they are well beyond the required age. They usually perform essential administrative tasks for the company but were not going to miss out on tonight's opportunity to catch a terrorist. I can't say that I blame them. With face paint almost covering his pale and wrinkled skin, Itzik is all smiles. He pats me on the back. He can't contain his joy. I know how he feels, but it is in my nature to appear more circumspect.

By the time we pull into the base, the guys are singing. I don't know the songs, but I am happy to listen. I am proud to be here with these men.

None of us has slept, but we don't seek out our beds. Instead, we all gather in groups to talk about the night. Some people are taking pictures, and that reminds me that I brought a disposable camera. I snap a few pictures of my own and we continue to chatter away like boys just back from their first coed dance.

When the company commander joins us, he asks us to form a circle. He thanks us for our service, and tells us that the commander of the special operations unit that joined us tonight complimented our stamina and professionalism.

Right now, those five prisoners are sitting together, their hands bound and their eyes covered, in a large shed that usually contains our food supplies. We'll be holding them here until the Shin Bet comes to take them away.

Once the self-congratulation is over, we're only too glad to put down our weapons, scrounge for food, take showers, and lie down to sleep for a few hours. The night's activities are over, but several other operations are already planned for today.

Looking at my watch, I see that it's 6:30 AM. It is still too early to call my family and Jennifer. I want to let them know that I'm okay, but it's almost midnight on the East Coast right now. Hopefully, they are all asleep.

I place my grenades in a small metal container outside our room, slip off my assault vest, take off my bulletproof vest, unlace my boots, take a last sip of water, pull off my shirt, slide out of my pants, and pile everything into a bundle. I stretch myself out on my bed, and say *"Liela tov"* to the guys who are also settling in, and fall into a deep, luxurious sleep that lasts for five whole hours. When I wake, I feel like a great weight has been lifted from my shoulders.

Epilogue

With Israel, the one thing you can depend on is rapid change. As of this writing, Israel has disengaged from Gaza, Ariel Sharon has been lauded by world leaders, and we have just enjoyed the least violent year since the second Intifadah began. Only three years ago, Israelis endured the worst spate of terrorism in its history, reasserted control over the West Bank, and saw Sharon vilified the world over.

Given the complexity and volatility of the Israeli–Palestinian relationship, I couldn't hazard a guess what will happen next year. Compared with those heady days following the signing of the Oslo Accords, I am less hopeful today. But my more cautious approach to Palestinian intentions and their leadership's ability to meet their obligations hasn't turned into pessimism.

One day Israelis and Palestinians will live as neighbors in peace, security, and prosperity. It might take time, but I believe that it is inevitable. Years ago, I volunteered to help a university professor and poet who ran a program designed to expose Israeli and Palestinian children to the elements of culture that both people share. In those classrooms, I saw friendships bloom.

I have been living and working in the United States for the last six years. I am grateful to the country of my birth, for it has succored my family for three generations. I am truly blessed. I have a wife who is generous with her love, parents and siblings who are my closest friends, individuals and communities that are dear to me, and an ever-expanding array of opportunities for professional and personal growth. And at the same time, my love and appreciation for the people and land of Israel deepens each day.

More than twenty years ago, I sensed that I belong to Israel and Israel belongs to me. That visceral understanding has, over time, been transformed into a reservoir of experience and emotion that is a source of great strength and at the core of my identity.

About the Author

ADAM HARMON grew up in New Hampshire and received his B.A. at American University's School of International Service in 1989. Within a year, he moved to Israel. He served with the 202nd Paratrooper Battalion for two years, and was invited to serve with an Israeli Special Operations reserve unit. Now living in the United States, he continues to serve with the Israeli reserves.

About the Type

This book was set in Garamond, a typeface originally designed by the Parisian typecutter Claude Garamond (1480–1561). This version of Garamond was modeled on a 1592 specimen sheet from the Egenolff-Berner foundry, which was produced from types assumed to have been brought to Frankfurt by the punchcutter Jacques Sabon.

Claude Garamond's distinguished romans and italics first appeared in *Opera Ciceronis* in 1543–44. The Garamond types are clear, open, and elegant.